FUNDAMENTALS OF WEB DEVELOPMENT

Fabio Guilherme da Silva

Toronto Academic Press

FUNDAMENTALS OF WEB DEVELOPMENT

Fabio Guilherme da Silva

Toronto Academic Press
4164 Lakeshore Road
Burlington ON L7L 1A4
Canada
www.tap-books.com

Email: orders@arclereducation.com

© 2025 Toronto Academic Press
ISBN: 978-1-77956-293-7

This book contains information obtained from highly regarded resources. Reprinted material sources are indicated and copyright remains with the original owners. Copyright for images and other graphics remains with the original owners as indicated. A Wide variety of references are listed. Reasonable efforts have been made to publish reliable data. Authors or Editors or Publishers are not responsible for the accuracy of the information in the published chapters or consequences of their use. The publisher assumes no responsibility for any damage or grievance to the persons or property arising out of the use of any materials, instructions, methods or thoughts in the book. The authors or editors and the publisher have attempted to trace the copyright holders of all material reproduced in this publication and apologize to copyright holders if permission has not been obtained. If any copyright holder has not been acknowledged, please write to us so we may rectify.

Notice: Registered trademark of products or corporate names are used only for explanation and identification without intent of infringement.

Toronto Academic Press publishes wide variety of books and eBooks. For more information about Toronto Academic Press and its products, visit our website at www.tap-books.com.

ABOUT THE AUTHOR

Fabio Guilherme da Silva is an academic, analyst, and software developer with over 25 years of experience in the field. He obtained a Bachelor's in Mathematics (with a specialisation in Informatics) from the State University of Rio de Janeiro (UERJ) in 1994, and began working as a software developer and business analyst right away. He worked on projects for numerous companies in Brazil, including giants such as TV Globo, Halliburton, UBS, and the government of the State of Rio de Janeiro. In 2010, he obtained his Master's in Information Systems from the Federal University of the State of Rio de Janeiro (UNIRIO), and in 2015, a Doctorate in Computer Science from the Pontifical Catholic University of Rio de Janeiro (PUC-Rio). His research was dedicated to the use of artificial intelligence in games and interactive storytelling, and for both of these latest two degrees, he was awarded a full scholarship from the Brazilian government. During his doctoral degree, he worked as a researcher at ICAD/IGames/VisionLab at PUC-Rio, producing reports that helped win some game copyright infringement cases in court, including one for Zynga. In 2012, he was awarded an Honourable Mention (Interactivity) by the International Telecommunication Union (ITU) for his work. He then worked as a lecturer at PUC-Rio and FUCAPE Business School before leaving Brazil in 2018 to work for companies in Argentina, Germany, the USA, and the UAE. He currently lives in Portugal where he works as a researcher and assistant professor at the European University of Lisbon, focusing his research and teaching on Artificial Intelligence, Games, and Programming Languages. In addition to his pursuits in Computer Science and IT, Fabio also holds a diploma in International Relations and is fluent in eight languages. In his free time, he enjoys travelling, sports and playing music, having already toured and played in multiple countries in Europe and the Americas.

Table of Contents

List of Figures — ix
List of Tables — xi
Preface — xiii

1 WEBSITE DEVELOPMENT: AN OVERVIEW — 1

- 1.1. Unit Introduction — 3
- 1.2. Evaluation of Website — 4
  - 1.2.1. Rapid Growth and Expansion of WWW with Browsers — 4
- 1.3. Website Usages — 7
- 1.4. HTTP and HTTPS Protocol — 9
  - 1.4.1. HTTP — 9
  - 1.4.2. HTTPs — 9
  - 1.4.3. Difference between HTTP and HTTPs — 10
- 1.5. Types of Websites — 11
- 1.6. Development of Website — 13
- 1.7. Web Frameworks — 15
  - 1.7.1. Types of Framework Architectures — 16
  - 1.7.2. User Authentication and Session Management — 16
  - 1.7.3. Data Persistence — 17
  - 1.7.4. Administrative Interface — 17
  - 1.7.5. Design Patterns — 17
  - 1.7.6. Maintenance — 18
- 1.8. Ingredients Required for Website Development — 19
- 1.9. Website Hosting — 21
  - 1.9.1. Types of Website Hosting — 21
  - 1.9.2. Web Hosting Alternatives — 23

Summary — 27
Multiple Choice Question — 27
Review Questions — 28
References — 29

2 HTML (HYPERTEXT MARKUP LANGUAGE) — 31

- 2.1. Unit Introduction — 34
- 2.2. Basics of HTML — 35
- 2.3. HTML Tags — 38
  - 2.3.1. Heading Tags — 38
  - 2.3.2. Paragraph Tag — 39
  - 2.3.3. Line Break Tag — 40
  - 2.3.4. Horizontal Lines — 41
  - 2.3.5. Preserve Formatting — 42
  - 2.3.6. Nonbreaking Spaces — 43
- 2.4. Elements of HTML — 45
  - 2.4.1. Nested HTML Elements — 45
  - 2.4.2. Empty HTML Elements — 47
- 2.5. HTML – ATTRIBUTES — 48
  - 2.5.1. Core Attributes — 49
  - 2.5.2. Internationalization Attributes — 51
- 2.6. HTML List Classes — 53
  - 2.6.1. OrderedList and OrderedListItem — 53
  - 2.6.2. UnorderedList and UnorderedListItem — 54
- 2.7. HTML List Types — 55

2.7.1. Unordered List	55
2.7.2. Ordered List	55
2.7.3. Definition List	56
2.8. HTML Formatting	**57**
2.9. Graphics to HTML Document	**61**
2.9.1. IMG Attributes	61
2.10. Creating Tables	**63**
2.10.1. Tables and the Border Attribute	65
2.10.2. Headings in a Table	65
2.10.3. Empty Cells in a Table	66
Summary	**72**
Multiple Choice Question	**72**
Review Questions	**74**
References	**74**

3 CASCADING STYLE SHEETS (CSS) 75

3.1. Unit Introduction	**78**
3.2. Basics of CSS	**79**
3.2.1. The "Cascade" Part of CSS	79
3.2.1.1. Who Creates and Maintains CSS?	80
3.2.2. Benefits of CSS	81
3.3. CSS Syntax	**82**
3.3.1. CSS Selectors	83
3.3.2. The CSS Grouping Selector	84
3.4. Types of CSS Styles	**86**
3.4.1. Inline Styles	87
3.4.2. Embedded Styles	88
3.4.3. External Style Sheets	89
3.5. CSS Properties	**92**
3.5.1. CSS Reference	92
3.5.2. Useful CSS Properties	92
3.5.3. CSS Box Model	94
3.5.4. CSS Units	95
3.6. CSS Layout	**98**
3.6.1. Normal Flow	99
3.6.2. Flexbox	100
3.6.3. Grid Layout	102
3.6.4. Floats	104
3.6.5. Positioning Techniques	105
3.6.6. Multi-Column Layout	110

Summary	**114**
Multiple Choice Question	**114**
Review Questions	**116**
References	**116**

4 JAVASCRIPT 119

4.1. Unit Introduction	**121**
4.2. Fundamentals of Javascript	**122**
4.2.1. The Java Connection	123
4.2.2. Client-Side JavaScript	124
4.2.3. JavaScript Development Tools	126
4.3. Document Object Model (DOM) Manipulation and Events	**127**
4.3.1. DOM and JavaScript	128
4.3.2. DOM Interfaces	132
4.3.3. Testing the DOM API	133
4.3.4. The Event Object	135
4.3.5. Event Phases	136
4.4. Pair Programming	**144**
4.4.1. Origins	145
4.4.2. Pairing Mechanics	145
4.5. Debugging	**149**
4.5.1. The Debugging Process	149
4.5.2. Common Debugging Tools	150
Summary	**156**
Multiple Choice Question	**156**
Review Questions	**158**
References	**158**

5 PHP 159

5.1. Unit Introduction	**161**
5.1.1. Common Uses of PHP	161
5.1.2. Characteristics of PHP	162
5.1.3. "Hello World" Script in PHP	162
5.2. PHP – Environment Setup	**163**
5.2.1. PHP ParserInstallation	163
5.2.2. PHP Installation on Linux or Unix with Apache	163
5.2.3. PHP Installation on Mac OS X with Apache	166

5.2.4. PHP Installation on Windows NT/2000/XP with IIS 167
5.3. PHP – Syntax Overview 168
   5.3.1. Escaping to PHP 168
   5.3.2. Commenting PHP Code 169
   5.3.3. PHP Is Whitespace Insensitive 170
   5.3.4. PHP Is Case Sensitive 170
   5.3.5. Statements Are Expressions Terminated by Semicolons 170
   5.3.6. Expressions Are Combinations of Tokens 171
   5.3.7. Braces Make Blocks 171
   5.3.8. Running PHP Script From Command Prompt 171
5.4. PHP – Variable Types 172
   5.4.1. Integers 173
   5.4.2. Doubles 173
   5.4.3. Boolean 174
   5.4.4. NULL 175
   5.4.5. Strings 175
   5.4.6. Variable Naming 177
   5.4.7. PHP – Variables 177
   5.4.8. PHP Local Variables 177
   5.4.9. PHP Function Parameters 178
   5.4.10. PHP Global Variables 179
   5.4.11. PHP Static Variables 179
5.5. PHP – Constants 181
   5.5.1. constant() Function 181
   5.5.2. Valid and Invalid Constant Names 182
   5.5.3. PHP Magic Constants 182
5.6. PHP – Operator Types 184
   5.6.1. Arithmetic Operators 184
   5.6.2. PHP Comparison Operators 185
   5.6.3. PHP Logical Operators 186
   5.6.4. PHP Conditional Assignment Operators 186
5.7. PHP Arrays 187
   5.7.1. Indexed or Numeric Arrays 187
   5.7.2. Associative Arrays 190
   5.7.3. Multidimensional Arrays 193
Summary 199
Multiple Choice Question 199
Review Questions 201
References 201

6 WORKING WITH AJAX 203

6.1. Unit Introduction 205
6.2. Concept of AJAX 206
   6.2.1. Characteristics of an AJAX Application 207
   6.2.2. Examples 209
6.3. AJAX: Rich Internet Applications 211
   6.3.1. Features of AJAX 211
   6.3.2. Architecture of Microsoft AJAX Applications 212
   6.3.3. How Does AJAX Work? 215
6.4. Common AJAX Attributes 217
   6.4.1. Data Processing 217
   6.4.2. Rendering 218
   6.4.3. Queuing and Traffic Control 220
   6.4.4. Events and JavaScript Interactions 220
6.5. Technologies Used in AJAX 223
   6.5.1. Steps of AJAX Operation 224
   6.5.2. AJAX Security 226
   6.5.3. AJAX Issues 227
   6.5.4. Uses of AJAX in Technologies 228
   6.5.5. Technical Aspects of AJAX 229
6.6. AJAX Application Server Performance 231
   6.6.1. The Application 231
   6.6.2. The HTML Application 232
   6.6.3. The AJAX Application 232
   6.6.4. Data Collection 233
6.7. Summary 237
Multiple Choice Question 237
Review Questions 239
References 239

7 WORKING WITH DATABASES 241

7.1. Unit Introduction 243
7.2. Databases And Web Development 244
7.3. Structured Query Language (SQL) 248
   7.3.1. Data Types and Constraints in MySQL 249
   7.3.2. SQL for Data Definition 251

7.3.3. SQL for Data Manipulation	253
7.3.4. Data Updation and Deletion	254
7.4. Database APIS	**256**
7.4.1. What Is an API?	256
7.4.2. How Does an API Work?	257
7.5. Managing a Mysql Database	**259**
7.5.1. Manage MySQL Databases From the Command Line	260
7.5.2. Tools for Managing MySQL DataBase Servers	263
7.6. Connect to Mysql Using PHP	**267**
7.6.1. Two Ways to Connect to MySQL Database Using PHP	267
7.6.2. Potential Errors with MySQLi and PDO	271
Summary	**278**
Multiple Choice Question	**278**
Review Questions	**280**
References	**280**

8 ERROR HANDLING 283

8.1. Unit Introduction	**285**
8.2. Handling Errors	**288**
8.2.1. Displaying Errors	288
8.2.2. Logging Errors	289
8.2.3. Ignoring Errors	290
8.2.4. Acting on Errors	290
8.3. Handling External Errors	**293**
8.4. Exceptions	**297**
8.4.1. Using Exception Hierarchies	300
8.4.2. A Typed Exceptions Example	302
8.4.3. Cascading Exceptions	311
8.4.4. Handling Constructor Failure	315
8.4.5. Installing a Top-Level Exception Handler	317
8.4.6. Data Validation	319
Summary	**328**
Multiple Choice Question	**328**
Review Questions	**330**
References	**330**

INDEX 331

List of Figures

Figure 1.1. Steps of website development process.

Figure 1.2. MVC model implementation in a web application.

Figure 3.1. CSS box model illustration.

Figure 4.1. Client-side and server-side JavaScript.

Figure 4.2. Document object model (DOM).

Figure 4.3. Architectural coverage of popular JavaScript web application components.

Figure 6.1. How AJAX works?

Figure 7.1. Example of Microsoft SQL server.

Figure 7.2. What API is and what does it do?

Figure 7.3. Example to show an API.

Figure 7.4. How applications use API to exchange data?

List of Tables

Table 1.1. Various software support internet applications

Table 1.2. Difference between HTTP and HTTPs

Table 3.1. Different CSS style linking

Table 4.1. Fundamental data types

Table 5.1. PHP constants along with their description

Table 7.1. Commonly used data types in MySQL

Table 7.2. Commonly used SQL constraints

PREFACE

The field of web development is fundamentally critical to the trajectory of a business, holding the potential to either catapult it to remarkable heights of success or cause it to plummet into failure. This area of expertise, when applied with strategic acumen, plays a pivotal role in attracting visitors to a website and effectively transforming these visitors into potential leads. Simply put, a website serves as an essential tool for the representation and advancement of a business, acting as a digital storefront that showcases the business's offerings to the world.

A web developer is tasked with the significant responsibility of creating, routinely updating, and maintaining a website to ensure its optimal performance and relevance. This role encompasses several key areas, including front-end development, which focuses on the aspects of a website that users interact with; back-end development, which deals with the server-side of the website, ensuring that it functions correctly; and full-stack development, a comprehensive role that involves handling both the front-end and back-end tasks. As we move forward, the demand for skilled web developers is expected to surge, highlighting the importance of mastery in languages such as HTML, CSS, JavaScript, and Python, which are the building blocks of web development.

The expertise in web development extends beyond mere website creation; it involves ensuring that the website offers a seamless and engaging user experience. Web developers must be proficient in managing server administration tasks, including but not limited to dealing with Global Web Services (GWS), managing DNS records, and implementing robust security measures to protect the website from potential threats. Furthermore, collaboration with hosting providers and database administrators is crucial for constructing a website that not only looks appealing but also performs flawlessly across a variety of devices, ensuring accessibility and a positive user experience for everyone.

This comprehensive approach to web development is instrumental in establishing a strong online presence for a business, underscoring the vital role that web developers play in the digital age.

This book "Fundamentals of Web Development" is designed with the primary goal of introducing students and aspiring web developers to the core principles, technologies, and best practices involved in developing websites and web applications. Targeted at beginners and intermediate learners, particularly undergraduate students in computer science, information technology, and related disciplines, this book aims to bridge the gap between theoretical knowledge and practical application in web development.

Covering a wide range of topics, including HTML, CSS, JavaScript, server-side programming, databases, user interface design, responsive web design, and web accessibility, the textbook provides a comprehensive overview of what is required to build functional, user-friendly, and accessible web applications. It emphasizes hands-on learning through examples, exercises, and projects that simulate real-world web development scenarios, enabling students to apply what they've learned in a practical context.

The aim is not only to equip readers with the technical skills necessary for web development but also to instill an understanding of the importance of web standards, usability, and ethical practices in the digital realm. This textbook serves as a foundational guide for those looking to pursue careers in web development, digital design, or related fields, offering the tools and knowledge needed to create impactful and efficient web solutions.

–Author

CHAPTER 1

Website Development: An Overview

LEARNING OBJECTIVES

After studying this chapter, you will be able to:

- Understand the evaluation of website;
- Discuss the usages of website;
- Define HTTP and HTTPS protocol;
- Describe various types of websites;
- Explain the development of website;
- Deal with web frameworks;
- Discuss the ingredients required for website development;
- Define the concept of website hosting

FUNDAMENTALS OF WEB DEVELOPMENT

INTRODUCTORY EXAMPLE

Static Web Page: A static web page, sometimes called a flat page or a stationary page, is a web page that is delivered to a web browser exactly as stored, in contrast to dynamic web pages which are generated by a web application.

Consequently, a static web page displays the same information for all users, from all contexts, subject to modern capabilities of a web server to negotiate content-type or language of the document where such versions are available, and the server is configured to do so. However, a webpage's JavaScript can introduce dynamic functionality which may make the static web page dynamic.

Static web pages are often HTML documents, stored as files in the file system and made available by the web server over HTTP (nevertheless URLs ending with ".html" are not always static). However, loose interpretations of the term could include web pages stored in a database and could even include pages formatted using a template and served through an application server, as long as the page served is unchanging and presented essentially as stored.

The content of static web pages remains stationary irrespective of the number of times it is viewed. Such web pages are suitable for the contents that rarely need to be updated, though modern web template systems are changing this. Maintaining large numbers of static pages as files can be impractical without automated tools, such as static site generators. Any personalization or interactivity has to run client-side, which is restricting.

Static site generators are applications that compile static websites – typically populating HTML templates in a predefined folder and file structure, with content supplied in a format such as Markdown or AsciiDoc.

1.1. UNIT INTRODUCTION

Usually, a website serves a specific function or topic, such as social networking, news, education, commerce, or entertainment. The navigation of the website, which typically begins with the home page, is guided by hyperlinks between web pages. Websites can be viewed on a variety of devices, such as smartphones, tablets, laptops, and desktop computers. On these devices, the software program is referred to as a web browser. The process of creating and managing websites is known as web development. In essence, it's the labor that goes on in the background to ensure that a website functions smoothly, looks amazing, and loads quickly. Web developers use a range of coding languages depending on the platforms they work on and the kind of tasks they are performing when developing websites.

1.2. EVALUATION OF WEBSITE

→ Learning Objectives
- Deal with rapid growth and expansion of WWW with browsers.
- Describe software support internet applications.

A website is an assemblage of web pages and related materials that are published on at least one web server, recognized by a general domain name. A website, sometimes referred to as a web site, is an assortment of web pages and associated material that is published on at least one web server and is recognized by a common domain name. On these devices, the software program is referred to as a web browser. In layman's terms, a website is essentially a collection of online data and information about a specific topic.

Websites may be used for a variety of purposes. Examples include personal websites for people's businesses or professions, corporate websites for businesses, government websites for any kind of organization, and other websites for organizations. Websites are usually devoted to a specific subject or objective and can be the creation of an individual, company, or other organization. Any website can have a hyperlink to any other website, making it possible for users to have trouble differentiating between different websites.

In 1989, Tim Berners-Lee and his associates at CERN, an international scientific organization situated in Geneva, Switzerland, started working on the creation of the World Wide Web (WWW). They developed the Hypertext Transfer Protocol (HTTP), a protocol that standardized server-to-client communication. In January 1992, their text-based Web browser was released to the public. CERN declared that anyone could use the World Wide Web for free. To retrieve individual files from a server prior to the introduction of the Hypertext Transfer Protocol (HTTP), other protocols like the File Transfer Protocol and the Gopher Protocol were utilized.

1.2.1. Rapid Growth and Expansion of WWW with Browsers

The development of the Web browser Mosaic, which was developed in the United States by Marc Andreessen and others and released in September 1993, contributed to the rapid acceptance of the WWW. Mosaic made it possible for users of the Web to perform "point-and-click" graphical manipulations, just like they could on personal computers. Andreessen cofounded Netscape Communications Corporation in April 1994, and shortly

WEBSITE DEVELOPMENT: AN OVERVIEW

after its December 1994 release, Netscape Navigator quickly rose to prominence as the most popular Web browser. The World Wide Web boasted millions of active users by the mid-1990s (Table 1.1).

Table 1.1. Various Software Support Internet Applications

Year of Origin	Internet Application	Logo and Parent Company	**Product Mandate**
1994	Launched on October 13, 1994, the web browser known as Mosaic Netscape 0.9 was the company's first offering. Three quarters of the browser market had already been captured by it in just four months since its release.	Netscape Communications Corporation	Netscape web browser was once dominant but lost to Internet Explorer and other competitors in the so-called first browser war, with its market share falling from more than 90% in the mid-1990s. Netscape advertised that "the web is for everyone" and stated one of its goals was to "level the playing field" among operating systems by providing a consistent web browsing experience across them.
1995 1996	Internet Explorer (IE), in 1995 as an add-on to the Windows 95 operating system. IE soon became the most popular web browser.	Microsoft Corporation	Internet Explorer is a series of graphical web browsers developed by Microsoft and included in the Microsoft Windows line of operating systems, starting since 1995. It was first released as part of the add-on package Plus! for Windows 95 that year. IE was integrated into the Windows operating system in 1996 and came "bundled" ready-to-use within the operating system of personal computers.
2002	Mozilla Firefox, or simply Firefox, is a free and open-source web browser developed by the Mozilla Foundation and its subsidiary, the Mozilla Corporation. Firefox uses the Gecko layout engine to render web pages, which implements current and anticipated web standards.		Firefox Browser for Android is automatically private and incredibly fast.

FUNDAMENTALS OF WEB DEVELOPMENT

2003 2005 2007	Apple's Safari is the default browser on Macintosh personal computers and later on iPhones (2007) and iPads (2010) Safari 2.0 was the first browser with a privacy mode.		Safari is a graphical web browser developed by Apple, based on the WebKit engine. First released on desktop in 2003 with Mac OS X Panther, a mobile version has been bundled with iOS devices since the iPhone's introduction in 2007.
2008	Google launched Chrome, the first browser with isolated tabs, which meant that when one tab is crashed, other tabs and the whole browser would still function.		By 2013 Chrome had become the dominant browser, surpassing IE, and Firefox in popularity.
2015	Microsoft discontinued Internet Explorer and replaced it with Edge.		Microsoft Edge is a cross-platform web browser developed by Microsoft. It was first released for Windows 10 and Xbox One in 2015, then for Android and iOS in 2017, for macOS in 2019, and as a preview for Linux in October 2020. Edge includes integration with Cortana and has extensions hosted on the Microsoft Store.

Source: https://egyankosh.ac.in/bitstream.

Keyword

Gopher protocol – It is a communication protocol designed for distributing, searching, and retrieving documents in Internet Protocol networks.

Early in the twenty-first century, smartphones started to resemble computers more and more, making it possible to use more sophisticated services like Internet access. Over half of all web browsing in 2016 was done on smartphones, as their use has been steadily rising.

Did you get it?

1. Is the website secure, with HTTPS encryption?
2. Which platform is best for personal website?

1.3. WEBSITE USAGES

→ Learning Objectives
- Know mobile-friendly responsive websites.
- How Web is helpful to reach customers?

The ease of access to the internet has made it possible for businesses to reach a wider audience and create new categories of web users as a result of the widespread use of mobile phones. Even though there are mobile apps available, audiences prefer mobile-friendly responsive websites, which are growing in popularity. A website gives buyers and sellers a quick and simple way to exchange information. In many respects, websites are helpful for both buyers and customers. Websites can be customized to meet the needs of the host. A website can offer a wealth of information, including contact details, opening hours, product or location photos, and AI-enabled contact forms that can be used to answer questions from prospective clients or get feedback from current ones. The following is a detailed explanation of the various uses for websites:

1. **24/7 Online Presence:** The service provider's website allows clients to get in touch with them from anywhere at any time. The website continues to attract and acquire new users even after business hours. The user benefits from 24/7 presence since it allows them to access the information, they need without feeling compelled to make purchases while remaining in the comfort of their own home or place of employment.

2. **Information Exchange:** A seller can give customers as much information as they need and desire via a website. Websites offer the simplest means for buyers and sellers to exchange information, which is extremely helpful to businesses looking to engage customers and make profitable sales.

3. **Credibility:** These days, having an online presence is essential for any kind of business. In one way or another, it helps them outperform their rivals. A significant number of well-known companies have a virtual presence, which contributes to their increased credibility and reputation among consumers. You can use a website to provide potential customers with all the what's and whys they might have. Furthermore, having a well-designed, user-friendly website gives them confidence that they will receive the same excellent service throughout the entire company.

4. **Market Expansion:** The target market can grow thanks to an online presence since it is reachable by people worldwide. Anybody, from any nation, can locate the business with ease, making them a potential client. In fact, having an online

presence allows businesses to greatly expand their market share and make significant financial gains that would not be possible otherwise.

5. **Consumer Insights:** These days, different customer analytics tools, like big data and artificial intelligence, assist in identifying typical customers as well as their demands, preferences, and behavior toward particular products. Businesses can also benefit from the wide range of data available, which spans 137 Website Development, by better understanding their potential clients and providing them with products that meet their needs.

6. **Advertising:** More accuracy and dependability can be achieved in reaching customers with tools like Facebook advertising and Google Ad Words than with conventional offline advertising. Online advertising and SEO are excellent ways to quickly raise awareness and increase traffic.

7. **Competitors Online:** It is quite possible that competitors who are not in the business world will have a website. This may result in passing up chances to become innovative and attract new clients. It is imperative that every prospect be acquired through competition and that no opportunity be lost. Therefore, every business needs to have an online presence in order to stay ahead of the competition and have a greater market presence.

8. **Customer Service Online:** Customer service can be handled more efficiently and easily with the help of websites. AI-enabled chat boxes can instantly respond to all inquiries, saving businesses money on hiring customer service personnel. Quick answers to consumer questions contribute to better customer relations with the service provider.

9. **Growth Opportunity:** All things considered; websites are excellent means of offering a location to which possible investors can be directed. It displays the company's goals, accomplishments to date, and potential going forward. Therefore, having a website offers a plethora of growth opportunities.

Did you get it?

1. How does a website help customer service?
2. What is the purpose of a website?

1.4. HTTP AND HTTPS PROTOCOL

→ Learning Objectives
- Load webpages HTTP and HTTPS protocol.
- Differentiate between HTTP and HTTPs.

All URL links starting with HTTP use a rudimentary version of the "hypertext transfer protocol." which Tim Berners-Lee developed in the early 1990s. Web browsers and servers can exchange data in order to communicate thanks to this network protocol. The secure version of HTTP, or Hyper Text Transfer Protocol, is called HTTPS. It is the protocol that your browser uses to send data to the website you are connected to "Secure" is what the final "S" in HTTPS stands for. It indicates that all correspondence is encrypted between the browser and the website.

1.4.1. HTTP

The HTTP protocol facilitates the retrieval of resources, including HTML documents. It is the basis for all data exchange on the Internet and is a client-server protocol, meaning that the Web browser, or other recipient, initiates requests. The various sub-documents that are retrieved—such as text, layout descriptions, photos, videos, scripts, and more—are assembled into a single document. It is an application-level protocol designed for hypermedia information systems that are distributed and collaborative.

Did you know?

The initial version of HTTP had no version number; it was later called 0.9 to differentiate it from later versions. HTTP/0.9 was extremely simple: requests consisted of a single line and started with the only possible method GET followed by the path to the resource. The full URL wasn't included as the protocol, server, and port weren't necessary once connected to the server.

1.4.2. HTTPs

An expansion of the Hypertext Transfer Protocol is the Hypertext Transfer Protocol Secure. It is popular on the Internet and used for safe computer network communication. With

HTTPS, Secure Sockets Layer (formerly known as Transport Layer Security) is used to encrypt the communication protocol.

1.4.3. Difference between HTTP and HTTPs

The protocol used to move hypertext across the Web is called HTTP. HTTP has been the most widely used protocol for data transfer over the Web because of its simplicity, but the data (i.e., HTTP-based hypertext exchange is not as secure as we would like it to be. More specifically, the information about a specific website is shared between the web server and the web browser via both HTTP and HTTPS. However, HTTPS differs from HTTP because it has an extra "s," which makes it more secure. Table 1.2 explains the key differences between HTTP and HTTPS in detail.

Table 1.2. Difference between HTTP and HTTPs

Basis	HTTP	HTTPs
Definition	It stands for hypertext transfer protocol.	It stands for hypertext transfer protocol secure.
Encryption	It does not encrypt the text.	It encrypts the text so that no one can access it.
Usage of SSL	They don't require secure socket layer at transport layer.	They use secure socket layer to encrypt the code.
Type	It is a default protocol.	It is not a default protocol.
Beginning	URL begins with http://	URL begins with https://
Security	It is an unsecure protocol.	It is a safe transfer protocol.
Validation	It does not require any validation.	It requires validation like domain verification.
Address bar	It has simple address bar.	It has green colored address bar that shows it is secure.
Hacking	It can be easily hacked.	It cannot be hacked easily.

Source: https://egyankosh.ac.in/bitstream/123456789/72091/1/.

Did you get it?

1. Why is HTTPS considered more secure than HTTP?
2. Describe the HTTP request/response cycle and explain how it works.

1.5. TYPES OF WEBSITES

→Learning Objectives
- Understand authority website;
- Discuss about utility website.

As far as we are aware, web hosting is a service that enables businesses and private users to publish websites or web pages on the World Wide Web. On specialized computers known as servers, websites are hosted or stored. All website visitors have to do to view a page is input the domain name or website address into their browser. The seller's requirements determine the kind of website to be chosen. Websites can be broadly divided into four categories: sales, lead generation, utility, and authority websites:

1. **Authority Website:** A reputable website with authority is a trustworthy information source. The business has an online presence thanks to the authority website. Prospective clients can visit this page to learn about the company's accomplishments and to find out how to contact someone about services and offline-generated leads. Visitors to the website are seeking further information, but they are already familiar with the business. Here, the website acts as an online placeholder, enhancing the company's perceived legitimacy with clients. As an illustration, Healthambition.com is a fantastic authority website in the health industry with dozens of product reviews that compare various items and make it simple for visitors to purchase the suggested items through affiliate links.

2. **Lead-Generation Website:** This website, as its name implies, is dedicated to using its internet presence to generate leads. A major factor in attracting new clients is SEO and focused marketing techniques. But sales still happen offline. Those with the intention of becoming buyers find these websites online. This indicates that the potential client is essentially prepared to make a purchase; all they need is persuasion that the company is the ideal location for them to make this purchase. For instance, Live Chat is a web-based customer support platform that combines web analytics, help desk software, and online chat features. It can be leveraged as a lead generation tool.

3. **Sales Website:** These are the websites that use e-commerce to sell goods or services. A website is classified as a sales website if it has a cart feature. Because all lead generation and sales are conducted entirely online, this website is particularly well-liked. If a company uses online scheduling and payment but offers the service in-person, its website can still be classified as sales.

4. **Utility Website:** A utility website performs tasks more akin to those of a tool than a typical website. These are the businesses whose websites and businesses are the same. Facebook and Air BNB are two instances of useful websites. They don't always produce online leads or sales. They are available to anyone who desires to use them, and they simply exist in the virtual world.

Remember

Before making any design or marketing decisions, one should determine what kind of website is necessary. This will help them avoid making costly mistakes and will also help them draw in the target audience.

Did you get it?

1. What are the different types of websites?
2. What is a lead generation website?

1.6. DEVELOPMENT OF WEBSITE

→Learning Objectives
- Discuss the steps of website development process;
- Explain the term quality assurance (QA).

The work required to create a website for the Internet, or an intranet is known as website development. Web development encompasses a wide range of tasks, from creating a basic static text page to creating intricate Web-based applications, electronic commerce, and social media platforms. Web development is the upkeep and creation of a website; in essence, it is the work done in the background to make a website appear massive, function quickly, and have perfect user knowledge.

Using a variety of coding languages, web developers carry out the extensive process of developing websites. The steps involved in the web development process are described in detail in Figure 1.1.

- **Step 1: Innovative Requirement:** The most important prerequisite for the web development process is innovation. This step is essentially conversation-based, where the client shares his ideas, needs, and requirements with the web developers. The developers then use their demands to generate creative suggestions that best meet the client's needs.
- **Step 2: Information Gathering:** Discovery phase is another name for the information gathering stage. This is the most crucial stage of the website design and development process, where the designer brings the client's vision to life in the document. Understanding the goal of building a website, the target market, and the content they seek out are crucial in this step. Determining these factors at the foundational stage of website design is very important.
- **Step 3: Planning: Good Website is the Result of Good Planning:** Planning is crucial after obtaining information. Setting work priorities to finish a website is the essence of planning. The website's sitemap, which includes the navigational system, menu, and contents, is created in this step. is the development of the websites.
- **Step 4: Web Design:** A website's web design is what gives it a nice appearance, distinct feel, and uniqueness. This stage of the website design process is creative. This is the stage where designers work to create a visually appealing

and distinctive website. In order to attempt to sketch the client's expectations, the designer must comprehend every single detail. In this step, templates, logo design, etc. are found.

Figure 1.1. *Steps of website development process.*

Source: https://egyankosh.ac.in/bitstream/123456789/72091/1/Unit-7.pdf.

- **Step 5: Web Development:** Following design, there is a phase of development called the "implementing phase." This is the stage where the website is actually put into use. The website design is likewise greatly influenced by the development phase. All of the data gathered in the first phase is integrated in this phase, which includes, among other things, the creation of a database, logic, and actual programming.
- **Step 6: Testing:** There is a testing and discovery phase that follows the development phase. In this stage, quality assurance (QA) is in charge of creating the test cases and conducting the testing. The different kinds of website testing consist of. Testing of design, functionality, and content, among other things.
- **Step 7: Maintenance:** The final stage is called maintenance, during which time the website is only maintained for a short while. Updating the website's content and design is referred to as maintenance. The company offers the maintenance facility for a set period of time; if the user wishes to extend the service, there will be additional costs.

Keyword

Web Development – It is the work involved in developing a website for the Internet (World Wide Web) or an intranet (a private network).

Did you get it?

1. How good website planning can save time and money?
2. What do web designers do?

1.7. WEB FRAMEWORKS

→Learning Objectives
- Explain the types of framework architectures;
- Describe user authentication and session management.

A web framework is a software architecture intended to facilitate the creation of web applications, encompassing web resources, web services, and web application programming interfaces. A standardized method for creating and launching web applications on the Internet is offered by web frameworks. The goal of web frameworks is to automate web development overhead related to routine tasks. For instance, a lot of web frameworks encourage code reuse and offer libraries for templating frameworks, database access, and session management. They are useful for static websites as well, even though they frequently focus on the development of dynamic websites.

Initially, hand-coded HTML text files that were hosted on web servers made up early hypertext since the World Wide Web's design was not intrinsically dynamic. The author of each published page was responsible for making any changes. In order to provide a dynamic web page that reflected user inputs, the Common Gateway Interface (CGI) standard was introduced in 1993 for integrating external applications with web servers.

The CGI interface's initial implementations, however, usually negatively impacted server load because each request initiated a different process. Newer versions use persistent processes in addition to other methods to minimize the resource footprint of the server and provide overall performance improvements.

The first fully integrated server/language development environments and new web-specific languages, like ColdFusion, PHP, and Active Server Pages, were introduced in 1995.

While libraries for common tasks are available in the vast majority of languages used to create dynamic web pages, web applications frequently need specific libraries for tasks like HTML creation (e.g., Jakarta Server Faces).

Mature, "full stack" frameworks started to emerge in the late 1990s. These frameworks frequently combined several web development-related libraries into a single, seamless software stack that was accessible to web developers.

1.7.1. Types of Framework Architectures

The model-view-controller (MVC) pattern is the foundation of the majority of web frameworks:

1. **Model-View-Controller (MVC):** A lot of frameworks divide the data model into the user interface (the "view") and business rules (the "controller") using the MVC architectural pattern. Since it encourages code reuse, modularizes the code, and permits the application of multiple interfaces, this is generally regarded as a good practice. This enables the presentation of multiple views in web applications, such as providing distinct web pages for mobile vs. desktop browsers or offering web service interfaces that are readable by machines.

2. **Push-based vs. Pull-based:** Many MVC frameworks adhere to a push-based architecture, also known as "action-based." These frameworks employ actions to carry out the necessary processing and then send the data to the view layer to display the outcomes. On the other hand, there is an alternative called pull-based architecture, sometimes referred to as "component-based." In this approach, the frameworks begin with the view layer, allowing it to retrieve results from various controllers whenever necessary. This architecture enables multiple controllers to be connected to a single view.

3. **Three-Tier Organization:** Applications are organized around three physical tiers in a three-tier organization: client, application, and database. Typically, the database is an RDBMS. The application, which runs on a server and uses HTTP to communicate with the client, contains the business logic. A web browser that runs HTML produced by the application layer serves as the client for web applications. The phrase should not be confused with MVC, where it is recommended to separate business logic from the controller, or "middle layer," in contrast to three-tier architecture.

> **Keyword**
>
> **Common Gateway Interface (CGI)** – It is an interface specification that enables web servers to execute an external program to process HTTP/S user requests.

1.7.2. User Authentication and Session Management

Web frameworks typically already provide user account management, so further implementation is not necessary. Furthermore, frameworks can utilize user authentication to automatically verify and mandate the user's authentication for a specific page. By limiting access to specific pages to only relevant users, this improves website security. Web frameworks also provide a common interface for database or disk storage, making caching implementation simpler. This is very helpful for enhancing the web application's responsiveness.

1.7.3. Data Persistence

The majority of the data in dynamic web applications is generated from persistent data before it is shown to the user. Persistent data can be managed in a number of ways, such as by establishing a core object structure, which gives all data a common, fundamental interface. A unified API will also be made available so that data from various storage systems can be accessed fast. Additionally, some web frameworks allow data objects to be automatically stored and retrieved.

1.7.4. Administrative Interface

The administrator can manage users and permissions, as well as alter the site's content, through the administrative interface. Web framework creates a navigation structure to accomplish this. Additionally, common form field interface elements are provided by web frameworks. Additionally, it enables web developers to use persistent data structures to automatically create, edit, and list pages. In addition to the essential elements, web frameworks enable web developers to download and apply particular functionalities with great speed. The specific way this is implemented varies depending on the web framework. Using Drupal modules is one such implementation. PHP is used to write Drupal, a content management system (CMS) and content management framework (CMF). Drupal's standard release includes the fundamental CMS features. After that, users can download modules—community-contributed add-ons—from the website. Every module has a unique set of features, and you can add or remove any module at any time, and it will update instantly on the page.

1.7.5. Design Patterns

Every web framework has a foundational design pattern, we'll concentrate on the model-view-controller (MVC) pattern, which is the most widely utilized design pattern for web application frameworks. By separating the domain logic from the user interface, the MVC pattern introduces abstraction and makes it possible to divide concerns between the two (Figure 1.2).

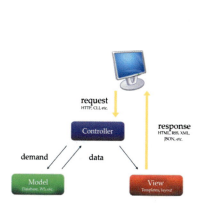
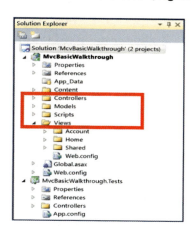

Figure 1.2. MVC model implementation in a web application.

Source: https://www.comp.nus.edu.sg/~seer/book/2e/Ch07.%20Web%20Development.pdf.

> **Keyword**
>
> **Model-View-Controller** – It is a software design pattern commonly used for developing user interfaces that divides the related program logic into three interconnected elements.

The MVC model's exact implementation in a web application created with a web framework is depicted in Figure 1.2. The framework's initial code responds to browser requests, like HTTP requests, and forwards them to the application controller. The controller then interacts with the model of the application, such as the database, to carry out the necessary operations. After that, the controller would give the response to the view so that it could be developed further. The client would then receive a copy of the response.

The existence of themes on websites is another illustration of structure. Web developers can rapidly integrate any web page theme and begin adding content to the web application by using web frameworks.

For every web framework, there are vast databases of themes that are tailored to a variety of uses and subjects. The web developer can reduce the amount of time spent coding in HTML or CSS by utilizing web page themes. Additionally, some web templates already have jQuery functionality included. All that's left to do for the web developer is tweak the application and add more features as needed.

1.7.6. Maintenance

The ability to maintain an existing web application is another fantastic benefit of web frameworks. First of all, it provides excellent extensibility, meaning that adding new features to any **web application** is incredibly simple. We've figured out how to accomplish this precisely in Drupal, where implementing particular functionalities only requires a checklist. Another way that web frameworks enhance maintenance is through the ongoing monitoring and correction of bugs that are typically present in the framework. Most web frameworks have extensive community support and are widely used, making it simple for users to track and report bugs. The bug can then be fixed by other users or developers. It enumerates the problem, its priority, and its current state. The issue can then be resolved by the module's developer or an authorized user, and all websites that use that specific module will also receive an update. This significantly reduces the amount of maintenance work needed.

Did you get it?

1. Describe MVC architectural pattern.
2. How to implement MVC model in a web application.

1.8. INGREDIENTS REQUIRED FOR WEBSITE DEVELOPMENT

→Learning Objectives
- Describe essential for the website;
- Understand multiple feedback channels.

The modern web is essentially unrecognizable from the days when it consisted solely of white pages with lists of blue links. These days, websites are planned with intricate layouts, superb fonts, and unique color palettes. Website interactivity is essential for remaining competitive, and incorporating some of these features calls for a more robust programming language. In reality, web design is a website's operation and the emotions it arouses in its visitors. With this enlarged viewpoint in mind, the following components—which are essential for the best website—are explained.

1. **Clean Navigation:** The site's navigation is what visitors notice right away. Excellent navigation makes it easy for users to navigate between pages and quickly find what they're looking for.
2. **Beautiful Typography:** Typography is a really big deal. A website that looks great always has beautiful typography. Typography starts with font choices, but goes far beyond into color, sizing, line height, paragraph margins and padding.
3. **White Space:** An amazing site requires proper spacing. It might even be the most crucial component. The spatial component of a message is just as important to its impact as its content. Without white space, a website will quickly become visually unappealing.
4. **Logical Layout:** Although the term "logical layout" is a little ambiguous, a website's connections must make sense. A well-designed layout will guide a potential customer through a journey while letting them go where they please. This is about making the appropriate presentation at the appropriate moment.
5. **Design with a Purpose:** The simplest design is the best design. This is a fundamental idea behind exquisitely designed websites. A great website should have everything working together cohesively to accomplish a single goal without

getting in the way of other things.

6. **Speed:** When it comes to the internet, speed wins. Consumers prefer to find what they need quickly and dislike having to wait around for it. Waiting to get the desired customers is essentially the same as losing forever. The website's speed needs to be properly considered; pages need to load quickly, and orders need to be fulfilled promptly.

7. **Detail:** The information that customers may search for on the website, such as product and service details, customer support information, etc., must be provided. The information offered must be simple to find and comprehensive enough to answer any questions prospective clients might have.

8. **Multiple Feedback Channels:** In order to enable visitors to quickly contact the relevant authority, the website should offer a variety of communication and feedback options, including a phone number, email address, live chat link, discussion board, and social media tools. In summary, the website should be excellent, but it should also highlight additional channels that make it simple for users to get in touch.

Did you get it?

1. What is the importance of website development?
2. How do you use typography on a website?

1.9. WEBSITE HOSTING

→Learning Objectives

- Explain the types of website hosting;
- Define web hosting alternatives.

One kind of Internet hosting service that lets people and businesses make their website accessible over the World Wide Web is called a web hosting service. Businesses that rent out their technologies and services to host websites on the internet are known as web hosts.

The hosting company allots space on a web server to hold the files. The files can be viewed online thanks to web hosting. Startups can concentrate on their apps and users by using web hosting, which offers the infrastructure and services needed to create, store, and launch globally accessible websites and web apps in the cloud.

Users can access the website by entering its web address, or domain name, in their web browser once it has been hosted by the hosting company. Their computer establishes a connection with the server that hosts the website when they take this action. In a practice known as co-location, web hosts can also offer data center space and Internet access to other servers housed in their data center. Web hosting is required for every website on the internet. The IP address of the web hosting company's computer is displayed when a user inputs the domain name into a browser. The files from the website are stored on this computer, which then forwards them to the users' browsers.

1.9.1. Types of Website Hosting

The different kinds of web hosting services are described in more detail below:

1. **Shared Hosting:** Entry-level website hosting is ideal for shared hosting. All domains using a shared hosting plan have access to the same server resources, including CPU (central processing unit) and RAM (random access memory). Shared hosting plans, however, are comparatively inexpensive because all resources are pooled, which makes them a great choice for novice website owners. Even so, website owners who use shared hosting benefit from a more straightforward online experience. This implies that the user experience on the website may eventually be impacted by spikes in usage. For website owners who do not receive a lot of traffic, shared hosting plans are perfect.

2. **Virtual Private Server (VPS) Hosting:** The best compromise between a dedicated server and a shared server is a virtual private server (VPS) hosting package. For website owners who require more control but do not necessarily require a dedicated server, it is perfect. Because each website is hosted in a separate area on the server, even though it still shares a physical server with other users, VPS hosting is distinct from other hosting options. Website owners can increase their customization and storage capacity with VPS hosting. Website owners who desire dedicated hosting but lack the necessary technical know-how typically use VPS hosting.

3. **Dedicated Server Hosting:** The most control over the server that hosts a website is provided by dedicated hosting. Dedicated servers are among the priciest web hosting solutions. Those who require total control over their servers and website owners with substantial website traffic are the main users of them. Additionally, the server's installation and continued management call for a high degree of technical proficiency. Since the user has complete administrative access to the server, the client is in charge of keeping his own dedicated server secure and up to date.

4. **Cloud Hosting:** The newest buzzword in the tech sector is cloud hosting. In the context of Web hosting, it refers to a large number of computers cooperating to run applications using their combined processing power. This eliminates the need for users to create and maintain their own computing infrastructure by enabling them to use as many resources as necessary. Because the resources are being distributed among multiple servers, there is less likelihood of any downtime brought on by a server malfunction. Because cloud-based hosting is scalable, a website can expand over time and use as many resources as necessary, with the website owner only having to pay for what they really need.

5. **Managed Hosting:** The user receives their own Web server, but they are not granted full control over it (root access for Linux, administrator access for Windows). Nevertheless, they can use other remote management tools, such as FTP, to manage their data. Complete control is denied to the user in order for the provider to ensure that the user won't change the server configuration or possibly cause issues with it. Usually, the user does not possess the server. The client leases the server.

6. **Co-Location Web Hosting Service:** Similar to dedicated web hosting, co-location web hosting allows users to own their co-servers; the hosting company provides the physical space needed for the server and manages it. This kind of web hosting service is the most potent and costly. Typically, the co-location provider merely offers the server's power, Internet access, and storage, with little to no direct support for the client's computer.

7. **Clustered Hosting:** Cluster hosting is an effective method of hosting where multiple servers are used to host the same content, resulting in improved utilization of resources. Clustered servers are an ideal choice for dedicated hosting with high availability or for creating a web hosting solution that can scale up easily. In a cluster setup, web serving and database hosting can be separated,

allowing for better efficiency. Shared hosting plans offered by web hosts often employ clustered hosting as it offers numerous advantages in managing a large number of clients.

8. **Grid Hosting:** It is a type of distributed hosting that is used when a server cluster, which is made up of several nodes, functions similarly to a grid and offers grid computing capabilities to its clients. Grid hosting reduces the possibility that a surge in resource requirements will force a website offline, much like cluster hosting does.

1.9.2. Web Hosting Alternatives

These days, websites are a crucial part of business. Website hosting might not be possible because of infrastructure, funding, technology, and ongoing updates. Content is stored on the web server (host) of the hosting company, which is known as web hosting. The host has dedicated IP addresses, power, and internet access, and it can be located anywhere in the world. The hardware and software required to provide connections via the Internet, Intranet, and Extranet are all present in the data center. When a client uses a co-location service—also spelled co-location—the service provider rents them a physical location where they can set up their own server hardware. With these features, your website is accessible 365 days a year. The service provider is responsible for maintaining the Web server hardware and software and provides the connection to the Internet through its routers and other network hardware. Since the whole world is moving from brick & Mortar system to click & Mortar system and due the usage of Smartphone the app-based business restricts to mobile hence the app is taken as a replacement to websites.

Did you get it?

1. What do you understand by internet hosting service?
2. What is a virtual private server (VPS)?

A CLOSER LOOK

- **World of Web Development:** In today's digital age, web developers play a significant role in crafting the online world. They are the individuals behind websites and web applications that shape our digital experiences. But what does it really mean to be a web developer, and what does this profession entail? Let's dive into the basics of what it means to be a web developer.
  - **The Language of the Web:** Web developers work with languages like HTML, CSS, and JavaScript, which they use to construct the structure, style, and functionality of websites. Utilizing these languages is the base of developing anything on the web, however, working from scratch is not always the best approach. Web Developers must also familiarize themselves with existing tools and platforms to achieve the desired result in the most efficient and functional way possible.

- **Front and Backstage Roles:** Web development encompasses two primary roles – front-end and back-end. Front-end developers focus on the visual aspects and visible functionality of a website, while back-end developers handle the behind-the-scenes aspects like servers, databases, and application logic. Many times, depending on the complexity of the project, these two types of development must work side by side to create seamless functionality and experience.

- **Problem Solving:** Web developers are constantly troubleshooting, debugging, reworking, and planning creative solutions to keep projects on track. This can be both the most rewarding and frustrating part of their job. Websites can feel unpredictable and complex. This means that it is crucial for a developer to understand all the inner workings of their project so that they can be ready to take action when something goes wrong.

- **The Journey of Constant Learning:** The digital landscape is in constant flux, and web developers must adapt to new tools, frameworks, and trends. This ongoing learning ensures their work remains relevant and up to date. Though this can seem a bit daunting, this is how many developers stay excited about their work.
- **Collaboration at Heart:** Web development is rarely a solitary endeavor. Developers work collaboratively with designers, project managers, clients, and many others to bring projects to life. Effective communication and teamwork are essential.
- **Paying Attention to the Details:** Detail-oriented by necessity, web developers carefully check their work. Even minor code or design issues can lead to errors. Much of being a web developer is not only building but maintaining websites. This means every time they go back to update a website, they must make sure that everything is double, or triple checked. Many aspects of a website or web application are intertwined, meaning changes in one thing could lead to unintentional changes somewhere else in the application.

Being a web developer can be an exciting and fulfilling career path. Every project gives you an interesting glimpse into a new industry. Being a web developer requires technical knowledge, the ability to see the big picture, the patience to pay attention to small details, and the ability to work with others. Though it can be difficult and frustrating sometimes, it is an ever-changing and exciting world to be a part of.

ROLE MODEL

TIM BERNERS-LEE: KNOWN FOR INVENTION OF THE WORLD WIDE WEB

Tim Berners-Lee is a British computer scientist. He is said to be the inventor of the World Wide Web. The World Wide Web allows people to see Web sites on a computer.

Berners-Lee proposed an information management system on 12 March 1989 and implemented the first successful communication between a Hypertext Transfer Protocol (HTTP) client and server via the Internet in mid-November. He devised and implemented the first Web browser and Web server and helped foster the Web's subsequent explosive development. He is the founder and director of the World Wide Web Consortium (W3C), which oversees the continued development of the Web. He co-founded (with Rosemary Leith) the World Wide Web Foundation. In April 2009, he was elected as Foreign Associate of the National Academy of Sciences.

- **Early Life:** Berners-Lee was born on June 8, 1955, in London, England. His parents were mathematicians and worked on the first commercial computer at the University of Manchester. As a child, Berners-Lee was fascinated by computers. He also enjoyed mathematics and electronics. He attended the University of Oxford and graduated in 1976 with a degree in physics.
- **Career:** Berners-Lee began his career as a computer software designer. He moved on to other positions in the computer industry. He worked at CERN, a physics laboratory in Geneva, Switzerland. While at CERN, Berners-Lee worked on a system that would allow different computers to communicate with each other. In 1989 he wrote a proposal for a system that would allow researchers to share and retrieve techniques, practices, and results with each other at any time using the Internet. He created the software for the World Wide Web in 1990–91.
- In 1994 Berners-Lee formed the World Wide Web Consortium (W3C) at the Massachusetts Institute of Technology, where he is a professor. He also co-wrote Weaving the Web: The Original Design and Ultimate Destiny of the World Wide Web by Its Inventor (1999).
- Awards and Honors: Berners-Lee was elected a fellow in the Royal Society in 2001. He was knighted by Queen Elizabeth II in 2004 and was awarded the Order of Merit in 2007. In 2004 Berners-Lee received the first Millennium Technology Prize, awarded by the Finnish Technology Award Foundation. He was inducted into the Internet Hall of Fame in 2012.

SUMMARY

- The navigation of the website, which typically begins with the home page, is guided by hyperlinks between web pages.
- The process of creating and managing websites is known as web development.
- A website is an assemblage of web pages and related materials that are published on at least one web server, recognized by a general domain name.
- In 1989, Tim Berners-Lee and his associates at CERN, an international scientific organization situated in Geneva, Switzerland, started working on the creation of the World Wide Web (WWW).
- The ease of access to the internet has made it possible for businesses to reach a wider audience and create new categories of web users as a result of the widespread use of mobile phones.
- The HTTP protocol facilitates the retrieval of resources, including HTML documents. It is the basis for all data exchange on the Internet and is a client-server protocol, meaning that the Web browser, or other recipient, initiates requests.
- An expansion of the Hypertext Transfer Protocol is the Hypertext Transfer Protocol Secure. It is popular on the Internet and used for safe computer network communication.
- A web framework is a software architecture intended to facilitate the creation of web applications, encompassing web resources, web services, and web application programming interfaces.
- For every web framework, there are vast databases of themes that are tailored to a variety of uses and subjects.
- One kind of Internet hosting service that lets people and businesses make their website accessible over the World Wide Web is called a web hosting service.

MULTIPLE CHOICE QUESTION

1. Which of the following factors can influence website usage statistics?
   a. User demographics;
   b. Website design;
   c. Content quality;
   d. All of the above.
2. Which port is typically used by HTTP?
   a. 80;
   b. 443;
   c. 8080;
   d. 22.

3. Which statement accurately describes the difference between HTTP and HTTPS?
   a. HTTP uses encryption while HTTPS does not;
   b. HTTPS uses encryption while HTTP does not;
   c. HTTP and HTTPS both use encryption;
   d. HTTP and HTTPS are completely unrelated protocols.
4. Which type of website primarily focuses on providing information and resources related to a specific topic or subject?
   a. Social networking website;
   b. E-commerce website;
   c. Educational website;
   d. Blogging website.
5. Which of the following is NOT a step in the website development process?
   a. Design;
   b. Testing;
   c. Deployment;
   d. Debugging.
6. Which of the following is NOT a web framework?
   a. Django;
   b. Flask;
   c. React;
   d. Ruby on rails.
7. Which of the following are essential ingredients for website development?
   a. Flour and eggs;
   b. HTML, CSS, and JavaScript;
   c. Milk and sugar;
   d. Paint and brushes.
8. What is a key component required for hosting a website?
   a. Database;
   b. HTML coding skills;
   c. A domain name;
   d. A library card.

REVIEW QUESTIONS

1. Briefly explain the origin of the website.
2. What are the various types of websites?

3. State the usages of websites.
4. State the differences between HTTP and HTTPs.
5. State the various phases of the website development process.
6. What are the various ingredients required for making a website?
7. What is web hosting? What are the various types of web hosting?

Answer to Multiple Choice Questions

1. (d); 2. (a); 3. (b); 4. (c); 5. (d); 6. (c); 7. (b); 8. (c)

REFERENCES

1. Al-Fedaghi, S., (2009). Flow-based description of conceptual and design levels. *IEEE International Conference on Computer Engineering and Technology*. Singapore.
2. Allen, C., Balkan, A. Grden, J., Arnold, W., & Cannasse, N., (2008). *The Essential Guide to Open Source Flash Development*. New York, NY A Press.
3. Canne, T., (2011). *Product-Focused Software Process Improvement: 12th International Conference, PROFES 2011: Lecture Notes in Computer Science / Programming and Software Engineering Series* (Vol. 6759). Italy: Springer Ltd.
4. Chai, L. G., (2012). The impact of website development on organization performance: Malaysia's perspective. *African Journal of Business Management, 6*(7), 22, 2435–2448.
5. De Castro, V., Vara, J. V., & Marcos, E., (2007). Model transformation for service-oriented web applications development. In: W*orkshop Proceedings of 7th International Conference on Web Engineering* (pp. 184–198).
6. Dewsbuy, G., Bruce, T., & Martin, E., (2001). *Design in Safe Smart Home Systems for Vulnerable People*. The 1st Dependability IRC Workshop.
7. Foster, H., Uchitel, H. S., Magee, J., & Kramer, J., (2003). Model-based verification of web service compositions. In: *18th IEEE International Conference on Automated Software Engineering*. Montreal, Canada.
8. Jovanovich, D., & Dogsa, T., (2003). Comparison of software development models. *Proceedings of the 7th International Conference* (pp. 587–592).
9. Koch, S., (2005). *Free/Open Source Software Development*. Pennsylvania, PA: Idea Group Publishers. Press.
10. Laura, C. R. M., Manuel, M., & Francisco, J. A., (2009). A descriptive/comparative study of the evolution of process models of software development life cycles. *Proceedings of the 2009 Mexican International Conference on Computer Science,* IEEE Computer Society Washington, DC, USA.
11. Meeker, H. J., (2008). *The Open Source Alternative: Understanding Risks and Leveraging Opportunities*. New Jersey, NJ: John Wiley & Sons Inc. Press.
12. Peng, W., & Cisna, J., (2000). HTTP cookies – a promising technology. *Online Information Review, 24*(2).

13. Walt, S., (2001). Process models in software engineering. Institute for Software Research, University of California, Irvine February 2001 Revised Version, May 2001, October 2001 Final Version to appear. In: Marciniak, J. J., (ed.), *Encyclopedia of Software Engineering* (2nd edn.). John Wiley and Sons, Inc, New York.

CHAPTER 2
HTML (HyperText Markup Language)

LEARNING OBJECTIVES

After studying this chapter, you will be able to:

- Explain the basics of HTML;
- Define the HTML tags;
- Describe the elements of HTML;
- Know HTML – attributes;
- Deal with HTML list classes;
- Discuss on HTML list types;
- Understand HTML formatting;
- Discuss the graphics to HTML document;
- Create tables using HTML

INTRODUCTORY EXAMPLE

Semantic HTML: With over 100 HTML elements, and the ability to create custom elements, there are infinite ways to mark up your content; but some ways—notably semantically—are better than others.

FUNDAMENTALS OF WEB DEVELOPMENT

Semantic means "relating to meaning." Writing semantic HTML means using HTML elements to structure your content based on each element's meaning, not its appearance.

This series hasn't covered many HTML elements yet, but even without knowing HTML, the following two code snippets show how semantic markup can give content context. Both use a word count instead of ipsum lorem to save some scrolling—use your imagination to expand "thirty words" into 30 words:

The first code snippet uses <div> and <span>, two elements with no semantic value.

```
<div>
<span>Three words</span>
<div>
<a>one word</a>
<a>one word</a>
<a>one word</a>
<a>one word</a>
</div>
</div>
<div>
<div>
<div>five words</div>
</div>
<div>
<div>three words</div>
<div>forty-six words</div>
<div>forty-four words</div>
</div>
<div>
<div>seven words</h2>
<div>sixty-eight words</div>
<div>forty-four words</div>
</div>
```

```
</div>
<div>
<span>five words</span>
</div>
```

Let's rewrite this code with semantic elements:

```
<header>
<h1>Three words</h1>
<nav>
<a>one word</a>
<a>one word</a>
<a>one word</a>
<a>one word</a>
</nav>
</header>
<main>
<header>
<h1>five words</h1>
</header>
<section>
<h2>three words</h2>
<p>forty-six words</p>
<p>forty-four words</p>
</section>
<section>
<h2>seven words</h2>
<p>sixty-eight words</p>
<p>forty-four words</p>
</section>
</main>
<footer>
<p>five words</p>
</footer>
```

2.1. UNIT INTRODUCTION

The standard markup language for documents intended for web browser display is called HyperText Markup Language, or HTML. It outlines the components and organization of web content. Programming languages like JavaScript and technologies like Cascading Style Sheets (CSS) frequently help with it.

Web browsers transform HTML documents into multimedia web pages after receiving them from a web server or local storage. Originally, HTML included cues for a page's appearance and provided a semantic description of the page's structure.

The fundamental units of an HTML page are HTML elements. Images and other objects, like interactive forms, can be embedded into the rendered page by using HTML constructs. By indicating structural semantics for text elements like headings, paragraphs, lists, links, quotes, and other items, HTML offers a way to create structured documents. Tags, which are written in angle brackets, are used to distinguish HTML elements. Tags such as <img> and <input> directly introduce content into the page. Other tags such as <p> and </p> surround and provide information about document text and may include sub-element tags. Browsers do not display the HTML tags but use them to interpret the content of the page.

Programs written in scripting languages like JavaScript can be embedded into HTML pages, changing their content and behavior. The appearance and organization of content are defined by the use of CSS. Since 1997, the World Wide Web Consortium (W3C), the organization that formerly oversaw the HTML standards and is currently in charge of the CSS standards, has promoted the usage of CSS over explicit presentational HTML. A form of HTML, known as HTML5, is used to display video and audio, primarily using the <canvas> element, together with JavaScript.

2.2. BASICS OF HTML

→Learning Objectives
- Describes the structure of Web pages using markup;
- Discuss the building blocks of HTML pages.

The collection of markup symbols or codes called HTML (Hypertext Markup Language) is added to a file with the intention of displaying it on a World Wide Web browser page. The markup instructs the Web browser on how to present the text and images on a Web page to the user. An element is a single piece of markup code (though many people also refer to it as a tag). Certain elements come in pairs that show the start and stop times of display effects.

The language used to create webpages is called HTML. The term "Hypertext" describes the hyperlinks that can be present on an HTML page. "Markup language" is the term used to describe the elements and page layout that are defined by tags.

An example of how to define a simple webpage with a title and one paragraph of text can be found below in HTML.

```
<!doctype html>

<html>

<head>

<title>TechTerms.com</title>

</head>

<body>

<p>This is an example of a paragraph in HTML.</p>

</body>

</html>
```

The first line defines what type of contents the document contains. "<!doctype html>" means the page is written in HTML5. Properly formatted HTML pages should include <html>, <head>, and <body> tags, which are all included in the example above. The page title, metadata, and links to referenced files are placed between the <head> tags. The actual contents of the page go between the <body> tags.

Over the past few decades, the web has undergone many changes, but HTML has remained the core language for creating webpages. Interestingly, HTML has gotten easier even though websites have become more sophisticated and interactive.

An HTML5 page would most likely have less code in its source when compared to a similar page written in XHTML 1.0 or HTML 4.01. This is due to the fact that almost every element on a page in modern HTML is formatted using either JavaScript or cascading style sheets.

- HTML is the standard markup language for creating Web pages.
- HTML stands for Hyper Text Markup Language.
- HTML describes the structure of Web pages using markup.
- HTML elements are the building blocks of HTML pages.
- HTML elements are represented by tags.
- HTML tags label pieces of content such as "heading," "paragraph," "table," and so on.
- Browsers do not display the HTML tags but use them to render the content of the page.

Keyword

Page Title – It is the title of a web page as it appears at the top of the browser window and in search engine results.

Example:

```
<!DOCTYPE html>
<html>
<head>
<title>Page Title</title>
</head>
<body>
<h1>My First Heading</h1>
<p>My first paragraph.</p>
</body>
</html>
```

Example Explained:

The <!DOCTYPE html> declaration defines this document to be HTML5

HTML (HYPERTEXT MARKUP LANGUAGE)

The <html> element is the root element of an HTML page

The <head> element contains meta information about the document

The <title> element specifies a title for the document

The <body> element contains the visible page content

The <h1> element defines a large heading

The <p> element defines a paragraph

Did you get it?

1. What are the basic rules of HTML?
2. Explain the structure of an HTML document.

2.3. HTML TAGS

→Learning Objectives
- Define heading tags;
- Explain line break tag.

HTML tags function similarly to keywords in that they specify how a web browser will format and present content. Web browsers are capable of telling the difference between simple and HTML content thanks to tags. Three main components make up an HTML tag: the opening tag, the content tag, and the closing tag.

However, some tags in HTML are not closed. When reading an HTML document, a web browser scans it from left to right and top to bottom. To create HTML documents and render their properties, use HTML tags. The properties of each HTML tag vary. A web browser needs to recognize certain essential tags in an HTML file in order to distinguish between plain text and HTML text. Depending on your code requirements, you can use as many tags as you like.

Did you know?

After the HTML and HTML+ drafts expired in early 1994, the IETF created an HTML Working Group. In 1995, this working group completed "HTML 2.0," the first HTML specification intended to be treated as a standard against which future implementations should be based.

2.3.1. Heading Tags

Example:

```
<!DOCTYPE html>
<html>
<head>
<title>Heading Example</title>
</head>
<body>
```

```
<h1>This is heading 1</h1>
<h2>This is heading 2</h2>
<h3>This is heading 3</h3>
<h4>This is heading 4</h4>
<h5>This is heading 5</h5>
<h6>This is heading 6</h6>
</body>
</html>
```

This will produce following result:

This is heading 1
This is heading 2
This is heading 3
This is heading 4
This is heading 5
This is heading 6

> **Keyword**
>
> **Closing Tag** – It is an instructional piece of code that ends a section of page content. It's nearly the same as an opening tag (e.g., "<p>") but it has a forward slash (e.g., "</p>") to let browsers know where to start and end different elements.

2.3.2. Paragraph Tag

The <p> tag offers a way to structure your text into different paragraphs. Each paragraph of text should go in between an opening <p> and a closing </p> tag as shown below in the example:

The <p> tag offers a way to structure your text into different paragraphs. Each paragraph of text should go in between an opening <p> and a closing </p> tag as shown below in the example:

Example:

```
<!DOCTYPE html>
<html>
<head>
<title>Paragraph Example</title>
</head>
<body>
```

```
<p>Here is a first paragraph of text.</p>

<p>Here is a second paragraph of text.</p>

<p>Here is a third paragraph of text.</p>

</body>

</html>
```

This will produce following result:

Here is a first paragraph of text.

Here is a second paragraph of text.

Here is a third paragraph of text.

2.3.3. Line Break Tag

Whenever you use the `<br/>` element, anything following it starts from the next line. This tag is an example of an empty element, where you do not need opening and closing tags, as there is nothing to go in between them.

The `<br/>` tag has a space between the characters 'br' and the forward slash. If you omit this space, older browsers will have trouble rendering the line break, while if you miss the forward slash character and just use `<br>` it is not valid in XHTML

Example:

```
<!DOCTYPE html>

<html>

<head>

<title>Line Break Example</title>

</head>

<body>

<p>Hello<br/>

You delivered your assignment ontime.<br/>

Thanks<br/>

Mahnaz</p>

</body>

</html>
```

This will produce following result:

Hello

You delivered your assignment on time.

Thanks

Mahnaz

- *Centering Content*: You can use <center> tag to put any content in the center of the page or any table cell.

Example:

```
<!DOCTYPE html>
<html>
<head>
<title>Centering Content Example</title>
</head>
<body>
<p>This text is not in the center.</p>
<center>
<p>This text is in the center.</p>
</center>
</body>
</html>
```

This will produce following result:

This text is not in the center.

This text is in the center.

2.3.4. Horizontal Lines

A document's sections can be visually divided using horizontal lines. The <hr> tag creates a line from the current position in the document to the right margin and breaks the line accordingly.

One possible approach would be to insert a line, as in the example below, to separate two paragraphs.

FUNDAMENTALS OF WEB DEVELOPMENT

Example:

```
<!DOCTYPE html>
<html>
<head>
<title>Horizontal Line Example</title>
</head>
<body>
<p>This is paragraph one and should be on top</p>
<hr/>
<p>This is paragraph two and should be at bottom</p>
</body>
</html>
```

This will produce following result:

This is paragraph one and should be on top

This is paragraph two and should be at bottom

Again <hr/> tag is an example of the empty element, where you do not need opening and closing tags, as there is nothing to go in between them.

The <hr/> element has a space between the characters 'hr' and the forward slash. If you omit this space, older browsers will have trouble rendering the Horizontal line, while if you miss the forward slash character and just use <hr> it is not valid in XHTML.

2.3.5. Preserve Formatting

There are times when you want your text to have the exact same format as the HTML document. In those cases, you can use the preformatted tag <pre>.

Any text between the opening <pre> tag and the closing </pre> tag will preserve the formatting of the source document.

Example:

<!DOCTYPE html>

> **Remember**
>
> In cases where you do not want the client browser to break text, you should use a nonbreaking space entity   instead of a normal space.

```
<html>
<head>
<title>Preserve Formatting Example</title>
</head>
<body>
<pre>
function testFunction(strText){
alert (strText)
}
</pre>
</body>
</html>
```

This will produce following result:

```
function testFunction(strText){
alert (strText)
}
```

Try using same code without keeping it inside <pre>...</pre> tags

2.3.6. Nonbreaking Spaces

Let's say you wish to say "12 Angry Men." Here, you wouldn't want the words "12, Angry" and "Men" to appear on two lines in a browser.

An example of this technique appears in the movie "12 Angry Men."

For example, when coding the "12 Angry Men" in a paragraph, you should use something similar to the following code:

Example:

```
<!DOCTYPE html>
<html>
<head>
<title>Nonbreaking Spaces Example</title>
```

```
</head>

<body>

<p>An example of this technique appears in the movie "12 Angry Men."</p>

</body>

</html>
```

This will produce the following result:

An example of this technique appears in the movie "12 Angry Men."

Did you get it?

1. What is the meaning of </p>?
2. What do you understand by preserve formatting?

2.4. ELEMENTS OF HTML

→Learning Objectives
- Understand nested HTML elements;
- Describe empty HTML elements.

After being parsed into the Document Object Model, an HTML element is a single part of an HTML document or web page. A tree of HTML nodes, including text nodes, makes up HTML. It is possible to specify HTML attributes for each node. Nodes may also contain text and other nodes as content. Many HTML nodes stand for meaning or semantics. The document's title, for instance, is represented by the title node.

An HTML element typically has two tags, a start tag and an end tag, and content inserted between them.

<tagname>Content goes here...</tagname>

The HTML element is everything from the start tag to the end tag:

<p>My first paragraph.</p>

2.4.1. Nested HTML Elements

HTML elements can be nested (elements can contain elements).

All HTML documents consist of nested HTML elements.

This example contains four HTML elements:

Example:

<!DOCTYPE html>

<html>

<body>

<h1>My First Heading</h1>

<p>My first paragraph.</p>

```
</body>

</html>
```

Example Explained:

The <html> element defines the whole document.

It has a start tag <html> and an end tag </html>.

The element content is another HTML element (the <body> element).

```
<html>

<body>

<h1>My First Heading</h1>

<p>My first paragraph.</p>

</body>

</html>
```

The <body> element defines the document body.

It has a start tag <body> and an end tag </body>.

The element content is two other HTML elements (<h1> and <p>).

```
<body>

<h1>My First Heading</h1>

<p>My first paragraph.</p>

</body>
```

The <h1> element defines a heading.

It has a start tag <h1> and an end tag </h1>.

The element content is: My First Heading.

```
<h1>My First Heading</h1>
```

The <p> element defines a paragraph.

It has a start tag <p> and an end tag </p>.

The element content is: My first paragraph.

```
<p>My first paragraph.</p>
```

> **Keyword**
>
> **HTML Document** – It is a text document saved with the extension .html or .htm that contains texts and some tags written between "< >" which give the instructions needed to configure the web page.

Do Not Forget the End Tag

Some HTML elements will display correctly, even if you forget the end tag:

Example:

```
<html>
<body>
<p>This is a paragraph
<p>This is a paragraph
</body>
</html>
```

2.4.2. Empty HTML Elements

Elements in HTML that are empty are those that contain no content.

 is an empty element without a closing tag (the <br> tag defines a line break).

    Empty elements can be "closed" in the opening tag like this: <br/>.

    HTML5 does not require the closure of empty elements. However, you must correctly close all HTML elements if you require stricter validation or if you need to make your document readable by XML parsers.

Did you get it?

1. How to select elements nested within an element?
2. What are empty tags in HTML?

2.5. HTML – ATTRIBUTES

→Learning Objectives
- Define core attribute;
- Discuss about internationalization attributes.

We have seen few HTML tags and their usage like heading tags <h1>, <h2>, paragraph tag <p> and other tags. We used them so far in their simplest form, but most of the HTML tags can also have attributes, which are extra bits of information.

An attribute is inserted inside the opening tag of an HTML element and is used to specify its properties. Every attribute consists of two components: a name and a value. Case insensitivity does not apply to attribute names or values. Nevertheless, in their HTML 4 recommendation, the World Wide Web Consortium (W3C) suggests using lowercase attributes and attribute values.

Example:

```
<!DOCTYPE html>
<html>
<head>
<title>Align Attribute Example</title>
</head>

<body>
<p align = "left">This is left aligned</p>
<p align = "center">This is center aligned</p>
<p align = "right">This is right aligned</p>
</body>
</html>
```

This will display the following result:

This is left aligned

This is canter aligned

This is right aligned

2.5.1. Core Attributes

Most HTML elements (but not all) can use the following four fundamental attributes:

- Id;
- Title;
- Class;
- Style.

2.5.1.1. The Id Attribute

Any element on an HTML page can be uniquely identified using the id attribute of an HTML tag. You might want to apply an id attribute to an element for two main reasons–

- If an element carries an id attribute as a unique identifier, it is possible to identify just that element and its content.
- If you have two elements of the same name within a Web page (or style sheet), you can use the id attribute to distinguish between elements that have the same name.

> **Keyword**
> **HTML Attribute** – It is a piece of markup language used to adjust the behavior or display of an HTML element.

Example:

<p id = "html">This para explains what is HTML</p>

<p id = "css">This para explains what is Cascading Style Sheet</p>

2.5.1.2. The Title Attribute

The element's suggested title is provided by the title attribute. The title attribute's syntax is the same as that of the id attribute–

Although it is frequently shown as a tooltip when the cursor is over the element or while the element is loading, the behavior of this attribute depends on the element that carries it.

Example:

<!DOCTYPE html>

```
<html>
<head>
<title>The title Attribute Example</title>
</head>
<body>
<h3 title = "Hello HTML!">Titled Heading Tag Example</h3>
</body>
</html>
```

This will produce the following result:

Titled Heading Tag Example

Try highlighting "Titled Heading Tag Example" with your cursor now, and you should notice that the title you entered in your code appears as a tooltip.

2.5.1.3. The Class Attribute

The class attribute indicates the type of element and is used to link it to a style sheet. When you learn about Cascading Style Sheets (CSS), you will become more familiar with the use of the class attribute. For the time being, you can avoid it.

The value of the attribute may also be a space-separated list of class names. For example:

```
class = "className1 className2 className3"
```

2.5.1.4. The Style Attribute

The style attribute allows you to specify Cascading Style Sheet (CSS) rules within the element.

```
<!DOCTYPE html>
<html>
<head>
<title>The style Attribute</title>
</head>
<body>
<p style = "font-family:arial; color:#FF0000;">Some text...</p>
```

</body>

</html>

This will produce the following result:

Some text...

Since we are not studying CSS at this time, let's move on without giving it any thought. Here, you must comprehend the meaning of HTML attributes and how to apply them to content formatting.

2.5.2. Internationalization Attributes

The majority of XHTML elements support the three internationalization attributes, though not all of them do:

- dir;
- lang;
- xml:lang.

2.5.2.1. The Dir Attribute

You can tell the browser which direction the text should flow in by using the dir attribute. The following table shows you the two possible values for the dir attribute:

Value	Meaning
ltr	Left to right (the default value).
rtl	Right to left (for languages such as Hebrew or Arabic that are read right to left).

Example:

<!DOCTYPE html>

<html dir = "rtl">

<head>

<title>Display Directions</title>

</head>

<body>

This is how IE 5 renders right-to-left directed text.

</body>

```
</html>
```

This will produce the following result:

This is how IE 5 renders right-to-left directed text.

When dir attribute is used within the <html> tag, it determines how text will be presented within the entire document. When used within another tag, it controls the text's direction for just the content of that tag.

2.5.2.2. The Lang Attribute

The main language used in a document can be indicated using the lang attribute; however, HTML only retains this attribute for backwards compatibility with previous HTML versions. In newer XHTML documents, the xml:lang attribute has taken the place of this attribute. The two-character ISO-639 standard language codes are the values of the lang attribute. For an exhaustive list of language codes, see HTML Language Codes: ISO 639.

Example:

```
<!DOCTYPE html>
<html lang = "en">
<head>
<title>English Language Page</title>
</head>
<body>
This page is using English Language
</body>
</html>
```

This will produce the following result:

This page is using English Language

2.5.2.3. The xml:lang Attribute

The XHTML equivalent of the lang attribute is the xml:lang attribute. An ISO-639 country code is what the xml:lang attribute should have as its value.

> **Did you get it?**
> 1. Which attributes can be used for all elements in HTML?
> 2. Which attribute can be added to most XHTML elements to identify?

2.6. HTML LIST CLASSES

→Learning Objectives
- Describe OrderedList and OrderedListItem;
- Understand UnorderedList and UnorderedListItem.

You can easily create lists inside of your HTML pages with the HTML List classes. These classes offer methods for getting and setting different lists' and lists' items' attributes.

Specifically, the parent class HTML List offers a way to generate a condensed list that arranges items in the smallest possible vertical space:

- Methods for HTML List include:
    - Compact the list;
    - Add and remove items from the list;
    - Add and remove lists from the list (making it possible to nest lists).
- Methods for HTML List Item include:
    - Get and set the contents of the item;
    - Get and set the direction of the text interpretation;
    - Get and set the language of the input element.

To create your HTML lists, use the HTML List and HTML List Item subclasses:

- OrderedList and OrderedListItem
- UnorderedList and UnorderedListItem

2.6.1. OrderedList and OrderedListItem

To create ordered lists in your HTML pages, use the OrderedList and OrderedListItem classes.

Methods for OrderedList include:
- Get and set the starting number for the first item in the list;
- Get and set the type (or style) for the item numbers.

Methods for OrderedListItem include:

- Get and set the number for the item;
- Get and set the type (or style) for the item number.

Did you know?

By using the methods in OrderedListItem, you can override the numbering and type for a specific item in the list.

2.6.2. UnorderedList and UnorderedListItem

To create unordered lists in your HTML pages, use the UnorderedList and UnorderedListItem classes.

Methods for UnorderedList include:

- Get and set the type (or style) for the items

Did you get it?

1. Explain the methods for HTML list.
2. Create unordered lists in your HTML pages.

2.7. HTML LIST TYPES

→Learning Objectives
- Define unordered list;
- Explain ordered list.

When creating a page, HTML offers three different types of lists: unordered, ordered, and definition lists. Unordered lists are made up of items for which the order is not crucial. On the other hand, ordered lists give great weight to item order. Definition lists are available when there is a list of terms and their descriptions, possibly for a glossary.

2.7.1. Unordered List

Unordered lists are just collections of related items without any sort of numbered or alphabetical list element; their order is irrelevant. The unordered list, ul, block level element in HTML is used to create an unordered list. The list item, li, block level element is used to mark up each list item individually within an unordered list.

Example:

```
<ul>
  <li>Tamilnadu</li>
  <li>Uttar Pradesh</li>
  <li>West-Bengal</li>
</ul>
```

2.7.2. Ordered List

When it comes to how each individual list item is created, the ordered list element, or ol, functions exactly like the unordered list element. An ordered list differs from an unordered list primarily in that it takes into account the representational order of the items in the list. An ordered list uses numbers as the default list item element rather than a dot. These numbers can then be converted to letters, Roman numerals, and other characters using CSS.

Example:

```
<ol type="1">
  <li>Tamilnadu</li>
  <li>Uttar Pradesh</li>
  <li>West-Bengal</li>
</ol>
```

2.7.3. Definition List

The dl element in HTML is used to create a definition list. The definition list actually requires two elements: the definition description element (dd) and the definition term element (dt), which are used to mark up list items instead of using the li element.

Several terms and definitions could appear one after the other in a list of definitions. Furthermore, there could be more than one term in a definition list and more than one description for each term. A single term may be defined differently depending on its context. On the other hand, one description might work for several terms.

<dl>

<dt>study</dt>

<dd>the devotion of time and attention to acquiring knowledge on an academic subject, esp. by means of books</dd>

<dt>design</dt>

<dd>a plan or drawing produced to show the look and function or workings of a building, garment, or other object before it is built or made</dd>

<dd>purpose, planning, or intention that exists or is thought to exist behind an action, fact, or material object</dd>

<dt>business</dt>

<dt>work</dt>

<dd>a person's regular occupation, profession, or trade</dd>

</dl>

Did you get it?

1. What is unordered list with example?
2. Which list is created using dl tag in HTML?

2.8. HTML FORMATTING

→Learning Objectives
- Describe categories for formatting tags in HTML;
- Understand HTML marked formatting.

Text can be formatted using HTML to give it a better appearance and feel. Text formatting is possible with HTML without the need for CSS. HTML contains a large number of formatting tags. Text can be underlined, bolded, or italicized using these tags. The way text appears in HTML and XHTML can be customized using nearly 14 different options.

There are two categories for formatting tags in HTML:

i. **Physical Tag:** These tags are used to provide the visual appearance to the text; and
ii. **Logical Tag:** These tags are used to add some logical or semantic value to the text.

We'll be learning about 14 HTML formatting tags in this section. The list of HTML formatting text is as follows:

Element Name	Description
<b>	This is a physical tag, which is used to bold the text written between it.
<strong>	This is a logical tag, which tells the browser that the text is important.
<i>	This is a physical tag which is used to make text italic.
<em>	This is a logical tag which is used to display content in italic.
<mark>	This tag is used to highlight text.
<u>	This tag is used to underline text written between it.
<tt>	This tag is used to appear a text in teletype. (not supported in HTML5).
<strike>	This tag is used to draw a strikethrough on a section of text (not supported in HTML5).

Tag	Description
<sup>	It displays the content slightly above the normal line.
<sub>	It displays the content slightly below the normal line.
<del>	This tag is used to display the deleted content.
<ins>	This tag displays the content which is added.
<big>	This tag is used to increase the font size by one conventional unit.
<small>	This tag is used to decrease the font size by one unit from base font size.

1. Bold Text:

HTML<b> and <strong> formatting elements

The HTML <b> element is a physical tag which display text in bold font, without any logical importance. If you write anything within <b>.........</b> element, is shown in bold letters.

See this example:

<p> <b>Write Your First Paragraph in bold text.</b></p>

Output:

Write Your First Paragraph in bold text.

The HTML <strong> tag is a logical tag, which displays the content in bold font and informs the browser about its logical importance. If you write anything between <strong>???????. </strong>, is shown important text.

Example:

<!DOCTYPE html>

<html>

<head>

<title>formatting elements</title>

</head>

<body>

```html
<h1>Explanation of formatting element</h1>
<p><strong>This is an important content</strong>, and this is normal content</p>
</body>
</html>
```

2. Italic Text:

HTML <i> and <em> formatting elements

The HTML <i> element is physical element, which display the enclosed content in italic font, without any added importance. If you write anything within <i>.........</i> element, is shown in italic letters.

```html
<!DOCTYPE html>
<html>
<head>
<title>formatting elements</title>
</head>
<body>
<h1>Explanation of italic formatting element</h1>
<p><em>This is an important content</em>, which displayed in italic font.</p>
</body>
</html>
```

3. HTML Marked Formatting: If you want to mark or highlight a text, you should write the content within <mark>.........</mark>.

See this example:

```html
<h2> I want to put a <mark> Mark</mark> on your face</h2>
```

4. Underlined Text:

If you write anything within <u>.........</u> element, is shown in underlined text.

```html
<p> <u>Write Your First Paragraph in underlined text.</u></p>
```

5. Strike Text:

Anything written within <strike>............</strike> element is displayed with strikethrough. It is a thin line which cross the statement.

```html
<p> <strike>Write Your First Paragraph with strikethrough</strike>.</p>
```

6. Monospaced Font:

If you want that each letter has the same width, then you should write the content within <tt>.........</tt> element.

- *Note:* Because different letters have varying widths, we are aware that the majority of fonts are referred to as variable-width fonts. As an illustration, 'w' is wider than 'i.' A monospaced font has equal spacing between each letter.

7. Superscript Text:

If you put the content within ^{.........} element, is shown in superscript; means it is displayed half a character's height above the other characters.

<p>Hello ^{Write Your First Paragraph in superscript.}</p>

8. Subscript Text:

If you put the content within _{.........} element, is shown in subscript; means it is displayed half a character's height below the other characters.

9. Deleted Text:

Anything that puts within <del>.........</del> is displayed as deleted text.

<p>Hello <del>Delete your first paragraph.</del></p>

10. Inserted Text:

Anything that puts within <ins>.........</ins> is displayed as inserted text.

<p> <del>Delete your first paragraph.</del><ins>Write another paragraph.</ins></p>

11. Larger Text:

If you want to put your font size larger than the rest of the text, then put the content within <big>.........</big>. It increase one font size larger than the previous one.

<p>Hello <big>Write the paragraph in larger font.</big></p>

12. Smaller Text:

If you want to put your font size smaller than the rest of the text then put the content within <small>.........</small>tag. It reduces one font size than the previous one.

<p>Hello <small>Write the paragraph in smaller font.</small></p

Did you get it?

1. Describe HTML tags for text formatting.
2. How to bold, italicize and format text in HTML

2.9. GRAPHICS TO HTML DOCUMENT

→Learning Objectives
- Define IMG attributes;
- Add graphics to HTML files.

Adding some graphics to your page is one of the best ways to make a statement. A web page can benefit from the addition of graphics, which can draw attention and hold viewers' interest by adding color, depth, and sparkle. An animated graphic image can convey information far more effectively than a thousand words. A plain, boring website can be made lively and captivating with the help of graphics and icons. An image that appears within a web browser is known as an "inline image."

Did you know?
To place a graphic image somewhere on a page, an empty "image" tag is used.

2.9.1. IMG Attributes

<IMG> indicates that an image—such as a photograph, icon, animation, cartoon, or other graphic—is to be displayed at that location.

The <IMG> tag should contain within its further parameters as part of the command:

- SRC= "URL/graphic .gif or .jpg" refers to the combination of the file name (graphic .gif or graphic .jpg) and the Uniform Resource Locator (URL). The image, icon, or other graphic is typically a "jpg" (Joint Photographic Experts Group image) or a "gif" (Graphics Interchange Format image), which are both supported by the majority of browsers. A "bmp" (Bitmap image) and a "tif" or "tiff" (Tag Image File Format image) are also recognized by some browsers.

    Usually, the location source of the graphic file is in an adjacent directory such as "graphics," or it possibly might be in the same directory. Assuming the image is a .jpg image, if the graphic is in an adjacent "graphics" directory, the tag would read: <IMG SRC= "graphics/graphic.jpg">. If the image is located within the same directory as the document, the tag would read simply: <IMG

SRC="graphic.jpg">. If the location of the image is somewhere else on the web, the tag might read something like this: <IMG SRC= "http://www.tedmontgomery.com/tutorial/graphics/graphic.gif">.

- ALIGN="LEFT"|"RIGHT"|"TOP"|"TEXTTOP"|"MIDDLE" | "ABSMIDDLE"|"BASELINE"|"BOTTOM"|"ABSBOTTOM": places the graphic image at a specified position, in relation either to the page margins or to the text. (Some browsers will not recognize all of these parameters.)

  "LEFT" aligns the image with the left margin of the page and allows text to wrap around the right side of the image. "RIGHT" aligns the image with the right margin of the page and allows the text to wrap around the left side of the image.

- *Note:* The only way to center a graphic horizontally on a page is to use <CENTER> & </CENTER> tags around the <IMG SRC> tag. However, centering a graphic in this manner will prevent text from being wrapped around either side of it. Also, any ALIGN="RIGHT" or ALIGN="LEFT parameter within the <IMG> tag will override the effect of the centering tags. "TOP" aligns the top of the image with the top of the tallest item in the line. "TEXTTOP" aligns the top of the image with the top of the tallest text in the line; usually, but not always, the same as the "TOP" parameter. "MIDDLE" aligns the middle of the image with the baseline of the current line. "ABSMIDDLE" aligns the middle of the image with the middle of the current line. "BASELINE" aligns the bottom of the image with the baseline of the current line. "BOTTOM" is the same as the "BASELINE" parameter. "ABSBOTTOM" aligns the bottom of the image with the bottom of the current line; usually, but not always, the same as the "BASELINE" or "BOTTOM" parameter.

Did you get it?

1. What do you understand by uniform resource locator (URL)?
2. Discuss the way to center a graphic horizontally on a page.

2.10. CREATING TABLES

→Learning Objectives
- Define tables and the border attribute;
- Explain empty cells in a table.

Tables are defined with the <table> tag. A table is divided into rows (with the <tr> tag), and each row is divided into data cells (with the <td> tag). The contents of a data cell is represented by the letters td, which stand for "table data." Text, pictures, lists, paragraphs, forms, horizontal rules, tables, and more can all be found inside a data cell.

Example:

    <table border="1">

    <tr>

    <th>Heading</th>

    <th>Another Heading</th>

    </tr>

    <tr>

    <td>row 1, cell 1</td>

    <td>row 1, cell 2</td>

    </tr>

    <tr>

    <td>row 2, cell 1</td>

    <td>row 2, cell 2</td>

    </tr>

    </table>

Output:

Heading	Another Heading
row 1, cell 1	row 1, cell 2
row 2, cell 1	row 2, cell 2

The basic structure of an HTML table consists of the following tags:

- **Table Tags:** <TABLE> </TABLE>
- **Row Tags:** <TR> </TR>
- **Cell Tags:** <TD> </TD>

Constructing an HTML table consists of describing the table between the beginning table tag, <TABLE>, and the ending table tag, </TABLE>. Between these tags, you then construct each row and each cell in the row. To do this, you would first start the row with the beginning row tag, <TR>, and then build the row by creating each cell with the beginning cell tag, <TD>, adding the Notes data for that cell, and then closing the cell with the ending cell tag, </TD>. When you finish all of the cells for a row, you would then close the row with the ending row tag, </TR>.

- *Example*: The following table is an example of a basic table with three rows and two columns of data.

  Data 1   Data 2

  Data 3   Data 4

  Data 5   Data 6

The codes that generated this table will look like this:

<TABLE>

<TR>

<TD>Data 1</TD>

<TD>Data 2</TD>

</TR>

<TR>

<TD>Data 3</TD>

<TD>Data 4</TD>

</TR>

<TR>

<TD>Data 5</TD>

<TD>Data 6</TD>

</TR>

</TABLE>

This table contains no border, title, or headings. If you wish to add any of these elements to your table, you need to include additional HTML codes.

2.10.1. Tables and the Border Attribute

The table will not have any borders when you don't specify a border attribute. Although this can be helpful at times, you usually want the borders to be visible.

To display a table with borders, you will have to use the border attribute:

<table border="1">

<tr>

<td>Row 1, cell 1</td>

<td>Row 1, cell 2</td>

</tr>

</table>

2.10.2. Headings in a Table

Headings in a table are defined with the <th> tag.

```
<table border="1">
    <tr>
    <th>Heading</th>
    <th>Another Heading</th>
    </tr>
    <tr>
    <td>row 1, cell 1</td>
    <td>row 1, cell 2</td>
    </tr>
    <tr>
    <td>row 2, cell 1</td>
    <td>row 2, cell 2</td>
    </tr>
    </table>
```

Output:

Heading	Another Heading
row 1, cell 1	row 1, cell 2
row 2, cell 1	row 2, cell 2

2.10.3. Empty Cells in a Table

Table cells with no content are not displayed very well in most browsers.

```
<table border="1">
<tr>
<td>row 1, cell 1</td>
<td>row 1, cell 2</td>
</tr>
<tr>
<td>row 2, cell 1</td>
<td></td>
</tr>
</table>
```

Output:

row 1, cell 1	row 1, cell 2
row 2, cell 1	

Note that the borders around the empty table cell are missing (NB! Mozilla Firefox displays the border).

To avoid this, add a non-breaking space () to empty data cells, to make the borders visible:

```
<table border="1">
<tr>
```

```
<td>row 1, cell 1</td>
<td>row 1, cell 2</td>
</tr>
<tr>
<td>row 2, cell 1</td>
<td> </td> Notes
</tr>
</table>
```

Output:

row 1, cell 1	row 1, cell 2
row 2, cell 1	

Did you get it?

1. How can you define headings in a table?
2. What are the uses of border attribute?

FOCUS ON CAREERS

Career in HTML: HTML full form is Hypertext Mark-Up language. It creates web pages, web applications, and sites. It mainly collaborates with CSS (Cascading style sheet), JavaScript, and another scripting language to provide the User interface for the website or the web application. It was initially released in the year 1993. W3C and WHATWG developed it. HTML elements represent tags and serve as the building blocks of HTML pages. Every browser and the elements like images, text, or other audible and visual web pages can interpret HTML language. With the help of CSS, the developer can change the feel and look of the website, or you can customize the web application accordingly.

- **Education Required for a Career in HTML:** HTML developers or programmers should have a bachelor's degree in computer science. Other graphic or web design certifications can be added on, and knowledge on the same. Many online portals, videos, and community forms are available for HTML developers and programmers to help upskill them in HTML. With the help of HTML, an individual can create web pages and websites for different vendors and their own.

  HTML developers or programmers mainly work with a team to create the website. They should be able to translate the change into the code and design the UI as requested. In learning HTML, you can learn other scripting languages that can embed the code, like JavaScript. Learning HTML is easy; you can check the output once the change is done on a web page.

- **Career Path in HTML:** An HTML developer or programmer has a well-defined career path. After learning HTML and having the degree, one can start their career at an entry-level position and, after getting experience in the same field for 3–5 years, can be at mid-level and then to senior-level positions. HTML and CSS is the critical skill for any front-end developer, whether that developer is working on the web application or web pages only.

  HTML developers can also find employment in software development to make the software product's design and look more user-friendly. Many employers are actively looking for HTML developers. These developers primarily work on applications that users can operate in a mobile browser such as Safari, Chrome, and others. Additionally, the same applications can also be used in a desktop browser. HTML gives the freedom and flexibility to use the application across different platforms.

- **Job Positions or Application Areas:** There are different job positions or application areas for careers in HTML developers: Web developer, Junior web developer, senior web developer, Graphic designer, Computer programmer, Web designer, web architect, and webmaster. Other roles require HTML skills, like JavaScript developer, Asp.Net developer, and MVC developer. These are also one of the main skills of HTML. Developers widely use different versions of HTML for application development. The other professions for this skill are social manager, website producer, website manager, content manager, Quality assurance engineer, etc. Understanding the different aspects of an application in the software industry requires every developer to have HTML knowledge.

- **Career Outlook in HTML:** There are good opportunities available for HTML developers or programmers. The HTML developers interested in visual and functional design can opt for web development. A web developer is a general term for careers like webmasters, web designers, etc. The qualities of web developers are having concentration as they have to write code longer. The other is Creativity; they ensure that the functional and UI parts appeal to the user.

The career of HTML developers is fast growing these days, and in the future as well, it will have good job opportunities. As we know, websites can be built anywhere in the world so the opportunities might go to the country with lower wages, but this is the second part. The HTML developers have the skill to develop the website effectively, and they can get the job through freelancing and from other areas.

A CLOSER LOOK

- **HTML Versions:** HTML has evolved into one of the most used and highly recommended markup languages. Web developers, both amateurs as well as professionals have tremendously benefited from the emergence of HTML. The frequent release of different HTML versions reflects the growing popularity of the language.

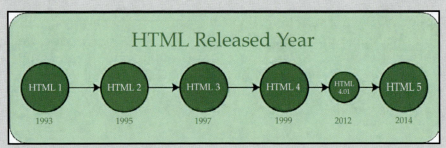

- **First Version – HTML:** Well, the very first version of HTML didn't come with a number. IT was just called "HTML" and was solely used for creating simple web pages. Marking its use way back in 1989–1995, this first version of HTML was later standardized by IETF and numbered as "HTML 2.0."

- **Second Version – HTML 2.0:** Considered as the very first definitive HTML version, the initial draft of HTML 2.0 was being re-written and revamped by Karen Muldrow in July 1994. After this, it was being presented at an IETF meeting in Toronto. The sole purpose of this draft was to capture the most common HTML practice in web browsers. Some of the features absent in HTML 2.0 include: support for tables or ALIGN attributes, Netscape/Microsoft extensions etc.

- **Third Version – HTML 3:** Released back in late 1995, HTML 3 was a result of the tireless efforts put in by Dave Raggett who was inclined on upgrading the features and utility of HTML. Although this version was never implemented, a majority of its features were being integrated in HTML's next official version which was known as HTML 3.2.

- Version 3.2 of HTML came equipped with an integrated support for images, Tables, heading and a variety of element ALIGN attributes. Serving as the current "universal" dialect, HTML 3.2 could be understood by all the major browsers. However, some features which went missing in HTML 3.2 comprised of EMBED, FRAMES and APPLET. This HTML version was being presented by World Wide Web Consortium (W3C) in the year 1997. Published in January 1997, HTML 3.2 included attribute alignment, tables, headings, images, and a lot more.

- **Fourth Version – HTML 4.0:** Considered as the next major release of HTML, version 4.0 was introduced in December 1997. As an extension to its existing feature set comprising of multimedia, text and hyperlink, this version of HTML included advanced multimedia options, style sheets, scripting languages, improved printing facilities and documents, which are accessible to users with specific disabilities. This version of HTML has also taken stride towards the internationalization of documents, with the sole aim of ensuring maximum evolution of the World Wide Web.

- **Fifth Version – HTML 5:** Assumed to be the last HTML version, HTML 5 was released in January 2008 and was published as a W3C Recommendation in October 2014. Equipped with its own HTML serialization, HTML 5 has a syntax which reminds us of the very popular SGML syntax. Plus, this HTML Version also comprises of an XML that's based on XHTML5 serialization. Although HTML5 isn't fully supported by some older browsers, there are polyfills which can easily use JavaScript for making specific features work in these browsers. For instance, html5shiv uses JavaScript for allowing older IE (Internet Explorer) versions to recognize and style specific HTML elements.

FUNDAMENTALS OF WEB DEVELOPMENT

SUMMARY

- The standard markup language for documents intended for web browser display is called HyperText Markup Language, or HTML.
- Web browsers transform HTML documents into multimedia web pages after receiving them from a web server or local storage.
- The fundamental units of an HTML page are HTML elements. Images and other objects, like interactive forms, can be embedded into the rendered page by using HTML constructs.
- The collection of markup symbols or codes called HTML (Hypertext Markup Language) is added to a file with the intention of displaying it on a World Wide Web browser page.
- HTML tags function similarly to keywords in that they specify how a web browser will format and present content.
- There are times when you want your text to have the exact same format as the HTML document. In those cases, you can use the preformatted tag <pre>.
- After being parsed into the Document Object Model, an HTML element is a single part of an HTML document or web page.
- Unordered lists are made up of items for which the order is not crucial. On the other hand, ordered lists give great weight to item order. Definition lists are available when there is a list of terms and their descriptions, possibly for a glossary.

MULTIPLE CHOICE QUESTION

1. **What does HTML stand for?**
   a. Hyper Transfer Markup Language
   b. Hyper Text Markup Language
   c. Home Tool Markup Language
   d. High Text Markup Language

2. **Which of the following tags is used to define a hyperlink in HTML?**
   a. <link>
   b. <a>
   c. <href>
   d. <hyperlink>

3. **Which tag is used to define an unordered list in HTML?**
   a. <ul>
   b. <list>
   c. <ol>
   d. <ulist>

HTML (HYPERTEXT MARKUP LANGUAGE)

4. **What does the <img> tag in HTML represent?**
   a. Image
   b. Link
   c. Text
   d. Audio

5. **Which attribute is used to define the alternative text for an image in HTML?**
   a. text
   b. title
   c. alt
   d. src

6. **Which tag is used to define a table row in HTML?**
   a. <row>
   b. <tr>
   c. <table-row>
   d. <tablerow>

7. **What does the <head> tag in HTML represent?**
   a. Heading
   b. Body
   c. Metadata
   d. Section

8. **Which tag is used to define the largest heading in HTML?**
   a. <h6>
   b. <h1>
   c. <header>
   d. <heading>

9. **Which of the following is the correct way to add a comment in HTML?**
   a. <!--This is a comment-->
   b. //This is a comment//
   c. /This is a comment/
   d. 'This is a comment'

10. **Which attribute is used to define the width of a table in HTML?**
    a. Size
    b. Table-width
    c. Colspan
    d. Width

REVIEW QUESTIONS

1. How to write HTML code.
2. Explain the essential and basic tags for creating an HTML.
3. Differentiate between tags vs elements in HTML
4. What are the classes in HTML? Explain.
5. What is ordered and unordered list in HTML?

Answer to Multiple Choice Questions

1. (b); 2. (b); 3. (a); 4. (a); 5. (c); 6. (b); 7. (c); 8. (b); 9. (a); 10. (d)

REFERENCES

1. Berners-Lee, T., (1991). Re: Status. Re: X11 BROWSER for WWW. *World Wide Web Consortium.*
2. Berners-Lee, T., Hendler, J., & Lassila, O., (2001). The semantic web. *Scientific American.*
3. Connolly, D., (1992). *Document Type Declaration Subset for Hyper Text Markup Language as Defined by the World Wide Web Project.* CERN.
4. Hendler, J., & Berners-Lee, T., (2010). From the semantic web to social machines: A research challenge for AI on the world wide web. *Artificial Intelligence, 174*(2), 156–161.
5. McCathie, N. C., (2017). HTML 5.2 is done, HTML 5.3 is coming. *World Wide Web Consortium.*
6. Philippe Le, H., (2016). HTML 5.1 is the gold standard. *World Wide Web Consortium.*
7. Raggett, D., (1993). *History for Draft-Raggett-Www-html-00.* IETF Datatracker.
8. Raggett, D., (2000). *A Review of the HTML+ Document Format. w3.* The hypertext markup language HTML was developed as a simple non-proprietary delivery format for global hypertext. HTML+ is a set of modular extensions to HTML and has been developed in response to a growing understanding of the needs of information providers. These extensions include text flow around floating figures, fill-out forms, tables, and mathematical equations.
9. Sauer, C., (2006). *WYSIWIKI – Questioning WYSIWYG in the Internet Age.* In: Wikimania.
10. Shankland, S., (2009). *An Epitaph for the Web Standard, XHTML 2.* CNET. CBS INTERACTIVE INC.
11. Spiesser, J., & Kitchen, L., (2004). Optimization of HTML automatically generated by WYSIWYG programs. In: *13th International Conference on World Wide Web* (pp. 355–364). WWW '04. ACM, New York, NY, U.S.

CHAPTER 3
Cascading Style Sheets (CSS)

LEARNING OBJECTIVES

After studying this chapter, you will be able to:

- Understand the basic concept of CSS;
- Define CSS syntax;
- Explain the types of CSS styles;
- Describe CSS properties;
- Know CSS layout.

INTRODUCTORY EXAMPLE

Putting the Style Sheet in a Separate File (HTML + CSS): We have an HTML file with an embedded style sheet. But if our site grows, we probably want many pages to share the same style. There is a better method than copying the style sheet into every page: if we put the style sheet in a separate file, all pages can point to it.

FUNDAMENTALS OF WEB DEVELOPMENT

To make a style sheet file, we need to create another empty text file. You can choose "New" from the File menu in the editor, to create an empty window. (If you are using TextEdit, don't forget to make it plain text again, using the Format menu.)

Then cut and paste everything that is inside the <style> element from the HTML file into the new window. Don't copy the <style> and </style> themselves. They belong to HTML, not to CSS. In the new editor window, you should now have the complete style sheet:

body {

padding-left: 11em;

font-family: Georgia, "Times New Roman,"

Times, serif;

color: purple;

background-color: #d8da3d }

ul.navbar {

list-style-type: none;

padding: 0;

margin: 0;

position: absolute;

top: 2em;

left: 1em;

width: 9em }

h1 {

font-family: Helvetica, Geneva, Arial,

SunSans-Regular, sans-serif }

ul.navbar li {

background: white;

margin: 0.5em 0;

padding: 0.3em;

border-right: 1em solid black }

ul.navbar a {

text-decoration: none }

a:link {

color: blue }

a:visited {

color: purple }

address {

margin-top: 1em;

padding-top: 1em;

border-top: thin dotted }

Choose "Save As…" from the File menu, make sure that you are in the same directory/folder as the mypage.html file, and save the style sheet as "mystyle.css."

Now go back to the window with the HTML code. Remove everything from the <style> tag up to and including the </style> tag and replace it with a <link> element, as follows:

<!DOCTYPE html PUBLIC "-//W3C//DTD HTML 4.01//EN">

<html>

<head>

<title>My first styled page</title>

<link rel="stylesheet" href="mystyle.css">

</head>

<body>

[etc.]

This will tell the browser that the style sheet is found in the file called "mystyle.css" and since no directory is mentioned, the browser will look in the same directory where it found the HTML file.

If you save the HTML file and reload it in the browser, you should see no change: the page is still styled the same way, but now the style comes from an external file.

3.1. UNIT INTRODUCTION

The presentation and styling of a document written in a markup language, such as HTML or XML (including XML dialects like SVG, MathML, or XHTML), can be specified using the style sheet language known as Cascading Style Sheets (CSS). The foundational technologies of the World Wide Web are HTML, JavaScript, and CSS.

Layout, color scheme, and font selection are just a few of the presentation elements that can be separated out thanks to CSS. This separation can reduce complexity and repetition in the structural content, improve content accessibility, give more flexibility and control in the specification of presentation characteristics, enable multiple web pages to share formatting by defining the relevant CSS in a separate .css file, and allow the .css file to be cached to speed up page loads between the pages that share the file and its formatting.

It is also possible to present the same markup page in multiple styles for various rendering methods, such as on-screen, print, voice (through a screen reader or speech-based browser), and on Braille-based tactile devices, when formatting and content are kept separate. In the event that the content is viewed on a mobile device, CSS also contains rules for alternative formatting.

The term "cascading" refers to the hierarchy that is defined to decide which property declaration, if multiple declarations that match an element, applies. This hierarchy of cascading priorities is foreseeable. The World Wide Web Consortium is responsible for maintaining the CSS specifications (W3C). RFC 2318 (March 1998) registered text/css as an Internet media type (MIME type) for use with CSS. For CSS documents, the W3C provides a free CSS validation service. Apart from HTML, CSS can also be used with other markup languages like XHTML, plain XML, SVG, and XUL. Furthermore, the GTK widget toolkit makes use of CSS.

3.2. BASICS OF CSS

→Learning Objectives
- Discuss the "Cascade" part of CSS;
- Understand the benefits of CSS.

The World Wide Web Consortium defined CSS, a standard that gives designers more precision and flexibility than standard HTML when defining the appearance of text and other formats. In essence, CSS gives web designers the ability to alter a webpage's look without changing the HTML structure. For instance, using standard HTML, you would have to manually alter each element on the page individually if you wanted to make all of the text in your document blue and all of the headlines green. With just one CSS command, it is possible to redefine all of the document's body elements to turn blue, and then take an additional step to change the headlines to green.

3.2.1. The "Cascade" Part of CSS

A cascading effect occurs when you use multiple styles. The browser loads the first style defined for an element; if another style affects the same element, it overrides the first if its attributes are the same; if not, it adds the new definition to the first definition, resulting in a combined style for the element. For example, consider a style that defines the text color for a paragraph (<p>) as black. Later you define another style that affects the <p> tag with a border of one pixel. The resulting style for the <p> tag now includes both a black text color and a border around the paragraph one-pixel thick. Thus, these styles cascade onto one another and are combined into a single style.

There is an inherent cascading order of importance (from most to least) in browsers that support CSS:

- User-defined styles — Some browsers allow for users to define their own styles. For example, a color-blind user may specify specific colors for hyperlinks and always use that in the browser to override styles on each Web page.
- Inline styles
- Embedded styles
- Linked styles
- Imported styles
- Default browser styles

3.2.1.1. Who Creates and Maintains CSS?

On October 10, 1994, Håkon Wium Lie extended an invitation for CSS, which is now maintained by the CSS Working Group, a W3C group. The CSS Working Group produces specifications in the form of documents. A specification becomes a recommendation after it has been deliberated and formally approved by W3C members. Since the W3C has no influence over how the language is actually implemented, these approved specifications are referred to as recommendations. That software is made by independent businesses and organizations.

3.2.1.2. CSS Versions

In December 1996, W3C released Cascading Style Sheets, Level 1 (CSS1) as a recommendation. This version includes a description of the CSS language along with a basic visual formatting model that applies to all HTML tags.

Building on CSS1, CSS2 was approved as a W3C recommendation in May 1998. Support for media-specific style sheets has been added in this version, e.g., printers, audio equipment, fonts that can be downloaded, element placement, and tables.

In June 1999, CSS3 was approved as a W3C recommendation, expanding upon previous iterations of CSS. It is separated into documentation sections referred to as modules, with new extension features defined in CSS2 for each module.

3.2.1.3. CSS3 Modules

The old CSS specifications and extension features are present in CSS3 modules:

- Selectors;
- Box model;
- Backgrounds and borders;
- Image values and replaced content;
- Text effects;
- 2D/3D transformations;
- Animations;
- Multiple column layout;
- User interface.

> **Keyword**
>
> CSS Declaration – It consists of a property and a value pair separated by a colon, followed by a semicolon to terminate it.

3.2.2. Benefits of CSS

One more benefit of CSS is that it only requires one definition, which is far more efficient than defining every element in HTML on each page. This means:

- Pages download faster, sometimes by as much as 50%;
- You have to type less code, and your pages are shorter and neater;
- The look of your site is kept consistent throughout all the pages that work off the same stylesheet;
- Updating your design and general site maintenance are made much easier, and errors;
- caused by editing multiple HTML pages occur far less often.

Well-written CSS also makes web content more accessible by ensuring that it can still be viewed by web users with disabilities and enabling access through a variety of devices (such as handheld PDAs). Additionally, it removes the need for tags and hacks unique to certain browsers, increasing the likelihood that your website will function properly in all of the major browsers.

Although it may seem intimidating at first, CSS is a beautiful, well-designed language. It is crucial for the future of web design and has played a major role in assisting designers in leaving behind the troublesome, hacker-ridden days of presentational HTML tags like and returning to the use of logical, structural elements that improve accessibility for websites.

In addition to all of that, stylesheet commands provide dozens of additional powerful formatting options and possibilities that are not possible with standard HTML.

> **Keyword**
>
> **CSS Selectors** – These are patterns used to select and style elements in an HTML document.

> **Keyword**
>
> **Grouping Selector** – This typically refers to a feature in programming or markup languages that allows you to select multiple elements or items based on certain criteria.

Did you get it?

1. Who maintains and governs CSS?
2. What are the major difference among CSS, CSS2, and CSS3?

3.3. CSS SYNTAX

→Learning Objectives
- Describe most basic CSS selectors;
- Define CSS grouping selector.

A declaration block and a selector make up a CSS rule-set:

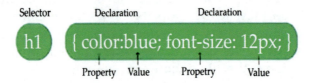

The HTML element you wish to style is indicated by the selector. One or more declarations are contained in the declaration block and are divided by semicolons. Each declaration consists of a value and the name of a CSS property, separated by a colon. Curly braces enclose declaration blocks, and a semicolon always marks the end of a CSS declaration.

In the following example all elements will be center-aligned, with a red text color:

Example:

p {

color: red;

text-align: center;

}

Despite being simple to use, CSS is a highly defined standard. This implies that the browser won't know what to do if you don't use proper grammar. Your style sheet may function unexpectedly, or it may not function at all. The components of a style sheet and an illustration of their assembly are shown above.

- Every statement must have a selector and a declaration. The declaration comes immediately after the selector and is contained in a pair of curly braces.
- The declaration is one or more properties separated by semicolons.
- Each property has a property name followed by a colon and then the value for

CASCADING STYLE SHEETS (CSS) 83

that property. There are many different types of values, but any given property can only take certain values as set down in the specification.

- Sometimes a property can take a number of values, as in the font family. The values in the list should be separated by a comma and a space.
- Sometimes a value will have a unit as well as the actual value, as in the 1.3em. You must not put a space between the value and its unit.
- As with HTML, white space can be used to make your style sheet easier to read and write.

Did you know?

Style sheets have existed in one form or another since the beginnings of Standard Generalized Markup Language (SGML) in the 1980s, and CSS was developed to provide style sheets for the web.

3.3.1. CSS Selectors

HTML elements can be "found" or selected using CSS selectors based on a variety of criteria, including element name, id, class, attribute, and more.

3.3.1.1. The Element Selector

Elements are chosen by the element selector according to their names. You can select all <p> elements on a page like this (in this case, all <p> elements will be center-aligned, with a red text color):

Example:

p {

text-align: center;

color: red;

}

3.3.1.2. The ID Selector

The id selector selects a particular HTML element by using its id attribute. The id selector is used to choose one unique element because each element's id should be distinct within a page! To designate an element with a particular id, type the element's id after the hash () character.

Example:

The CSS rule below will be applied to the HTML element with id="para1":

```
#para1 {
text-align: center;
color: red;
}
```

3.3.1.3. The Class Selector

Elements possessing a particular class attribute are chosen by the class selector. To designate elements belonging to a particular class, affix a period (. character is listed first, then the class name. All HTML elements with class="center" in the example below will be center-aligned and red.

```
.center {
text-align: center;
color: red;
}
```

You can also specify that only specific HTML elements should be affected by a class.

In the example below, only <p> elements with class="center" will be center-aligned:

```
p.center {
text-align: center;
color: red;
}
```

Additionally, HTML elements can relate to multiple classes.

In the example below, the <p> element will be styled according to class="center" and to class="large":

3.3.2. The CSS Grouping Selector

All of the HTML elements with the same style definitions are chosen by the grouping selector.

Look at the following CSS code (the h1, h2, and p elements have the same style definitions):

```
h1 {
text-align: center;
```

```
color: red;

}

h2 {

text-align: center;

color: red;

}

p {

text-align: center;

color: red;

}
```

Grouping the selectors will help reduce the amount of code. Put a comma between each selector to group them together.

Example:

In this example we have grouped the selectors from the code above:

```
h1, h2, p {

text-align: center;

color: red;

}
```

Did you get it?

1. What are CSS selectors and how do they work?
2. How would you target elements that are direct children of an element using CSS selectors?

3.4. TYPES OF CSS STYLES

→Learning Objectives
- Understand inline styles;
- Describe embedded styles;
- Explain external style sheets.

There are three methods you can use to add CSS styles to your website. One may utilize either an "internal stylesheet," "external stylesheet," or "inline style." Using each will yield different benefits depending on how you are using the Style. The differences between them are shown in Table 3.1.

Table 3.1. Different CSS Style Linking

Internal Stylesheet	An internal stylesheet holds the CSS code for the webpage in the head section of the particular file. This makes it easy to apply styles like classes or id's in order to reuse the code. The downside of using an internal stylesheet is that changes to the internal stylesheet only effect the page the code is inserted into.
External Stylesheet	The External Stylesheet is a .css file that you link your website to. This makes it so that whatever you change in the .css sheet, will affect every page in your website. This prevents you from having to make many code changes in each page. This is for "global" site changes.
Inline Styles	The Inline style is specific to the tag itself. The inline style uses the HTML "style" attribute to style a specific tag. This is not recommended, as every CSS change has to be made in every tag that has the inline style applied to it. The Inline style is good for one an individual CSS change that you do not use repeatedly through the site

Source: https://www.inmotionhosting.com/support/website/linking-your-css-to-your-website/.

3.4.1. Inline Styles

Styles that are written directly within an HTML document's tag are known as inline styles. Only the specific tag to which they are applied is impacted by inline styles. An illustration of an inline style applied to a regular link, or anchor, tag can be found here.

```
!DOCTYPE html>
<html>
<head>
<title>Inline CSS</title>
<style>
p {
color:#009900;
font-size:50px;
font-style:italic;
text-align:center;
}
</style>
</head>
<body>
<p>
GeeksForGeeks
</p>
</body>
</html>
```

> **Keyword**
>
> **Embedded Style Sheets** – These are a way of applying CSS (Cascading Style Sheets) styles directly within an HTML document.

This particular link's standard underline text decoration would be disabled by this CSS rule. But it wouldn't affect any other link on the page. One of the drawbacks of inline styles is this. To create a real page design, you would have to overuse these styles in your HTML since they only apply to a single item. It is not recommended to do that. In actuality, it is a step away from the time when web pages mixed structure and style with "font" tags.

Additionally, inline styles have a very high specificity. Because of this, it is very difficult to overwrite them with non-inline styles. For instance, inline styles on an element will make it very difficult to use media queries to make a site responsive and alter how an element appears at specific breakpoints. In the end, inline styles should only be utilized extremely infrequently.

3.4.1.1. Creating an Inline Stylesheet

If you want to apply a style to just one instance of an element, use inline stylesheets. Only the specific tags that they declare are affected by inline stylesheets. The style attribute is used to declare inline stylesheets.

> **Keyword**
>
> **CSS Files** – These are documents containing styling information used to control the presentation and layout of web pages written in HTML and XHTML.

Example:

```
<p style="color:gray">This text will be gray.
</p>
```

In this example, we are indicating that the text within a paragraph will be gray by using the stylesheet command color.

Output:

This text will be gray.

3.4.2. Embedded Styles

Styles that are incorporated into the document's head are known as embedded styles. Only the tags on the page in which they are embedded are impacted by embedded styles. When creating a stylesheet internally in the web page, you will need to use the <style></style> HTML tags in the Head section of your webpage. All the code for the Internal CSS stylesheet is contained between the <head></head> section of your websites code. You can define all of the styles for a specific HTML document in one location by using an embedded stylesheet. This is done by embedding the <style></style> tags containing the CSS properties in the head of your document. When HTML documents need a different style from the other documents in your project, embedded style sheets come in handy. Instead of using separate **embedded style sheets**, you should link to an external style sheet if the styles need to be applied to multiple documents. There is a clear benefit to using embedded stylesheets as opposed to inline styles, which can only handle one HTML element at a time.

```html
<!DOCTYPE html>
<html>
<head>
<title>Page Title</title>
<!--Embedded stylesheet-->
<style>
h2 {
font-size: 1.5rem;
color: #2f8d46;
text-align: center;
}
p {
font-variant: italic;
}
</style>
</head>
<body>
<h2>Welcome To GFG</h2>
<p>This document is using an embedded stylesheet!</p>
<p>This is a paragraph</p>
<p>This is another paragraph</p>
</body>
</html>
```

3.4.3. External Style Sheets

These days, external style sheets are used by most websites. Styles that are created in a different document and then added to different web documents are known as external styles. If you have a 20-page website and every page uses the same style sheet (which is usually the case), you can make a visual change to every single page by just editing the external style sheet. This is because external style sheets can affect any document to which they are attached.

This greatly simplifies long-term site management. The drawback of external style sheets is that in order to load and fetch these external files, pages are needed. Many pages will load a much larger CSS page than they actually need because not every page will use every style in the CSS sheet.

Although there is a performance penalty associated with external CSS files, it can be minimized. Since CSS files are essentially just text files, they are typically not very big in the first place. One CSS file for the entire website gives you the added benefit of that document being cached once it loads. This implies that there might be a small performance hit on the first page for some users, but that hit would be minimized because later pages will use the CSS file that was cached.

3.4.3.1. Creating an External Stylesheet

Applying a single style to numerous pages requires the use of an external stylesheet. Any changes you make to an external stylesheet will be reflected universally on all pages that use it.

An external file with the .css extension contains the declaration of an external stylesheet. Pages whose interface it will impact call it. Using the tag, which belongs in the HTML document's head section, external stylesheets are called. We need three attributes for this tag.

Attributes of the <link> tag:

- **rel:** When using an external stylesheet on a webpage, this attribute takes the value «stylesheet»
- **type:** When using an external stylesheet on a webpage, this attribute takes the value «text/css»
- **href:** Denotes the name and location of the external stylesheet to be used.

Example:

```
<html>
<head>
<link rel="stylesheet" type="text/css" href="style1.css" />
</head>
<body>
<p>
The text in this paragraph will be blue.
</p>
</body>
</html>
```

Output:

The text in this paragraph will be blue

The code from style1.css:

```
p {color:blue}
```

Did you get it?

1. How to Create an inline stylesheet?
2. How to use an external style sheet for CSS3 programming?

3.5. CSS PROPERTIES

→Learning Objectives
- Describe CSS reference;
- Understand useful CSS properties.

We should look at a few more CSS properties so we can truly use them to accomplish something with CSS. There are far too many properties to introduce all at once (or even to remember all of them and how they work).

3.5.1. CSS Reference

For every CSS component, we will use a CSS Reference, just as we did with HTML elements and the HTML Reference. We'll cover some important properties now, but you should still pay attention to the references. As we've seen, text-align can be found in the CSS reference. You will see a brief description of the property and the possible values for it, similar to the HTML reference.

Additionally, a section on "browser support" can be found on the reference page for every CSS property. With plan HTML, this wasn't much of a problem, but with CSS, we need to know which properties are supported by popular web browsers. New CSS versions bring with them new features, not all of which are fully supported by all browsers.

We'll only talk about the ones that have good support here, but if you're looking for others, quickly check the compatibility table to make sure it will function as advertised.

3.5.2. Useful CSS Properties

Again, we won't cover every interesting CSS property in this article, but we can introduce some of the more interesting ones (with links to the CSS reference for each).

text-align

It is evident that altering the text justification is possible with text-align. The following values are possible: justify (for complete justification with to ragged left or right margin), center, right, and left.

font-style

Used to control italic text: possible values include italic and normal (for non-italics).

font-weight

Used to control bold text: possible values include bold and normal (for non-bold).

color

Used to set the color (usually of the text) for the element. For example, "color: green;." We will discuss color values more in Colors in CSS.

background-color

Used to set the background color (behind the text) for the element. For example, "background-color: black;"

border-width

border-style

border-color

These (line width, line type, and line color, respectively) are used to control the border surrounding an element. These properties can be used independently, or you can combine them into a single line (giving the three values in any order) by using a shorthand property border. These two items are interchangeable.

figure {

border-style: solid;

border-width: 3px;

border-color: red;

}

figure {

border: solid red 3px;

}

line-height

Controls the amount of vertical space each line of text takes up (which you might know as "leading"). For example, "line-height:

Remember

The <style> tag is NOT used in an external stylesheet, and neither are HTML comments.

1.5;" sets the spacing between single- and double-spaced (and is probably a good default value.

font-family

Sets the font for the text. You should give a list of fonts that are tried in-order until the browser finds one available on the user's system. There are five generic font families, and your list must end with one of them since it's guaranteed to work. For example, "font-family: "Garamond," "Times," serif."

3.5.3. CSS Box Model

Using the CSS box model, a number of properties in CSS are frequently combined to form box properties, which regulate how browsers arrange pages (Figure 3.1).

Although these properties aren't very complex, they might not be immediately apparent. Suppose we have an element on the page (like a <h2>Element Contents</h2>). Here are the parts of its "box" when drawn:

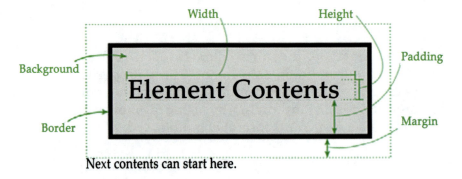

Figure 3.1. CSS box model illustration.

Source: https://www2.cs.sfu.ca/.

So, this CSS code:

h2 {

padding: 1em;

border: medium dashed black;

background-color: gray;

}

… will make the <h2> have a gray background, with 1em of space between the text and the border. The space inside the border (even if it's invisible because you don't have one) is covered with the background color and is controlled by the padding properties.

We would need to increase the margin values if we wanted more space between this element (and its border) and the surrounding material.

Errors in margin and padding are common, particularly in cases where background color and border are absent. Try setting both margin and padding to zero and work from there if you are trying to change the space surrounding an element (especially if the browser's default CSS has some space there).

ul {

margin: 0em;

padding: 0em;

}

3.5.4. CSS Units

You probably noticed the measurement 1em above. The em is a unit of (length) measurement in CSS. Here are some common units that need a little explanation:

em

The current font size: if the current text is 12 points, then this will be 12 points. Another unit, an ex is half the text size.

px

One screen pixel (dot) on the display. (Note: for some very high-resolution devices, real "pixels" are very small, so this length is adjusted to be close to the size of a pixel on a traditional display.)

mm

A millimeter. In addition, there are units for centimeters, inches, etc. Note: Depending on the display, projector, phone, and other device scaling, this may not be an accurate estimation based solely on the browser. When using a projector, for instance, the "millimeter" suddenly enlarges significantly.).

As much as possible, we suggest you specify measurements using ems and exs. These are the only units that don't require some kind of note describing when they are a lie. If you think in ems, you will be thinking properly about the way a page might scale depending on the current screen/font/whatever size.

The one exception is when dealing with bitmapped images: they are inherently sized in pixels, so that probably makes the most sense.

p {

line-height: 1.5em;

```
}
blockquote {
margin-left: 2em;
border-left: 0.25em solid black;
}
img#ourlogo {
width: 120px;
height: 160px;
float: left;
margin-left: 1em;
}
```

Example:

Here is an example page that we can style with some of the properties above:

```
<!DOCTYPE html>
<html>
<head>
<meta charset="UTF-8"/>
<title>CSS Properties</title>
<link rel="stylesheet" href="css-prop.css"/>
</head>
<body>
<h1>CSS Properties</h1>
<h2>Goals</h2>
<p>This is a page that we're using to demonstrate various CSS properties and techniques. Because of that, it's probably going to be ugly.</p>
<h2>Results</h2>
<p>Yup, it's turning out rather ugly, but it's important to demonstrate some CSS stuff.
```

Here are some of the new things:</p>

<ul>

<li>more CSS properties</li>

<li>the box model</li>

<li>the units of length used</li>

</ul>

</body>

</html>

... and a CSS to go with it:

body {

font-family: "Helvetica," sans-serif;

}

h1 {

text-align: center;

font-weight: bold;

background-color: silver;

color: teal;

padding: 0.25em;

}

h2 {

border: medium dotted teal;

font-weight: normal;

padding: 0.1em;

}

Did you get it?

1. In the CSS Box Model, which component directly surrounds the content of the element?
2. Which CSS property allows you to change the position of an element without disrupting the normal flow of the document?

3.6. CSS LAYOUT

→Learning Objectives
- Define normal flow layout;
- Understand Flexible Box Layout CSS module;
- Explain positioning techniques;
- Describe multi-column layout.

We've now covered the basics of CSS, text styling, and styling and working with the boxes that contain your content. It's time to examine how to properly align your boxes with respect to the viewport and each other now. Now that the prerequisites have been covered, let's get into CSS layout and examine a variety of features, including positioning, different display settings, and contemporary layout tools like flexbox and CSS grid. We'll also cover some legacy techniques that you may still find useful.

With the help of CSS page layout techniques, we can manipulate an element's position on a web page with respect to its default position in the normal layout flow, surrounding elements, parent container, and main viewport/window. We'll go into greater detail about the following page layout strategies in this module:

- Normal flow;
- The display property;
- Flexbox;
- Grid;
- Floats;
- Positioning;
- Table layout;
- Multiple-column layout.

Every technique has applications, benefits, and drawbacks. It is not intended for any technique to be utilized alone. You'll be in a good position to determine which layout method is best for each task if you know what each method is intended for.

3.6.1. Normal Flow

When you leave page layout settings unmodified, the browser will automatically layout HTML pages according to normal flow. Let's examine a brief example of HTML:

```
<p>I love my cat.</p>

<ul>

<li>Buy cat food</li>

<li>Exercise</li>

<li>Cheer up friend</li>

</ul>

<p>The end!</p>
```

By default, the browser will display this code as follows:

- I love my cat.
- Buy cat food
- Exercise
- Cheer up friend

The end!

Observe that the elements of the HTML are arranged exactly as they appear in the source code, with the first paragraph, the unordered list, and the second paragraph all stacked on top of one another.

The elements that appear one below the other are described as block elements, in contrast to inline elements, which appear beside one another like the individual words in a paragraph.

- *Note:* The Block Direction is the direction in which the contents of a block element are arranged. In languages with a horizontal writing mode, like English, the Block Direction is vertical. In any language that has a vertical writing mode, like Japanese, it would run horizontally. The direction that inline contents, like a sentence, would run is known as the corresponding Inline Direction. The natural flow of many of the elements on your page will produce the ideal layout for you. But for more intricate layouts, you'll need to change this default behavior with some of the CSS tools at your disposal. It is crucial that you start with a well-structured HTML document so that you can work with the default layout rather than against it. The methods that can change how elements are laid out in CSS are:
    1. **The Display Property:** Standard values such as block, inline or inline-block can change how elements behave in normal flow, for example, by making a block-level element behave like an inline-level element. We also have entire layout

methods that are enabled via specific display values, for example, CSS Grid and Flexbox, which alter how child elements are laid out inside their parents.

2. **Floats:** Applying a float value such as left can cause block-level elements to wrap along one side of an element, like the way images sometimes have text floating around them in magazine layouts.

3. **The Position Property:** Allows you to precisely control the placement of boxes inside other boxes. static positioning is the default in normal flow, but you can cause elements to be laid out differently using other values, for example, as fixed to the top of the browser viewport.

4. **Table Layout:** Features designed for styling parts of an HTML table can be used on non-table elements using display: table and associated properties.

5. **Multi-Column Layout:** The Multi-column layout properties can cause the content of a block to lay out in columns, as you might see in a newspaper.

3.6.2. Flexbox

The Flexible Box Layout CSS module, also known by its shorter name, flexbox, was created to make it simple for us to arrange elements in one dimension, either as a row or a column. Applying display: flex to the parent element of the elements you wish to arrange will make all of its direct children become flex items when you use flexbox. We can observe this in a basic illustration.

3.6.2.1. Setting Display: Flex

The HTML markup below gives us a containing element with a class of wrapper, inside of which are three <div> elements. By default, these would display as block elements, that is, below one another in our English language document.

Nevertheless, the three items now arrange themselves into columns if we add display: flex to the parent. This is because they turn into flex items and are influenced by some initial values that the flex container's flexbox sets. Because the parent element's property flex-direction has an initial value of row, they are shown in a row. Because their parent elements align-items property has an initial value of stretch, they all seem to stretch in height. This indicates that the items stretch to the flex container's height, which is determined in this instance by the tallest item. Any remaining space at the end of the row is left by the items aligning at the beginning of the container.

CSS

.wrapper {

display: flex;

}

HTML

```
<div class="wrapper">
<div class="box1">One</div>
<div class="box2">Two</div>
<div class="box3">Three</div>
</div>
```

| One | Two | Three |

3.6.2.2. Setting the Flex Property

There are properties that can be applied to flex items in addition to properties that can be applied to a flex container. These characteristics, among other things, can alter how an item flexes, allowing it to enlarge or decrease in size in accordance with available space.

We can add the flex property and set its value to 1 to all of our child items as a basic example. As a result, instead of leaving room at the end of the container, every item will grow and fill it. The objects will get broader in the presence of more space and narrower in the absence of it. Furthermore, the items collectively continue to occupy all the space; if you add another element to the markup, the other items will all shrink to make room for it.

CSS

```
.wrapper {
display: flex;
}
.wrapper > div {
flex: 1;
}
```

HTML

```
<div class="wrapper">
<div class="box1">One</div>
<div class="box2">Two</div>
```

```html
<div class="box3">Three</div>
</div>
```

One	Two	Three

3.6.3. Grid Layout

Grid Layout is intended for two dimensions, or aligning objects in rows and columns, whereas Flexbox is intended for one-dimensional layout.

3.6.3.1. Setting Display: Grid

Grid Layout is enabled with its unique display value, display: grid, just like flexbox. The markup in the example below is comparable to that of the flex example; it has a container and a few child elements. We use the grid-template-rows and grid-template-columns properties to define some row and column tracks for the parent in addition to display: grid. We have two rows of 100 pixels each and three columns, each measuring 1fr. The child elements enter the cells that our grid has created automatically; we don't need to apply any rules to them.

CSS

```css
.wrapper {
display: grid;
grid-template-columns: 1fr 1fr 1fr;
grid-template-rows: 100px 100px;
gap: 10px;
}
```

HTML

```html
<div class="wrapper">
<div class="box1">One</div>
<div class="box2">Two</div>
<div class="box3">Three</div>
<div class="box4">Four</div>
<div class="box5">Five</div>
<div class="box6">Six</div>
```

</div>

3.6.3.2. Placing Items on the Grid

Instead of depending on the auto-placement behavior shown above, you can explicitly place your items on the grid once you've created one. We've defined the same grid with three child items in the following example. Using the grid-column and grid-row properties, we have determined the beginning and ending lines of each item. The items now span several tracks as a result.

CSS

.wrapper {

display: grid;

grid-template-columns: 1fr 1fr 1fr;

grid-template-rows: 100px 100px;

gap: 10px;

}

.box1 {

grid-column: 2/4;

grid-row: 1;

}

.box2 {

grid-column: 1;

grid-row: 1/3;

}

.box3 {

grid-row: 2;

grid-column: 3;

}

HTML

<div class="wrapper">

<div class="box1">One</div>

<div class="box2">Two</div>

<div class="box3">Three</div>

</div>

The remaining sections cover additional layout techniques that, while not as crucial to the overall design of your page, can still be useful for completing particular tasks. Once you comprehend the nature of each layout task, you will quickly discover that the best kind of layout for a given aspect of your design will frequently be obvious when you look at it.

3.6.4. Floats

An element that is floating alters both its own behavior and that of the block level elements that follow it in a typical flow. The surrounding content floats around the floated element, which is moved to the left or right and taken out of the regular flow.

The float property has four possible values:

i. Left: Floats the element to the left.

ii. Right: Floats the element to the right.

iii. None: Specifies no floating at all. This is the default value.

iv. Inherit: Specifies that the value of the float property should be inherited from the element's parent element.

In the example below, we float a <div> left and give it a margin on the right to push the surrounding text away from it. This gives us the effect of text wrapped around the boxed element and is most of what you need to know about floats as used in modern web design.

HTML

```
<h1>Simple float example</h1>
<div class="box">Float</div>
<p>
Lorem ipsum dolor sit amet, consectetur adipiscing elit. Nulla luctus aliquam dolor, eu lacinia lorem placerat vulputate. Duis felis orci, pulvinar id metus ut, rutrum luctus orci. Cras porttitor imperdiet nunc, at ultricies tellus laoreet sit amet. Sed auctor cursus massa at porta. Integer ligula ipsum, tristique sit amet orci vel, viverra egestas ligula. Curabitur vehicula tellus neque, ac ornare ex malesuada et. In vitae convallis lacus. Aliquam erat volutpat. Suspendisse ac imperdiet turpis. Aenean finibus sollicitudin eros pharetra congue. Duis ornare egestas augue ut luctus. Proin blandit quam nec lacus varius commodo et a urna. Ut id ornare felis, eget fermentum sapien.
</p>
```

CSS

```
.box {
float: left;
width: 150px;
height: 150px;
margin-right: 30px;
}
```

3.6.5. Positioning Techniques

An element can be positioned to be in a different place than where it would normally be in a normal flow. Positioning is more about controlling and fine-tuning the position of individual items on a page than it is about designing a page's primary layouts.

   An element can be positioned to be in a different place than where it would normally be in a normal flow. Positioning is more about controlling and fine-tuning the position of individual items on a page than it is about designing a page's primary layouts.

There are five types of positioning you should know about:

- Static positioning is the default that every element gets. It just means "put the element into its normal position in the document layout flow — nothing special to see here."
- Relative positioning allows you to modify an element's position on the page, moving it relative to its position in normal flow, as well as making it overlap other elements on the page.
- Absolute positioning moves an element completely out of the page's normal layout flow, like it's sitting on its own separate layer. From there, you can fix it to a position relative to the edges of its closest positioned ancestor (which becomes <html> if no other ancestors are positioned). This is useful for creating complex layout effects, such as tabbed boxes where different content panels sit on top of one another and are shown and hidden as desired, or information panels that sit off-screen by default, but can be made to slide on screen using a control button.
- Fixed positioning is very similar to absolute positioning except that it fixes an element relative to the browser viewport, not another element. This is useful for creating effects such as a persistent navigation menu that always stays in the same place on the screen as the rest of the content scrolls.
- Sticky positioning is a newer positioning method that makes an element act like position: relative until it hits a defined offset from the viewport, at which point it acts like position: fixed.

3.6.5.1. Simple Positioning Example

To provide familiarity with these page layout techniques, we'll show you a couple of quick examples. Our examples will all feature the same HTML structure (a heading followed by three paragraphs), which is as follows:

HTML

```
<h1>Positioning</h1>

<p>I am a basic block level element.</p>

<p class="positioned">I am a basic block level element.</p>

<p>I am a basic block level element.</p>
```

This HTML will be styled by default using the following CSS:

CSS

```
body {

width: 500px;

margin: 0 auto;
```

```css
}
p {
background-color: rgb(207 232 220);
border: 2px solid rgb(79 185 227);
padding: 10px;
margin: 10px;
border-radius: 5px;
}
.positioned {
background: rgb(255 84 104/30%);
border: 2px solid rgb(255 84 104);
}
```

The rendered output is as follows:

Positioning

I am a basic block level element.

I am a basic block level element.

I am a basic block level element.

3.6.5.2. Relative Positioning

You can move an object away from its default location in a normal flow by using relative positioning. This implies that you could accomplish an icon's downsizing to align it with a text label, for example. We could incorporate relative positioning by adding the following rule to achieve this:

CSS

```css
.positioned {
position: relative;
top: 30px;
```

left: 30px;

}

Here, we assign a position value of relative to our middle paragraph. Since this is ineffective on its own, we additionally add the top and left properties. These function to shift the impacted element to the right and downward. Although this may appear to be the opposite of what you were expecting, you should consider it as the element being pushed downward and to the left, which causes it to move downward and to the right.

Adding this code will give the following result:

Relative positioning

I am a basic block level element.

This is my relatively positioned element.
I am a basic block level element.

3.6.5.3. Absolute Positioning

When an element is completely positioned using offsets from the edges of a containing block, it is removed from the normal flow. This is known as absolute positioning.

Going back to our original non-positioned example, we could add the following CSS rule to implement absolute positioning:

CSS

.positioned {

position: absolute;

top: 30px;

left: 30px;

}

We now assign an absolute position value to our middle paragraph and maintain the same top and left properties. The following outcome will be obtained by adding this code:

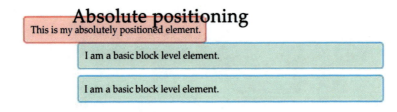

This is a major change: the positioned element now rests on top of the rest of the page layout, fully isolated from it. Now, the other two paragraphs coexist as though their positioned sibling never happened. When it comes to absolutely positioned elements, the top and left properties work differently than when it comes to relatively positioned elements. The offsets in this instance have been determined starting from the left and top of the page.

3.6.5.4. Fixed Positioning

Our element is removed from the document flow in the same manner as absolute positioning by fixed positioning. Nevertheless, the offsets are applied from the viewport rather than the container. We can create effects like a menu that stays in place even when the page scrolls beneath it because the item stays fixed in relation to the viewport.

In this case, the HTML includes a box with the property position: fixed and three paragraphs of text that allow us to scroll through the page.

HTML

```
<h1>Fixed positioning</h1>

<div class="positioned">Fixed</div>

<p>

Lorem ipsum dolor sit amet, consectetur adipiscing elit. Nulla luctus aliquam

dolor, eu lacinia lorem placerat vulputate. Duis felis orci, pulvinar id metus

ut, rutrum luctus orci.

</p>

<p>

Cras porttitor imperdiet nunc, at ultricies tellus laoreet sit amet. Sed

auctor cursus massa at porta. Integer ligula ipsum, tristique sit amet orci

vel, viverra egestas ligula. Curabitur vehicula tellus neque, ac ornare ex

malesuada et.

</p>

<p>

In vitae convallis lacus. Aliquam erat volutpat. Suspendisse ac imperdiet

turpis. Aenean finibus sollicitudin eros pharetra congue. Duis ornare egestas

augue ut luctus. Proin blandit quam nec lacus varius commodo et a urna. Ut id
```

ornare felis, eget fermentum sapien.

</p>

CSS

```
.positioned {
position: fixed;
top: 30px;
left: 30px;
}
```

3.6.5.5. Sticky Positioning

The last positioning technique we have available is sticky positioning. It combines fixed and relative positioning. An item with position: sticky will scroll normally until it encounters offsets from the specified viewport. It then becomes "stuck," acting as though position: fixed were applied.

CSS

```
.positioned {
position: sticky;
top: 30px;
left: 30px;
}
```

3.6.6. Multi-Column Layout

Content can be arranged in columns using the multi-column layout CSS module, which mimics the way text appears in newspapers. Even though users must scroll up and down to read columns that go up and down on a web page, organizing content into columns can still be a helpful strategy.

Using either the column-count or column-width properties, we can make a block into a multi-column container by telling the browser how many columns we want or how many columns of a given width we want to see inside the container.

HTML

<div class="container">

<h1>Multi-column Layout</h1>

```
<p>
Lorem ipsum dolor sit amet, consectetur adipiscing elit. Nulla luctus
aliquam dolor, eu lacinia lorem placerat vulputate. Duis felis orci,
pulvinar id metus ut, rutrum luctus orci. Cras porttitor imperdiet nunc, at
ultricies tellus laoreet sit amet. Sed auctor cursus massa at porta.
</p>
<p>
Nam vulputate diam nec tempor bibendum. Donec luctus augue eget malesuada
ultrices. Phasellus turpis est, posuere sit amet dapibus ut, facilisis sed
est. Nam id risus quis ante semper consectetur eget aliquam lorem.
</p>
<p>
Vivamus tristique elit dolor, sed pretium metus suscipit vel. Mauris
ultricies lectus sed lobortis finibus. Vivamus eu urna eget velit cursus
viverra quis vestibulum sem. Aliquam tincidunt eget purus in interdum. Cum
sociis natoque penatibus et magnis dis parturient montes, nascetur ridiculus
mus.
</p>
</div>
```

We're using a column-width of 200 pixels on that container, causing the browser to create as many 200-pixel columns as will fit. Whatever space is left between the columns will be shared.

CSS

```
.container {

column-width: 200px;

}
```

Did you get it?

1. Discuss the methods that can change how elements are laid out in CSS.
2. Write the CSS rule to implement absolute positioning.

A CLOSER LOOK

CSS SOFTWARE

To use CSS effectively, you need to know some of the popular CSS software in use:

- **PostCSS:** Through JavaScript, PostCSS enables you to add and manage CSS. PostCSS is more than just one CSS tool; it's a potent combination of features and packages that improves your CSS process. The grid in PostCSS is incredibly flexible and adaptable.

- **Visual Studio:** Microsoft created Visual Studio Code, an open-source CSS editor. It has built-in support for TypeScript, JavaScript, and Node.js. This CSS editor tool offers the IntelliSense feature, which delivers intelligent completions based on crucial modules, variable types, and function definitions.

- **Notepad++:** Popular free CSS code editor Notepad++ is created in C++. Pure Win32 API is used, which allows faster program execution. All the standard code editor capabilities, such as tabbed editing, find and replace, and autocompletion, are present in Notepad++.

- **Koala:** It is a complete GUI program that manages CoffeeScript, Compass, Less, and Sass compilations from a single location. Windows, Linux, and macOS all support its use. Koala offers developers a selection of project parameters, extra compilation choices, and personalized error messages.

- **Komodo Edit:** It is a traditional CSS tool. It is a robust and user-friendly tool for modifying code. It enables developers to debug, perform unit testing, refactor code, and perform other tasks. Additionally, it offers code profiles and connections with other technologies like Grunt.

ROLE MODEL

HÅKON WIUM LIE: KNOWN FOR CASCADING STYLE SHEETS

Håkon Wium Lie is a Norwegian web pioneer, a standards activist, and the chairman of YesLogic, developers of Prince CSS-based PDF rendering software. He was the Chief Technology Officer of Opera Software from 1998 until the browser was sold to new owners in 2016. He is best known for developing Cascading Style Sheets (CSS) while working with Tim Berners-Lee and Robert Cailliau at CERN in 1994.

- **Education and Career:** Håkon Wium Lie attended Østfold University College, West Georgia College, and MIT Media Lab, receiving an MS in Visual Studies in 1991.

  On February 17, 2006, he successfully defended his PhD thesis at the University of Oslo. His PhD thesis is background to the origins of CSS and a rationale to some of the design decisions behind it – particularly as to why some features were not included and why CSS avoids trying to become DSSSL. He has worked for, among others, the W3C, INRIA, CERN, MIT Media Lab, and Norwegian telecom research in Televerket.

- **Awards and Recognition:** In 1999, he was named to the MIT Technology Review TR100 as one of the top 100 innovators in the world under the age of 35.

In 2001, he was a Technology Pioneer at the World Economic Forum in Davos.

In 2017, Wium Lie held a keynote at the WeAreDevelopers Conference 2017, talking about his contributions to the web today with the creation of CSS, and how it has evolved together with the web itself up to its current state.

SUMMARY

- The presentation and styling of a document written in a markup language, such as HTML or XML (including XML dialects like SVG, MathML, or XHTML), can be specified using the style sheet language known as Cascading Style Sheets (CSS).
- The World Wide Web Consortium defined CSS, a standard that gives designers more precision and flexibility than standard HTML when defining the appearance of text and other formats.
- Building on CSS1, CSS2 was approved as a W3C recommendation in May 1998. Support for media-specific style sheets has been added in this version, e.g., printers, audio equipment, fonts that can be downloaded, element placement, and tables.
- The id selector selects a particular HTML element by using its id attribute.
- There are three methods you can use to add CSS styles to your website. One may utilize either an "internal stylesheet," "external stylesheet," or "inline style."
- Styles that are written directly within an HTML document's tag are known as inline styles.
- These days, external style sheets are used by most websites. Styles that are created in a different document and then added to different web documents are known as external styles.
- Using the CSS box model, a number of properties in CSS are frequently combined to form box properties, which regulate how browsers arrange pages.

MULTIPLE CHOICE QUESTION

1. **Which HTML tag is used to link an external CSS file to an HTML document?**
   a. <style>
   b. <link>
   c. <css>
   d. <script>

2. **Which CSS property is used to change the text color of an element?**
   a. color
   b. font-color
   c. text-color
   d. font-style

3. **In CSS, which property is used to set the background color of an element?**
   a. color
   b. background
   c. bg-color

d. background-color

4. **Which CSS property is used to add space between the border and the content of an element?**
   a. padding
   b. margin
   c. spacing
   d. border-spacing

5. **How can you select an element with the id "header" in CSS?**
   a. .header
   b. #header
   c. header
   d. *header

6. **Which CSS property is used to make text bold?**
   a. font-weight
   b. bold
   c. font-style
   d. text-decoration

7. **What does the CSS property "display: none;" do?**
   a. Shows the element
   b. Changes the font style
   c. Hides the element
   d. Adds a border to the element

8. **How do you comment in CSS?**
   a. <!–Comment–>
   b. /* Comment */
   c. //Comment
   d. **Comment**

9. **Which CSS property is used to control the size of text?**
   a. text-size
   b. font-size
   c. size
   d. text-font

10. **Which CSS property is used to make an element float to the left or right?**
    a. align
    b. position
    c. display
    d. float

REVIEW QUESTIONS

1. What are the elements of the CSS box model?
2. Differentiate between CSS3 and CSS2.
3. How can CSS be integrated into an HTML page?
4. Explain a few advantages of CSS.
5. What are the different types of Selectors in CSS?

Answer to Multiple Choice Questions

1. (b); 2. (a); 3. (d); 4. (a); 5. (b); 6. (a); 7. (c); 8. (b); 9. (b); 10. (d)

REFERENCES

1. Adewumi, A., Misra, S., & Ikhu-Omoregbe, N., (2012). Complexity metrics for cascading style sheets. In: *International Conference on Computational Science and Its Applications* (pp. 248–257). Berlin, Heidelberg.
2. Barton, J. J., & Odvarko, J., (2010). Dynamic and graphical web page breakpoints. In: *Proceedings of the 19th International Conference on World Wide Web, WWW '10* (pp. 81–90). New York, NY, USA, ACM.
3. Basci, D., & Misra, S., (2011a). Metrics suite for maintainability of XML web-services. *IET Software, 5*(3), 320–341.
4. Bos, B., Celik, T., Hickson, I., & Lie, H. W., (2011). Cascading style sheets level 2 revision 1 (CSS 2.1) specification. *W3C Recommendation, World Wide Web Consortium.*
5. Celik, T., Etemad, E. J., Glazman, D., Hickson, I., Linss, P., & Williams, J., (2011). Selectors level 3. *W3C Recommendation, World Wide Web Consortium.*
6. Eberlein, K. J., Anderson, R. D., & Joseph, G., (2010). *Darwin Information Typing Architecture (DITA) Version 1.2*. Oasis standard, OASIS.
7. Genev`es, P., Laya¨ıda, N., & Schmitt, A., (2007). Efficient static analysis of XML paths and types. In: *PLDI '07: Proceedings of the ACM SIGPLAN Conference on Programming Language Design and Implementation* (pp. 342–351).
8. Henley, C., (2015). *Better CSS with Sass*. UK: Five Simple Steps. ISBN: 978-3-863730-81-9.
9. Keller, M., & Nussbaumer, M., (2009). Cascading style sheets: A novel approach towards productive styling with today's standards. In: *Proceedings of the 18th International Conference on World Wide Web, WWW '09* (pp. 1161, 1162). New York, NY, USA. ACM.
10. Lie, H. W., & Bos, B., (2005). *Cascading Style Sheets: Designing for the Web* (3rd edn.). Boston, MA, USA: Addison-Wesley Professional.
11. Lincke, R., Lundberg, J., & Löwe, W., (2008). Comparing software metrics tool. In:

ACM Proceedings of the 2008 International Symposium on Software Testing and Analysis (pp. 131–142).

12. Mazinanian, D., & Tsantalis, N., (2016). An empirical study on the use of CSS preprocessors. In: *2016 IEEE 23rd International Conference on Software Analysis, Evolution, and Reengineering (SANER)* (Vol. 1, pp. 168–178).

13. Misra, S., Adewumi, A., Fernandez-Sanz, L., & Damasevicius, R., (2018). A Suite of object oriented cognitive complexity metrics. *IEEE Access, 6*, 8782–8796.

14. Muketha, G. M., Ghani, A. A. A., Selamat, M. H., & Atan, R., (2010b). Complexity metrics for executable business processes. *Information Technology Journal, 9*(7), 1317–1326.

15. Ogheneovo, E. E., (2014). On the relationship between software complexity and maintenance costs. *Journal of Computer and Communications, 2*(14), 1–16.

16. Pichler, C., Strommer, M., & Huemer, C., (2010). Size matters!? measuring the complexity of xml schema mapping models. In: *2010 6th World Congress on Services* (pp. 497–502). IEEE.

17. Tamayo, A., Granell, C., & Huerta, J., (2011). Analyzing complexity of XML schemas in geospatial web services. In: *Proceedings of the 2nd International Conference on Computing for Geospatial Research & Applications* (p. 17). ACM.

18. Wolf, D., & Henley, A. J., (2017). Cascading style sheets (CSS). In: *Java EE Web Application Primer* (pp. 115–118). A Press, Berkeley, CA.

CHAPTER 4

JavaScript

LEARNING OBJECTIVES

After studying this chapter, you will be able to:

- Understand fundamentals of JavaScript;
- Describe document object model (DOM) manipulation and events;
- Explain pair programming;
- Define the term debugging.

INTRODUCTORY EXAMPLE

POPUP Message Using Event: Display a simple message "Welcome!!!" on your demo webpage and when the user hovers over the message, a popup should be displayed with a message "Welcome to my WebPage!!!."

```html
<html>
<head>
<title>Event!!!</title>
<script type="text/javascript">
function trigger() {
document.getElementById("hover").addEventListener("mouseover," popup);
function popup() {
alert("Welcome to my WebPage!!!");
}
}
</script>
<style>
p{
font-size: 50px;
position: fixed;
left: 550px;
top: 300px;
}
</style>
</head>
<body onload="trigger();">
<p id="hover">Welcome!!!</p>
</body>
</html>
```

4.1. UNIT INTRODUCTION

Along with HTML and CSS, JavaScript is a programming language and a fundamental component of the World Wide Web. By 2024, 98.9% of websites will have client-side JavaScript for webpage behavior, frequently utilizing third-party libraries. A specific JavaScript engine is built into every major web browser to run the code on users' devices.

JavaScript is an ECMAScript-compliant high-level language that is frequently compiled just in time. It features first-class functions, prototype-based object orientation, and dynamic typing. It supports imperative, functional, and event-driven programming paradigms and is multi-paradigm. It supports working with text, dates, regular expressions, standard data structures, and the Document Object Model (DOM) through application programming interfaces (APIs).

No input/output (I/O) functionality, such as networking, storage, or graphics capabilities, is included in the ECMAScript standard. In reality, JavaScript APIs for I/O are provided by the web browser or another runtime system. Originally limited to use in web browsers, JavaScript engines are now essential parts of many servers and applications. Node is the most widely used runtime system for this purpose. Js. Despite sharing similarities in name, syntax, and standard libraries, Java and JavaScript are two very different languages with very different designs.

4.2. FUNDAMENTALS OF JAVASCRIPT

→Learning Objectives
- Understand the connection of JavaScript with Java;
- Describe client-side JavaScript;
- Discuss about JavaScript development tools.

JavaScript is a powerful dynamic programming language that can be used to create dynamic webpage interactivity within an HTML document. Brendan Eich, a co-founder of the Mozilla Corporation, the Mozilla Foundation, and the Mozilla project, invented it.

JavaScript has enormous versatility. You can begin modestly by experimenting with carousels, picture galleries, dynamic layouts, and button click responses. You'll be able to make animated 2D and 3D graphics, games, extensive database-driven apps, and much more with more experience.

You really don't need to set up any particular environment in order to learn JavaScript because it is installed on every modern web browser. For instance, all current browsers such as Chrome, Mozilla Firefox, Safari, and others support JavaScript.

You can create incredibly stunning and blazingly fast websites with JavaScript. You can create a website that has the look and feel of a console to provide the best Graphical User Experience for your visitors. Game developers, desktop app developers, and mobile app developers are now using JavaScript.

The wonderful thing about JavaScript is that there are a ton of pre-made frameworks and libraries available that you can use right away to speed up the development of your software.

1. **Client-Side Validation:** It is crucial to confirm any user input before sending it to the server, and JavaScript is a key component in front-end validation of user input.
2. **Manipulating HTML Pages:** JavaScript facilitates dynamic HTML page manipulation. This makes it simple to add and remove any HTML tag using JavaScript, and you can alter your HTML to adjust its appearance and feel to suit various devices and needs.

3. **User Notifications:** JavaScript can be used to display dynamic pop-ups on your website so that users can receive various kinds of notifications.
4. **Back-End Data Loading:** AJAX is a library provided by JavaScript that facilitates the loading of back-end data while performing other processing tasks. Your website visitors will have an incredible experience thanks to this.
5. **Presentations:** Additionally, JavaScript offers the ability to create presentations, which enhance the appearance and feel of websites. RevealJS and BespokeJS are JavaScript libraries that are used to create web-based slide shows.
6. **Server Applications:** The JavaScript runtime in Chrome is the foundation of Node JS, which is used to create scalable and quick network apps. This library, which is event-based, aids in the development of extremely complex server applications, such as web servers.

> **Keyword**
>
> **Scripting Language** – It is a programming language that is interpreted. It is translated into machine code when the code is run, rather than beforehand.

The JavaScript language is quite small and highly adaptable. On top of the fundamental JavaScript language, developers have created a wide range of tools that enable a significant amount of additional functionality with little effort. These include:

- Browser application programming interfaces (APIs) — web browser-integrated applications programming interfaces (APIs) that offer features like dynamic HTML creation and CSS style settings, video stream collection and manipulation, and the creation of 3D graphics and audio samples.
- Third-party APIs to let developers add features from other content providers, like Facebook or Twitter, to their websites.
- You can add third-party frameworks and libraries to your HTML to quickly create websites and applications.

4.2.1. The Java Connection

Understandably, JavaScript's connection with Java is regularly misunderstood. They are not the same thing.

- Similar to C++, Java is a comprehensive computer programming language developed by Sun Microsystems that can be used to create extensive, full-fledged programs.
- Conversely, Netscape is the company that created JavaScript. Although the code syntax is quite similar to Java, it was partially inspired by Java, though it is hardly ever utilized for purposes other than web browsing. It was actually going to be called "Live Script," but Netscape changed the name

for marketing purposes due to Java's rising popularity at the time.

One way to conceptualize a scripting language is a lightweight programming language, meaning it doesn't require compilation in order to be interpreted by a browser. In reality, the script consists of a few commands that the browser must execute.

There are numerous parallels between the two. The fact that they are both types of object-oriented programming, and OOP, is the most notable of these. This implies that you work with tiny pieces that are assembled into larger pieces.

You may be familiar with Java's use in conjunction with HTML through the use of applets. Although these small-scale apps can be integrated into pages for highly sophisticated effects, their huge file sizes and lack of additional usefulness make them somewhat impractical. On the other hand, JavaScript has many benefits.

4.2.1.1. Versions

JavaScript has been released in versions, much like almost every other tool we use to create websites. Version 1.0 of JavaScript first appeared in Netscape Navigator 2. JavaScript was upgraded to versions 1.1, 1.2, and 1.3 in later iterations. Microsoft attempted to support JavaScript 1.0 in Internet Explorer 3, but the result was incredibly unreliable and riddled with bugs. Microsoft gave their version the name "Jscript." Browsers from the most recent generation support JavaScript 1.3 fairly well.

A standardized version of JavaScript, sometimes referred to as ECMAScript after its standardizers, the ECMA, was eventually brought about by the dismay of coders over the incompatibilities caused by the two browsers' varying levels of support. This standard is well supported by contemporary browsers such as IE8, Firefox, and Safari, and there has been a lot of recent work to make sure that all browsers are using the same DOM.

4.2.2. Client-Side JavaScript

The most widely used version of the language is client-side JavaScript. For the code to be interpreted by the browser, the script needs to be a part of or referenced by an HTML document. This implies that a web page does not have to be static HTML; instead, it can contain applications that manage the browser, communicate with the user, and generate HTML content on the fly. The JavaScript client-side mechanism provides many advantages over traditional

> **Keyword**
>
> **Scripting Language** – It is a programming language that is interpreted. It is translated into machine code when the code is run, rather than beforehand.

CGI server-side scripts. For example, you might use JavaScript to check if the user has entered a valid e-mail address in a form field.

When a user submits a form, JavaScript code is run; only then is the form submitted to the web server if every entry is valid.

User-initiated events, such as button clicks, link navigation, and other actions the user performs either explicitly or implicitly, can be captured using JavaScript (Figure 4.1).

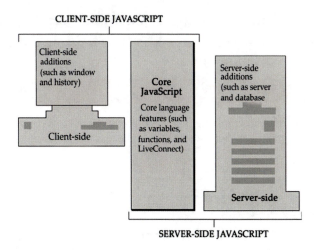

Figure 4.1. Client-side and server-side JavaScript.

Source: https://docs.oracle.com/cd/E19957-01/816-6409-10/graphics/lang.gif.

> **Keyword**
>
> **Web Browser** – It is used to access information on the World Wide Web using the Internet. Read on for the types, functions, and questions on web browsers.

4.2.2.1. Advantages of JavaScript

The merits of using JavaScript are:

1. **Less Server Interaction:** You can validate user input before sending the page off to the server. This saves server traffic, which means less load on your server
2. **Immediate Feedback to the Visitors:** They do not have to wait for a page reload to see if they have forgotten to enter something.
3. **Increased Interactivity:** You can create interfaces that react when the user hovers over them with a mouse or activates them via the keyboard.
4. **Richer Interfaces:** You can use JavaScript to include such items as drag-and-drop components and sliders to give a Rich Interface to your site visitors.

4.2.2.2. Limitations of JavaScript

As a programming language, JavaScript cannot be considered complete. It lacks the following important features:

- Client-side JavaScript does not allow the reading or writing of files. This has been kept for security reason.
- JavaScript cannot be used for networking applications because there is no such support available.
- JavaScript does not have any multithreading or multiprocessor capabilities.

Once again, you can add interactivity to otherwise static HTML pages with JavaScript, a lightweight, interpreted programming language.

Did you know?

The choice of the JavaScript name has caused confusion, implying that it is directly related to Java. At the time, the dot-com boom had begun, and Java was a popular new language, so Eich considered the JavaScript name a marketing ploy by Netscape.

4.2.3. JavaScript Development Tools

The fact that JavaScript doesn't require pricey development tools is one of its main advantages. A basic text editor like Notepad can be used as a starting point. You don't even need to purchase a compiler because it is an interpreted language that runs within a web browser.

To make our life simpler, various vendors have come up with very nice JavaScript editing tools. Some of them are listed here:

1. **Microsoft FrontPage:** Microsoft has developed a popular HTML editor called FrontPage. FrontPage also provides web developers with a number of JavaScript tools to assist in the creation of interactive websites.
2. **Macromedia Dreamweaver MX:** It is a very popular HTML and JavaScript editor in the professional web development crowd. It provides several handy prebuilt JavaScript components, integrates well with databases, and conforms to new standards such as XHTML and XML.
3. **Macromedia HomeSite 5:** HomeSite 5 is a well-liked HTML and JavaScript editor from Macromedia that can be used to manage personal websites effectively.

Did you get it?

1. What are the advantages of JavaScript?
2. Differentiate between client-side and server-side JavaScript.
3. Discuss the limitations of JavaScript.

4.3. DOCUMENT OBJECT MODEL (DOM) MANIPULATION AND EVENTS

→Learning Objectives
- Understand DOM and JavaScript;
- Describe DOM interfaces.

The programming interface called the Document Object Model (DOM) is used for HTML and XML documents. It provides a representation of the page, allowing programs to modify the structure, style, and content of the document. Nodes and objects are used by the DOM to represent the document, enabling programming languages to interact with the page.

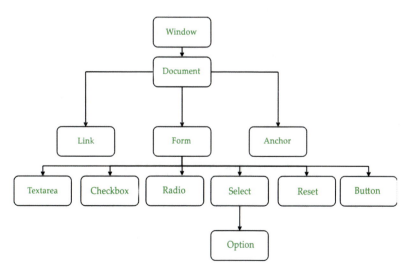

Figure 4.2. Document object model (DOM).

Source: https://media.geeksforgeeks.org/wp-content/uploads/DOM.png.

FUNDAMENTALS OF WEB DEVELOPMENT

A document is a Web page. This document can be seen as the HTML source or as it opens in a browser window. However, the document is the same in both instances. That same document is represented by the Document Object Model (DOM), which allows for manipulation. An object-oriented representation of the web page, known as the Document Object Model (DOM), is modifiable using scripting languages like JavaScript (Figure 4.2).

In most contemporary browsers, the W3C and WHATWG DOM standards are implemented. When using browsers on the web, where documents may be viewed by multiple browsers with different DOMs, caution must be taken because many of them extend the standard.

For example, the standard DOM specifies that the getElementsByTagName method in the code below must return a list of all the <P> elements in the document:

For example, the DOM specifies that the querySelectorAll method in this code snippet must return a list of all the <p> elements in the document:

JS

const paragraphs = document.querySelectorAll("p");

//paragraphs[0] is the first <p> element

//paragraphs[1] is the second <p> element, etc.

alert(paragraphs[0].nodeName);

Objects contain all of the attributes, functions, and events needed to manipulate and create web pages. Objects include, for instance, the document object, which is a representation of the document, any table objects that provide access to HTML tables via the HTMLTableElement DOM interface, and so on.

Keyword

Document Object Model (DOM) – It is the data representation of the objects that comprise the structure and content of a document on the web.

4.3.1. DOM and JavaScript

This brief example is in JavaScript, as are almost all of the examples in this reference. In other words, even though it's written in JavaScript, it accesses the document and its components through the DOM. Although the Document Object Model (DOM) is not a programming language, without it, JavaScript would lack a model or concept for web pages, HTML documents, XML documents, and their constituent elements (e.g., components). All of a document's elements, including the head, tables inside the document, table headers, and text within table cells, are components of the document object model, and as such, they can all be accessed and modified with the help of the Document Object Model (DOM) and a scripting language such as JavaScript. JavaScript and the DOM were closely related at first, but they gradually separated into different things. The page content is stored in the DOM and may be accessed and manipulated via JavaScript, so that we may write this approximative equation:

API (HTML or XML page) = DOM + JS (scripting language)

Because the DOM was created to be independent of any specific programming language, the document's structural representation could be accessed through a single, standardized API. While this reference documentation primarily focuses on JavaScript, it is possible to create DOM implementations for any language, as this Python example shows.

PYTHON

Python DOM example

import xml.dom.minidom as m

doc = m.parse(r"C:\Projects\Py\chap1.xml")

doc.nodeName # DOM property of document object

p_list = doc.getElementsByTagName("para")

4.3.1.1. Accessing the DOM

To start using the DOM, there is nothing special you need to do. In JavaScript, you can use the API directly from within a script, which is a browser-run program.

When you create a script, whether inline in a <script> element or included in the web page, you can immediately begin using the API for the document or window objects to manipulate the document itself, or any of the various elements in the web page (the descendant elements of the document). Your DOM programming may be something as simple as the following example, which displays a message on the console by using the console.log() function:

HTML

<body onload="console.log('Welcome to my home page!');">

...

</body>

> **Remember**
>
> JavaScript form validation only provides convenience for users, not security. If a site verifies that the user agreed to its terms of service, or filters invalid characters out of fields that should only contain numbers, it must do so on the server, not only the client.

The JavaScript components will be grouped here and kept apart from the HTML because it is generally not advised to combine the HTML-written page structure with the JavaScript-written DOM manipulation. For example, the following function creates a new h1 element, adds text to that element, and then adds it to the tree for the document:

HTML

```
<html lang="en">
<head>
<script>
//run this function when the document is loaded
window.onload = () => {
//create a couple of elements in an otherwise empty HTML page
const heading = document.createElement("h1");
const headingText = document.createTextNode("Big Head!");
heading.appendChild(headingText);
document.body.appendChild(heading);
};
</script>
</head>
<body></body>
</html>
```

4.3.1.2. Important Data Types

This reference attempts to provide the most straightforward description of the different types and objects. However, you should be aware that the API passes around a variety of different data types. This API reference's syntax examples usually refer to nodes as elements for simplicity's sake, arrays of nodes as nodeLists (or just elements), and attribute nodes as attributes.

Table 4.1 briefly describes these data types.

Table 4.1. Fundamental Data Types

Data Type (Interface)	Description
Document	When a member returns an object of type document (e.g., the ownerDocument property of an element returns the document to which it belongs), this object is the root document object itself. The DOM document Reference chapter describes the document object.
Node	Every object located within a document is a node of some kind. In an HTML document, an object can be an element node but also a text node or attribute node.
Element	The element type is based on node. It refers to an element or a node of type element returned by a member of the DOM API. Rather than saying, for example, that the document.createElement() method returns an object reference to a node, we just say that this method returns the element that has just been created in the DOM. element objects implement the DOM Element interface and also the more basic Node interface, both of which are included together in this reference. In an HTML document, elements are further enhanced by the HTML DOM API's HTMLElement interface as well as other interfaces describing capabilities of specific kinds of elements (for instance, HTMLTableElement for <table> elements).
NodeList	A nodeList is an array of elements, like the kind that is returned by the method document.querySelectorAll(). Items in a nodeList are accessed by index in either of two ways: • list.item(1) • list[1] These two are equivalent. In the first, item() is the single method on the nodeList object. The latter uses the typical array syntax to fetch the second item in the list.
Attr	When an attribute is returned by a member (e.g., by the createAttribute() method), it is an object reference that exposes a special (albeit small) interface for attributes. Attributes are nodes in the DOM just like elements are, though you may rarely use them as such.
NamedNodeMap	A namedNodeMap is like an array, but the items are accessed by name or index, though this latter case is merely a convenience for enumeration, as they are in no particular order in the list. A namedNodeMap has an item() method for this purpose, and you can also add and remove items from a namedNodeMap.

Source: https://developer.mozilla.org/en-US/docs/Web/API/Document_Object_Model/Introduction.

4.3.2. DOM Interfaces

It is all about the actual tools and objects that you can use to work with the DOM hierarchy. There are numerous places where it can be difficult to understand how these operate. For instance, the HTMLFormElement interface provides the object representing the HTML form element with its name property, while the HTMLElement interface provides the object with its className property. The desired property is just in that form object in both situations.

However, there can be a lack of clarity regarding the relationship between objects and the DOM interfaces they implement, so this section aims to clarify the actual DOM interfaces and their availability.

4.3.2.1. Interfaces and Objects

Numerous objects take cues from multiple interfaces. For instance, the table object implements a customized HTML Table Element Interface with methods like insertRow and createCaption. However, because table is an HTML element as well, it implements the Element interface that the DOM element describes. Lastly, the table element implements the more fundamental Node interface, from which Element derives, since an HTML element is also, as far as the DOM is concerned, a node in the tree of nodes that comprise the object model for an HTML or XML page.

Perhaps unknowingly, you use all three of these interfaces interchangeably on a regular basis when you get a reference to a table object, as shown in the following example.

JS

```
const table = document.getElementById("table");
const tableAttrs = table.attributes;//Node/Element interface
for (let i = 0; i < tableAttrs.length; i++) {
//HTMLTableElement interface: border attribute
if (tableAttrs[i].nodeName.toLowerCase() === "border") {
table.border = "1";
}
}
//HTMLTableElement interface: summary attribute
table.summary = "note: increased border";
```

4.3.2.2. Core Interfaces in the DOM

A selection of the DOM's most popular interfaces are listed in this section. The purpose of this is to give you an idea of the kinds of methods and properties you will frequently encounter when using the DOM, rather than to explain what these APIs do in detail.

In DOM programming, the objects whose interfaces you typically use the most are the document and window objects. To put it simply, the document object is the actual document root, and the window object is a representation of something akin to the browser. Many of the properties and methods you use on individual elements are provided by these two interfaces together, which the element inherits from the generic Node interface.

The following is a brief list of common APIs in web and XML page scripting using the DOM:

- document.querySelector()
- document.querySelectorAll()
- document.createElement()
- Element.innerHTML
- Element.setAttribute()
- Element.getAttribute()
- EventTarget.addEventListener()
- HTMLElement.style
- Node.appendChild()
- window.onload
- window.scrollTo()

> **Keyword**
> **Pair Programming** – It is a concept where two developers use just one machine to work, meaning they work simultaneously on a single block of code.

4.3.3. Testing the DOM API

This document provides samples for every interface that you can use in your own web development. In some cases, the samples are complete HTML pages, with the DOM access in a <script> element, the interface (e.g., buttons) necessary to fire up the script in a form, and the HTML elements upon which the DOM operates listed as well. When this is the case, you can cut and paste the example into a new HTML document, save it, and run the example from the browser.

Nonetheless, there are certain instances where the examples are shorter. It might be helpful to set up a test page where interfaces are easily accessible from scripts, so that examples can be run that just show the fundamental relationship between the interface and the HTML elements. The following very simple web page provides a <script> element in the header in which you can place functions that test the interface, a few HTML elements with attributes that you can retrieve, set, or otherwise manipulate, and the web user interface necessary to call those functions from the browser.

To test and observe how the DOM interfaces you are interested in function on the browser platform, you can use this test page or make one that is similar. You can add elements, make more buttons, and change the contents of the test() function as needed.

```
<html>
<head>
<title>DOM Tests</title>
<script type="application/x-JavaScript">
function setBodyAttr(attr,value){
if(document.body) eval('document.body.'+attr+'="'+value+'"');
else notSupported();
}
</script>
</head>
<body>
<div style="margin: .5in; height="400"">
<p><b><tt>text</tt> color</p>
<form>
<select onChange="setBodyAttr('text,'
this.options[this.selectedIndex].value);">
<option value="black">black
<option value="darkblue">darkblue
</select>
<p><b><tt>bgColor</tt></p>
<select onChange="setBodyAttr('bgColor,'
this.options[this.selectedIndex].value);">
<option value="white">white
```

```html
<option value="lightgray">gray
</select>
<p><b><tt>link</tt></p>
<select onChange="setBodyAttr('link,'
this.options[this.selectedIndex].value);">
<option value="blue">blue
<option value="green">green
</select>  <small>
<a href="http://www.brownhen.com/dom_api_top.html" id="sample">
(sample link)</a></small><br>
</form>
<form>
<input type="button" value="version" onclick="ver()"/>
</form>
</div>
</body>
</html>
```

You can build a test page with a console full of buttons, textfields, and other HTML elements to test a lot of interfaces on a single page—for instance, a "suite" of properties that change a web page's color scheme.

In this illustration, the dropdown menus dynamically change the color of the text (text), the hyperlinks' (aLink) and background (bgColor) on the webpage, among other DOM-accessible elements. Testing the interfaces as you read about them is a crucial step in mastering the use of the DOM, regardless of how you construct your test pages.

4.3.4. The Event Object

The event object is created at the beginning of the event and follows the event through the DOM. The event object is passed as the first argument to the function that we designate as a callback to an event listener. With the help of this object, we can learn a great deal about the incident that has happened:

- **type (string):** This is the name of the event.
- **target (node):** This is the DOM node where the event originated.

- **currentTarget (node):** This is the DOM node that the event callback is currently firing on.
- **bubbles (Boolean):** This indicates whether this is a "bubbling" event.
- **preventDefault (function):** This prevents any default behavior from occurring that the user agent (i.e., browser) might carry out in relation to the event (for example, preventing a click event on an <a> element from loading a new page).
- **stopPropagation (function):** This prevents any callbacks from being fired on any nodes further along the event chain, but it does not prevent any additional callbacks of the same event name from being fired on the current node.
- **stopImmediatePropagation (function):** This prevents any callbacks from being fired on any nodes further along the event chain, including any additional callbacks of the same event name on the current node.
- **cancelable (Boolean):** This indicates whether the default behavior of this event can be prevented by calling the event.preventDefault method.
- **defaultPrevented (Boolean):** This states whether the preventDefault method has been called on the event object.
- **isTrusted (Boolean):** An event is said to be "trusted" when it originates from the device itself, not synthesized from within JavaScript.
- **eventPhase (number):** This number represents the phase that the event is currently in: none (0), capture (1), target (2) or bubbling (3). We'll go over event phases next.
- **timestamp (number):** This is the date on which the event occurred.

The event object has a lot more properties, but they are unique to the particular kind of event. To show where the pointer is in the viewport, mouse events, for instance, will have clientX and clientY properties on the event object.

Using a console or the debugger in your preferred browser is the best option. log to examine the event object's properties in greater detail.

4.3.5. Event Phases

In your application, when a DOM event fires, it doesn't stop there; instead, it starts a three-phase journey. To put it briefly, the event moves from the root of the document to the target (i.e., capture phase), flows back to the document's root (bubbling phase), and then fires on the event target (target phase).

4.3.5.1. Capture Phase

The capture phase is the first stage. Beginning at the document's root, the event fires on each node along the way as it makes its way through the DOM layers and arrives at the event target. Building the propagation path that the event will retrace during the bubbling phase is the responsibility of the capture phase. You can listen to events in the capture phase by setting the third argument of addEventListener to true. You could potentially prevent any clicks from firing in a certain element if the event is handled in the capture phase.

    var form = document.querySelector('form');

    form.addEventListener('click,' function(event) {

    event.stopPropagation();

    }, true);//Note: 'true'

If you are unsure, listen for events in the bubbling phase by setting the useCapture flag to false or undefined.

4.3.5.2. Target Phase

The target phase is the time after an event reaches the target. After the event fires on the target node, it propagates back to the outermost document level by going back and retracing its steps.

In the case of nested elements, mouse and pointer events are always targeted at the most deeply nested element. If you have listened for a click event on a <div> element, and the user actually clicks on a <p> element in the div, then the <p> element will become the event target. The fact that events "bubble" means that you are able to listen for clicks on the <div> (or any other ancestor node) and still receive a callback once the event passes through.

4.3.5.3. Bubbling Phase

An event doesn't end when it fires on the intended target. It rises (or spreads) through the Document Object Model (DOM) and eventually reaches the document root. This indicates that until there is no parent node left to pass the event onto, the same event is fired on the parent node of the target, then the parent's parent, and so on.

Consider the event target as the center of an onion, with the DOM serving as the outer layer. The event penetrates each layer of the onion during the capture phase. The event reverses course and climbs back up through each layer after firing (the target phase) when it reaches the core (the propagation phase). The event's journey comes to an end when it resurfaces.

Talking is helpful. By listening on an element higher up the DOM tree, we are freed from listening for an event on the exact element from which it originated and can instead wait for it to reach us. In the event that events did not bubble, we might need to listen for an event on a variety of different elements in order to catch it.

Most events bubble, but not all of them. Events that don't catch on typically have good reasons behind them.

1. **Stopping Propagation:** Changing the course of the event at any time during its travels (i.e., it is possible to do so by simply invoking the stopPropagation method on the event object during the capture or bubbling phase. After that, when the event passes through nodes en route to the target and back to the document, it will stop calling listeners on those nodes.

child.addEventListener('click,' function(event) {

event.stopPropagation();

});

parent.addEventListener('click,' function(event) {

//If the child element is clicked

//this callback will not fire

});

If there are multiple listeners for the same event, calling event .stopPropagation() won't stop any more from being called on the current target. Use the more aggressive event if you want to stop the current node from calling any additional listeners. use the stopImmediatePropagation() function.

child.addEventListener('click,' function(event) {

event.stopImmediatePropagation();

});

child.addEventListener('click,' function(event) {

//If the child element is clicked

//this callback will not fire

});

2. **Prevent The Browser's Default Behavior:** The browser has built-in default actions that activate in response to specific events within the document. Clicking on a link is the most frequent occurrence. The browser interprets the href attribute and reloads the window at the new address when a click event happens on an element, bubbling up to the document level of the DOM.

Developers typically want to control the navigation within Web applications themselves, without forcing the page to reload. We must override the browser's default action in response to clicks in order to accomplish this. We use event .preventDefault() to accomplish this. event.preventDefault().

anchor.addEventListener('click,' function(event) {

```
event.preventDefault();

//Do our own thing

});
```

Numerous other browser default behaviors can be stopped. For instance, we could stop clicks from selecting text or space bar presses from scrolling the page in an HTML5 game.

Only callbacks attached further down the propagation chain will not be fired if event .stopPropagation() is called here. It won't stop the browser from operating as intended.

3. Custom DOM Events: DOM events can be initiated by more than just the browser. We are able to generate our own unique events and apply them to any document element. An event of this kind would act exactly like a typical DOM event.

```
var myEvent = new CustomEvent("myevent," {

detail: {

name: "Wilson"

},

bubbles: true,

cancelable: false

});

//Listen for 'myevent' on an element

myElement.addEventListener('myevent,' function(event) {

alert('Hello ' + event.detail.name);

});

//Trigger the 'myevent'

myElement.dispatchEvent(myEvent);
```

Synthesizing "untrusted" DOM events on elements (for example, click) to simulate user interaction is also possible. This can be useful when testing DOM-related libraries.

Note the following:

- The CustomEvent API is not available in IE 8 and below.
- The Flight framework from Twitter makes use of custom events to communicate between modules. This enforces a highly decoupled, modular architecture.

4. Delegate Event Listeners: A single event listener can be used to listen for events on many DOM nodes more efficiently and conveniently by using delegation event listeners. For instance, we could query the DOM to retrieve every item in the list and attach an event listener to each one if the list had 100 items and each item needed to react to a click event in the same way. There would be 100 distinct event listeners as a result. The click event listener would need to be added to the list each time a new item was added. This not only runs the risk of becoming costly, but it is also difficult to maintain.

Delegate event listeners can make our lives a lot easier. Instead of listening for the click event on each element, we listen for it on the parent <ul> element. When an <li> is clicked, then the event bubbles up to the <ul>, triggering the callback. We can identify which <li> element has been clicked by inspecting the event.target. Below is a crude example to illustrate:

```
var list = document.querySelector('ul');

list.addEventListener('click,' function(event) {

var target = event.target;

while (target.tagName !== 'LI') {

target = target.parentNode;

if (target === list) return;

}

//Do stuff here

});
```

This is preferable since it eliminates the need to attach a new event listener each time an item is added to the list, reducing overhead to that of a single event listener. The idea is quite straightforward but incredibly helpful.

Make use of a JavaScript event delegate library, like ftdomdelegate from FT Lab. If you are using jQuery, you can use event delegation with ease by giving the .on() method a selector as the second parameter.

```
//Not using event delegation

$('li').on('click,' function(){});

//Using event delegation

$('ul').on('click,' 'li,' function(){});
```

4.3.5.4. Useful Events

1. LOAD: Any resource that has completed loading—including any dependent resources—triggers the load event. An image, style sheet, script, audio file, video, document, or window could be this.

```
image.addEventListener('load,' function(event) {

image.classList.add('has-loaded');

});
```

2. ONBEFOREUNLOAD: window.onbeforeunload enables developers to ask the user to confirm that they want to leave the page. This can be useful in applications that require the user to save changes that would get lost if the browser's tab were to be accidentally closed.

window.onbeforeunload enables developers to ask the user to confirm that they want to leave the page. This can be useful in applications that require the user to save changes that would get lost if the browser's tab were to be accidentally closed.

```
window.onbeforeunload = function() {

if (textarea.value != textarea.defaultValue) {

return 'Do you want to leave the page and discard changes?';

}

};
```

Note that assigning an onbeforeunload handler prevents the browser from caching the page, thus making return visits a lot slower. Also, onbeforeunload handlers must be synchronous.

3. Stopping Window Bounce in Mobile Safari: At the Financial Times, we use a simple event.preventDefaulttechnique to prevent mobile Safari from bouncing the window when it is scrolled.

```
document.body.addEventListener('touchmove,' function(event) {

event.preventDefault();

});
```

However, it should be noted that this will also stop any native scrolling from functioning (like overflow: scroll). We listen for the same event on the scrollable element and set a flag on the event object to enable native scrolling on a subset of elements that require it. Depending on whether the isScrollable flag is present, we determine in the callback at the document level whether to stop the touch event's default behavior.

```
//Lower down in the DOM we set a flag

scrollableElement.addEventListener('touchmove,' function(event) {

event.isScrollable = true;
```

});

//Higher up the DOM we check for this flag to decide

//whether to let the browser handle the scroll

document.addEventListener('touchmove,' function(event) {

if (!event.isScrollable) event.preventDefault();

});

Manipulating the event object is not possible in IE 8 and below. As a workaround, you can set properties on the event.target node.

4. Resize: When creating intricate responsive layouts, it's quite helpful to pay attention to the window object's resize event. It is not always possible to achieve a layout using CSS by itself. JavaScript occasionally has to assist us in determining and setting the size of elements. We would probably need to readjust these sizes if the device's orientation changed, or the window was resized.

window.addEventListener('resize,' function() {

//update the layout

});

It is recommended to use a debounced callback to normalize the callback rate and prevent extreme thrashing in the layout.

5. Transitionend: Most transitions and animations in applications today are powered by CSS. However, there are situations in which we still require the completion time of a specific animation.

el.addEventListener('transitionEnd,' function() {

//Do stuff

});

Note the following:

- If you are using @keyframe animations, use the animationEndevent name, instead of transitionEnd.
- Like a lot of events, transitionEnd bubbles. Remember either to call event.stopPropagation() on any descendant transition events or to check the event.target to prevent callback logic from running when it's not supposed to.
- Event names are still widely vendor-prefixed (for example, webkitTransitionEnd, msTransitionEnd, etc.). Use a library such as Modernizr to get the event name's correct prefix.

6. Animationiteration: Each time an animating element finishes an iteration, the animationiteration event will be triggered. This is helpful if we wish to halt an animation before it ends.

function start() {

div.classList.add('spin');

}

function stop() {

div.addEventListener('animationiteration,' callback);

function callback() {

div.classList.remove('spin');

div.removeEventListener('animationiteration,' callback);

}

}

7. Error: We may want to take action if a resource loads with an error, particularly if users are experiencing unstable connections. The Financial Times makes use of this event to identify and instantly hide any images that might not have loaded properly in an article. We have two options for handling the error event now that it has been redefined to "not bubble" per the "DOM Level 3 Events" specification.

imageNode.addEventListener('error,' function(event) {

image.style.display = 'none';

});

Sadly, not all use cases are covered by addEventListener. Unfortunately, using (often discouraged) inline event handlers is the only way to ensure that image error event callbacks are executed. Fortunately, my colleague Kornel has graciously directed me to an example that demonstrates this.

<img src="https://example.com/image.jpg" onerror="this.style.display='none';"/>

This is because there's no guarantee that the code binding the error event handler will run prior to the error event actually occurring. By using inline handlers, our error listeners will be attached when the markup is parsed, and the image is requested.

Did you get it?

1. Explain the core interfaces in the DOM.
2. What do you understand by Event Object?

4.4. PAIR PROGRAMMING

→Learning Objectives
- Explain the concept of pair programming;
- Describe pairing mechanics.

Pair programming consists of two programmers sharing a single workstation (one screen, keyboard, and mouse among the pair). It is customary for the two programmers to switch roles every few minutes or so. The programmer at the keyboard is known as the "driver," while the other is known as the "navigator," and both are actively involved in the programming task but concentrate more on overall direction.

Two persons collaborate at a single computer to write all code that is sent into production. Pair programming improves the quality of software without affecting delivery time. Contrary to popular belief, two persons using a single computer can accomplish the same functionality as two working separately, but the output will be of far higher quality. Later in the project, significant savings are associated with higher quality.

- The best way to pair program is to just sit side by side in front of the monitor. Slide the keyboard and mouse back and forth. Both programmers concentrate on the code being written.
- Pair programming is a social skill that takes time to learn. You are striving for a cooperative way to work that includes give and take from both partners regardless of corporate status. The best pair programmers know when to say, "let's try your idea first." Do not expect people to be good at it from the start. It helps if you have someone on your team with experience to show everyone what it should feel like.

Actively sharing the input devices can be challenging in that style: aside from a few multiplayer games, it's difficult to find software that allows two people to type and click simultaneously. Pairs naturally decide who gets to use the keyboard and mouse at any given time to avoid confusion and needless backspace key presses, though these arrangements can vary greatly based on a variety of factors.

For us, one of the most crucial aspects of these agreements is what to do in the event that a programmer is not typing. The word "navigator," which means "driver's opposite," probably originated from rallying, where a navigator usually sits next to the pilot or driver and provides directions and alerts them to potential trouble spots.

Much like in racing though, the driver gets a disproportionate share of the credit and attention, and often, the mechanics of good navigation have been somewhat neglected.

4.4.1. Origins

Anecdotes of John Von Neumann, Fred Brooks, Jerry Weinberg, Richard Gabriel, or Edsger Dijkstra using pair programming are intriguing but occasionally difficult to substantiate. The names of numerous celebrities have been invoked in an attempt to give the practice an aura of necessity, if not sanctity. The chronology of credible sources that follows, however, does seem to indicate that pair programming in its current incarnation predates the Agile movement:

- **1992:** "Dynamic Duo" is the term coined by Larry Constantine, reporting on a visit to Whitesmiths Inc., a compiler vendor started by P.J. Plauger, one of the implementors of C: "At each terminal were two programmers! Of course, only one programmer was actually cutting code at each keyboard, but the others were peering over their shoulders." Whitesmiths existed from 1978 to 1988.
- **1993:** "The benefits of collaboration for student programmers" by Wilson is one early empirical study indicating benefits of pairing for programming tasks specifically. Posterior studies are more abundant and driven by the desire to "validate" pair programming after it had already gained popularity through Extreme Programming.
- **1995:** The pattern "Developing in Pairs" is given a brief description, in Alexandrian pattern form, in Jim Coplien's chapter "A Generative Development-Process Pattern Language" from the first patterns book, "Pattern Languages of Program Design."
- **1998:** In "Chrysler goes to Extremes," the earliest article about Extreme Programming, pair programming is presented as one of the core practices of the C3 team; it is later described formally as one of XP's original "twelve practices"
- **2000 (or Earlier):** The roles of Driver and Navigator are introduced to help explain pair programming; the earliest known reference is a mailing list posting; note however that the reality of these roles has been disputed, for instance Sallyann Bryant's article "Pair programming and the mysterious role of the navigator"
- **2002:** "Pair Programming Illuminated," by Laurie Williams and Robert Kessler, is the first book devoted exclusively to the practice and discusses its theory, practice, and the various studies up to that date
- **2003:** An anonymous article on the C2 Wiki describes Ping-Pong Programming, a moderately popular variant which marries pairing with test-driven development.

4.4.2. Pairing Mechanics

Two programmers working at the same workstation is known as pairing. While the other programmer "navigates," observing, learning, asking questions, conversing, and offering suggestions, one programmer "drives," using the keyboard.

The driver, in theory, concentrates on the syntax, semantics, and algorithm of the code in question. Less emphasis is placed on that by the navigator, who instead concentrates on higher abstraction levels such as the test they are attempting to pass, the next technical task to be completed, the amount of time since the last repository commit, the time elapsed since all tests were run, and the overall design quality. According to the theory, pairing produces better designs, fewer bugs, and a far better knowledge distribution within a development team, all of which add up to more functionality per unit of time over the long run.

4.4.2.1. Spreading Knowledge

Pairing is undoubtedly the best mentoring mechanism available. Pairing efficiently distributes a variety of knowledge across the team when partners switch off on a regular basis (as they should). This knowledge includes knowledge of the codebase, design and architecture, features and problem domains, language, development platforms, frameworks and tools, refactoring, and testing. It is widely accepted that pairing, as opposed to more informal approaches and traditional code reviews, is a better way to disseminate this kind of knowledge. What productivity cost do you incur, if any, for your excellent knowledge dissemination?

4.4.2.2. Pairing and Productivity

Anecdotal reports and research findings seem to indicate that while short-term productivity may decline slightly (roughly 15%), long-term productivity increases due to the significantly improved code produced. It also depends on how and over what period of time productivity is measured. Productivity in an agile setting is frequently gauged by the number of functional, tested features that are actually delivered each iteration and release. It is possible for a team that tracks productivity in lines of code per week to discover that pairing reduces this. If this results in fewer lines of code for each tested and operational feature, that is undoubtedly a positive development.

4.4.2.3. Productivity and Staff Turnover

Pairing proponents assert that pairing begins to demonstrate even greater value if productivity is measured over a long enough period of time to account for hiring and firing of staff. In numerous mainstream projects, knowledge tends to gather in "islands of expertise." Individual programmers frequently possess a wealth of knowledge that other programmers lack. There could be a significant delay in the project, if any of these islands decides to leave the team. According to the theory of pairing, management is less vulnerable to the ongoing risk of employee turnover when a team has a wide variety of knowledge. The number of team members who would need to be struck by a truck in order for the project to fail is referred to as the "Truck Number" in Extreme Programming. The goal of Extreme Programming projects is to maintain the Truck Number as near to the team size as feasible. If an individual departs, there are typically multiple individuals to assume their position. While specialization does exist, everyone is undoubtedly more knowledgeable about everything that is happening. Productivity should be higher if measured in terms of features delivered by such a team over multiple releases than if pairing.

4.4.2.4. Pairing Strategies

In by-the-book Extreme Programming, all production code is written by pairs. Pairing is not used at all by many non-XP agile teams. However, there is a lot of room for compromise between never pairing and always pairing. When mentoring new hires, taking on exceptionally risky tasks, starting a project from scratch with a fresh design, implementing new technology, or on a rotating monthly or weekly basis, consider utilizing pairing. Pairing is optional for programmers; those who don't want to can choose not to. Although it is common practice to use code reviews in place of pairing altogether, there is no reason why pairing shouldn't be tried at least once. There is growing evidence that it is a beneficial best practice and no plausible reason to believe it harms a team or a project.

4.4.2.5. Skill Levels

Passivity is one of the main problems preventing successful pairing. One variation of test-driven development known as "ping-pong programming" promotes more frequent role switching when used concurrently with the methodology: one programmer writes a unit test that fails, then hands the keyboard to another who writes the corresponding code and moves on to a new test. This variation can be used as a playful alternative by seasoned programmers, or it can be used solely for educational purposes.

Beginner:

- Able to participate as navigator, in particular to intervene appropriately;
- Able to participate as driver, in particular to explain code while writing it;
- Intermediate;
- Can tell the right moment to give up the keyboard and switch roles;
- Can tell the right moment to "steal" the keyboard and switch roles;
- Advanced;
- Able to "drop in" when another pair has been working on a task and pick up the navigator role smoothly.

4.4.2.6. Signs of Use

- The room's furniture and workstations are set up so as to encourage pairing (in teams new or hostile to pairing, obvious mistakes are tolerated, such as desks with too little room for two chairs)
- The room's noise level is controlled: the muted conversations from several simultaneous pairs create a background hum but do not rise to the level where they would disturb anyone's work

- If, on entering the room, you spot any programmer wearing an audio headset, take that as a "negative" sign – not only is pairing probably not practiced in the team but the conditions for successful adoptions are likely not met

4.4.2.7. Expected Benefits

- Increased code quality: "programming out loud" leads to clearer articulation of the complexities and hidden details in coding tasks, reducing the risk of error, or going down blind alleys
- Better diffusion of knowledge among the team, in particular when a developer unfamiliar with a component is pairing with one who knows it much better
- Better transfer of skills, as junior developers pick up micro-techniques or broader skills from more experienced team members
- Large reduction in coordination efforts, since there are N/2 pairs to coordinate instead of N individual developers
- Improved resiliency of a pair to interruptions, compared to an individual developer: when one member of the pair must attend to an external prompt, the other can remains focused on the task and can assist in regaining focus afterwards

Did you get it?

1. What do you understand by ping-pong programming?
2. Explain the benefits of pair programming

4.5. DEBUGGING

→Learning Objectives
- Understand the debugging process;
- Describe common debugging tools.

The process of finding and fixing errors, sometimes known as "bugs," in software code that could lead to unexpected behavior, or a crash is known as debugging. Debugging is the process of identifying and fixing errors or defects in software or systems in order to prevent improper operation. Debugging becomes more difficult when subsystems or modules are closely coupled because changes made to one module may result in additional bugs popping up in other modules. Occasionally, debugging a program requires more time than coding it.

4.5.1. The Debugging Process

In order to debug a program, a user must first identify the issue, isolate its source code, and then resolve it. It is expected of a user of a program to be knowledgeable about problem analysis, including how to solve problems. The program is operational once the bug has been fixed. During different phases of development, coding errors are found using debugging tools, also known as debuggers. They are used to replicate the error-causing circumstances, analyze the program's state at the moment, and identify the root cause. By analyzing the values of the variables and pausing the program execution when necessary to obtain the values of the variables or reset the program variables, programmers can track the execution of a program step-by-step. A debugger is a tool that some programming language packages offer to check code for errors as it is being written and during runtime. Debugging in software development is the process of identifying and fixing coding errors in a computer program. A crucial component of the software development lifecycle, debugging is a step in the software testing process. Debugging begins as soon as code is written and progresses through different phases as code is assembled with other programming elements to create software. Using techniques like unit tests, code reviews, and pair programming can streamline the debugging process in large programs with thousands or even millions of lines of code.

Finding the error in the code itself is required once it has been identified. At this point, using an integrated development environment's (IDE) debugging component or a standalone debugger tool can be helpful, as can examining the code's logging. Generally speaking, the most frequently used functions have their bugs discovered and fixed first. Sometimes the line of code itself is not obvious, but the module presenting the issue is. Debugging can then be aided by unit tests, such as JUnit and xUnit, which let the programmer run a particular function with a given set of inputs.

Typically, a "breakpoint" is set up and the program is executed until that point is reached, at which point it stops. Programmers can view memory and variables, run the program to the next breakpoint, execute just the next line of code, and, in certain situations, modify the value of variables or even the contents of the line of code that is about to be executed, thanks to the debugging feature of an IDE.

4.5.2. Common Debugging Tools

Debugging can also benefit from the use of source code analyzers, which include security, complexity, and common code errors analyzers. Modules that are so complex that they are challenging to comprehend, and test can be found using a complexity analyzer. To help with debugging, certain tools can actually examine a test run to determine which lines of code were not run. Advanced logging and simulators that let programmers simulate how an app will look and act on a mobile device are two more debugging tools.

Debugging certain tools—particularly scripting languages and open-source tools—requires a more manual approach because they don't run in an IDE. Some examples of such techniques are the dropping of values into a log, the addition of lengthy "print" statements during code execution, or the use of hard-coded "wait" commands that wait for keyboard input at predetermined intervals to simulate a breakpoint.

In engineering, the term "bug" was first used to refer to an error. Admiral Grace Hopper, a pioneer in computer programming who was also well-known for her wry sense of humor, is credited with coining the term, applying it to computers, and providing the idea for the synonym debugging. When a real bug—a moth—got stuck between electrical relays and created an issue in the U.S. Admiral Hopper and her group "debugged" the Navy's first computer and preserved the moth.

4.5.2.1. Use a JavaScript Debugger

A debugger is an application that gives the programmer complete control over how a script is executed. Debuggers give you fine-grained control over the script's state by enabling you to inspect, modify, and control the execution flow through an interface.

A script can be told to stop at specific breakpoints or run one line at a time after it has been loaded into a debugger. The programmer can check the script's state and its variables after stopping execution to see if there is a problem. Variables can also be monitored for changes in value.

4.5.2.2. Useful Tips for Developers

To cut down on errors in your scripts and streamline the debugging process, bear in mind the following advice:

- Use plenty of comments. Comments enable you to explain why you wrote the script the way you did and to explain particularly difficult sections of code.
- Always use indentation to make your code easy to read. Indenting statements also makes it easier for you to match up beginning and ending tags, curly braces, and other HTML and script elements.
- Write modular code. Whenever possible, group your statements into functions. Functions let you group related statements, and test and reuse portions of code with minimal effort.
- Be consistent in the way you name your variables and functions. Try using names that are long enough to be meaningful and that describe the contents of the variable or the purpose of the function.
- Use consistent syntax when naming variables and functions. In other words, keep them all lowercase or all uppercase; if you prefer CamelBack notation, use it consistently.
- Test long scripts in a modular fashion. In other words, do not try to write the entire script before testing any portion of it. Write a piece and get it to work before adding the next portion of code.
- Use descriptive variable and function names and avoid using single character names. Watch your quotation marks. Remember that quotation marks are used in pairs around strings and that both quotation marks must be of the same style (either single or double).
- Watch your equal signs. You should not use a single = for comparison purpose.
- Declare variables explicitly using the var keyword.

Keyword
Debugging – It is the process of finding and fixing errors or bugs in the source code of any software.

Did you get it?

1. How to use a JavaScript debugger?
2. How to identify and fix errors or defects in software?

A CLOSER LOOK

JAVASCRIPT: A CLOSER LOOK AT CLOSURES WITH CODE EXAMPLES

JavaScript is a powerful programming language that has become an essential tool for web development. One of the key features of JavaScript is its ability to create closures, which are functions that have access to the variables in their parent scope. In this blog, we will take a closer look at closures and how they can be used in JavaScript.

A closure is a function that has access to the variables in its parent scope, even after the parent function has returned. This allows the closure to "remember" the values of the variables at the time it was created and continue to use them even after the parent function has been completed. Closures are created when a function is defined inside another function, and the inner function references a variable from its parent scope.

One of the main benefits of closures is that they provide a way to maintain the state in a program. For example, in an event-driven program like a web page, a closure can be used to keep track of the state of a button or other UI element. The closure can store the current state of the button and update it as the user interacts with the page. This allows the program to maintain a consistent state across different interactions, without having to use global variables.

Another benefit of closures is that they can be used to create private variables and methods. By using closures, we can create variables and functions that are not accessible from outside the closure, which can help to protect sensitive data and logic from being modified or accessed by other parts of the program.

Closures can also be used to create function factories, which are functions that return other functions. This can be useful for creating similar functions with slightly different behavior, without having to duplicate code. For example, a function factory could be used to create a set of functions that each perform a different mathematical operation, such as addition, subtraction, multiplication, and division.

Closures can also be used to create closures within closures, which allows for even more powerful functionality.

It's important to note that closures have their own unique set of rules and considerations, such as memory management and the potential for creating circular references that can cause memory leaks.

You can also see how closures can be used to maintain the state:

```
function createCounter() {
    let count = 0;
    return function increment() {
        count++;
        return count;
    }
}

let counter = createCounter();
console.log(counter()); // Output: 1
console.log(counter()); // Output: 2
console.log(counter()); // Output: 3
```

Here, the createCounter the function returns a closure that maintains the state of a count variable. Each time we call the closure, it increments the count by 1 and returns the new value.

CASE STUDY

- **Modularity of JavaScript Libraries and Frameworks in Modern Web Applications:** JS is a scripting language derived from the ECMAScript Standard, which was adopted by the international standard ISO/IEC 16262. It supports object-oriented and functional programming paradigms and employs dynamic typing. The JavaScript Object Notation (JSON) has become a lightweight and flexible communication standard for web-based information systems. The basic language constructs are very simple, which could be the reason for the languages' popularity. Today, JS is used for nearly every dynamic user interface on the web with jQuery being the most popular.Design patterns are reliable solutions for common design problems in a specific context and have specific purposes (creational, structural, and behavioral). One of the most prevalent architectural principles of web applications is the separation of concerns, which is implemented by the design pattern Model-View-Controller (MVC) respectively Model-ViewViewModel (MVVM). Separation of concerns is also associated with the concept of "modularity." Modularity in a software system means to provide multiple functional units while keeping dependencies between the units low. These units, or modules, should have high cohesion and low coupling.

  The used design patterns have a significant impact at least on the following non-functional properties of the resulting product: changeability, interoperability, efficiency, reliability, testability, and reusability. A high degree of fulfillment of these characteristics makes the software product easier to code, debug, test, extend and maintain while lowering the costs for these tasks.

- **Evaluation of JavaScript Application Architecture:** The design of the application's architecture involves the earliest and many of the most crucial decisions in the software development process. As web technologies like JS become ever more important for the frontend layer of enterprise applications, these decisions must also be evaluated for the use of libraries and frameworks to provide fast and highly interactive applications on the web. A "library" in this discussion is considered a closed functional package that is tailored to provide a solution for a specific problem, e.g., plotting, dragand-drop or DOM manipulation (document object model). Balzert calls it "small-scale reuse." The term "framework" is referred to as a generic solution for a set of common problems which employs good design practices and can comprise libraries and architectural patterns (ibid.).

  Currently, there are lots of JS libraries and frameworks with different scopes as can be seen in Figure 4.3. The introduction of new non-standard functionality in JS applications can usually be achieved by integrating a suitable library. The libraries can be combined almost arbitrarily, e.g., different widget libraries can be used together. Frameworks have a more fundamental impact on the application structure due to their architectural implications and therefore cannot be combined as easily as libraries. So, the combination of frameworks is possible, but must be well-conceived as their roles in the MVC pattern may overlap. Recently, there also has been a shift of the usage of JS to the backend side of the software architecture resulting in the possibility of full-stack JS-based web applications. In practice, a popular combination with the acronym "MEAN" is emerging as a typical JS-based web application stack: MongoDB (database), Express (backend framework), AngularJS (frontend framework), Node.js (backend platform). The user interface (UI) respectively widget libraries are easier to replace and therefore are not included.

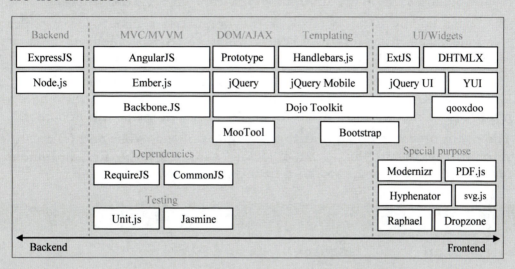

Figure 4.3. Architectural coverage of popular JavaScript web application components.

Source: https://www.researchgate.net/publication/265914279_Modularity_of_JavaScript_Libraries_and_Frameworks_in_Modern_Web_Applications.

The order of inclusion plays a significant role for the working of the different scripts. For example, many scripts are based on jQuery and therefore must be included after it in the source code to work as intended. Beside the implicit dependencies of JS modules, problems include namespace pollution and the use of global variables. That is why there are components for organizing the dependencies between modules. The organization of JS modules is often achieved by using asynchronous module definition, a JS API applying the "inversion of control" pattern. The asynchronous loading of needed resources improves performance. The problem is that every "module" (or bean) has to be loaded as a single file to resolve dependencies which can increase network protocol overhead.

SUMMARY

- Along with HTML and CSS, JavaScript is a programming language and a fundamental component of the World Wide Web.
- JavaScript is an ECMAScript-compliant high-level language that is frequently compiled just in time. It features first-class functions, prototype-based object orientation, and dynamic typing.
- JavaScript is a powerful dynamic programming language that can be used to create dynamic webpage interactivity within an HTML document.
- The most widely used version of the language is client-side JavaScript. For the code to be interpreted by the browser, the script needs to be a part of or referenced by an HTML document.
- The programming interface called the Document Object Model (DOM) is used for HTML and XML documents. It provides a representation of the page, allowing programs to modify the structure, style, and content of the document.
- The event object is created at the beginning of the event and follows the event through the DOM. The event object is passed as the first argument to the function that we designate as a callback to an event listener.

MULTIPLE CHOICE QUESTION

1. **JavaScript is an _____ language?**
   a. Object-Oriented
   b. Object-Based
   c. Procedural
   d. None of the above

2. **Which of the following keywords is used to define a variable in JavaScript?**
   a. var
   b. let
   c. Both (a) and (b)
   d. None of the above

3. **Which of the following methods is used to access HTML elements using JavaScript?**
   a. getElementbyId()
   b. getElementsByClassName()
   c. Both (a) and (b)
   d. None of the above

4. **Upon encountering empty statements, what does the JavaScript Interpreter do?**
   a. Throws an error
   b. Ignores the statements

c. Gives a warning
   d. None of the above
5. **Which of the following methods can be used to display data in some form using JavaScript?**
   a. document.write()
   b. console.log()
   c. window.alert()
   d. All of the above
6. **How can a datatype be declared to be a constant type?**
   a. const
   b. var
   c. let
   d. constant
7. **What will be the output of the following code snippet?**
   ```
   <script type="text/JavaScript">
   a = 5 + "9";
   document.write(a);
   </script>
   ```
   a. Compilation Error
   b. 14
   c. Runtime Error
   d. 59
8. **When the switch statement matches the expression with the given labels, how is the comparison done?**
   a. Both the datatype and the result of the expression are compared.
   b. Only the datatype of the expression is compared.
   c. Only the value of the expression is compared.
   d. None of the above.
9. **What is the use of the <noscript> tag in JavaScript?**
   a. The contents are displayed by non-JS-based browsers.
   b. Clears all the cookies and cache.
   c. Both A and B.
   d. None of the above.
10. **What does the JavaScript "debugger" statement do?**
    a. It will debug all the errors in the program at runtime.
    b. It acts as a breakpoint in a program.

c. It will debug error in the current statement if any.
d. All of the above.

REVIEW QUESTIONS

1. What are the different data types present in JavaScript?
2. Why do we use the word "debugger" in JavaScript?
3. How do you add JavaScript code to a website?
4. What are the key differences between Java and JavaScript?/How is JavaScript different from Java?
5. How to use external JavaScript file?

Answer to Multiple Choice Questions

1. (a); 2. (c); 3. (c); 4. (b); 5. (d); 6. (a); 7. (d); 8. (a); 9. (a); 10. (b)

REFERENCES

1. Aho, A., Lam, M., Sethi, R., & Ullman, J., (2006). *Compilers: Principles, Techniques, and Tools.* Addison-Wesley Longman Publishing Co., Inc. Boston, MA, USA.
2. Anderson, C., Giannini, P., & Drossopoulou, S., (2005). Towards type inference for JavaScript. In: *19th European Conference on Object-Oriented Programming* (pp. 428–453).
3. Balzert, H., (2001). *Lehrbuch Der Software-Technik* (2nd edn., p. 840). Heidelberg, Berlin: Spektrum Verlag.
4. Das, M., (2000). Unification-based pointer analysis with directional assignments. *Proceedings of the ACM SIGPLAN 2000 Conference on Programming Language design and Implementation* (pp. 35–46).
5. Hind, M., & Pioli, A., (2000). Which pointer analysis should I use? *ACM SIGSOFT Software Engineering Notes, 25*(5), 113–123.
6. International Organization for Standardization (ISO) and International Electrotechnical Commission (IEC), (2011). *Information Technology — Programming Languages, Their Environments and System Software Interfaces — ECMAScript Language Specification.* Switzerland: ISO/IEC.
7. Rountev, A., Milanova, A., & Ryder, B., (2001). Points-to analysis for Java using annotated constraints. *Proceedings of the 16th ACM SIGPLAN Conference on Object Oriented Programming, Systems, Languages, and Applications* (pp. 43–55).
8. Thiemann, P., (2005). Towards a type system for analyzing JavaScript programs. *European Symposium on Programming,* 408–422.

CHAPTER 5
PHP

LEARNING OBJECTIVES

After studying this chapter, you will be able to:

- Understand PHP – environment setup;
- Describe PHP syntax;
- Know about variables in PHP;
- Explain PHP constants;
- Define PHP operators.

INTRODUCTORY EXAMPLE

Your First PHP-Enabled Page: Create a file named hello.php and put it in your web server's root directory (DOCUMENT_ROOT) with the following content:

<!DOCTYPE html>

<html>

<head>

<title>PHP Test</title>

</head>

<body>

<?php echo '<p>Hello World</p>'; ?>

</body>

</html>

Use your browser to access the file with your web server's URL, ending with the/hello.php file reference. When developing locally this URL will be something like http://localhost/hello.php or http://127.0.0.1/hello.php but this depends on the web server's configuration. If everything is configured correctly, this file will be parsed by PHP and the following output will be sent to your browser:

<!DOCTYPE html>

<html>

<head>

<title>PHP Test</title>

</head>

<body>

<p>Hello World</p>

</body>

</html>

This program is extremely simple, and you really did not need to use PHP to create a page like this. All it does is display: Hello World using the PHP echo statement. Note that the file does not need to be executable or special in any way. The server finds out that this file needs to be interpreted by PHP because you used the ."php" extension, which the server is configured to pass on to PHP. Think of this as a normal HTML file which happens to have a set of special tags available to you that do a lot of interesting things.

If you tried this example and it did not output anything, it prompted for download, or you see the whole file as text, chances are that the server you are on does not have PHP enabled or is not configured properly. Ask your administrator to enable it for you using the Installation chapter of the manual. If you are developing locally, also read the installation chapter to make sure everything is configured properly. Make sure that you access the file via http with the server providing you the output. If you just call up the file from your file system, then it will not be parsed by PHP. If the problems persist anyway, do not hesitate to use one of the many » PHP support options.

5.1. UNIT INTRODUCTION

PHP is a versatile scripting language designed primarily for web development. Programmer Danish-Canadian programmer Rasmus Lerdorf, originally created it in 1993, and it was made available in 1995. The PHP Group is now responsible for producing the PHP reference implementation. Originally standing for Personal Home Page, PHP is now an acronym for PHP: Hypertext Preprocessor, a recursive initialism. PHP interpreters, which can be implemented as modules, daemons, or Common Gateway Interface (CGI) executables, are typically used on web servers to process PHP code. The outcome of the interpreted and run PHP code on a web server could be any kind of data, including binary image data or generated HTML, and it could make up all or part of an HTTP response. There are several web content management systems, web template systems, and web frameworks available that can be used to coordinate or expedite the creation of that response. PHP is also useful for a wide range of programming tasks that are not related to the web, like controlling robotic drones and creating standalone graphical applications. It is also possible to run PHP code straight from the command line.

PHP began as a modest open-source project and grew in size as more and more users realized how beneficial it was. In 1994, Rasmus Lerdorf released the initial version of PHP.

- PHP is a recursive acronym for "PHP: Hypertext Preprocessor."
- PHP is a server-side scripting language that is embedded in HTML. It is used to manage dynamic content, databases, session tracking, even build entire e-commerce sites.
- It is integrated with a number of popular databases, including MySQL, PostgreSQL, Oracle, Sybase, Informix, and Microsoft SQL Server.
- PHP is pleasingly zippy in its execution, especially when compiled as an Apache module
- on the Unix side. The MySQL server, once started, executes even very complex queries with huge result sets in record-setting time.
- PHP supports a large number of major protocols such as POP3, IMAP, and LDAP. PHP4 added support for Java and distributed object architectures (COM and CORBA), making n-tier development a possibility for the first time.
- PHP is forgiving PHP language tries to be as forgiving as possible.
- PHP Syntax is C-Like.

5.1.1. Common Uses of PHP

PHP performs system functions, i.e., from files on a system it can create, open, read, write, and close them. The other uses of PHP are:

- PHP can handle forms, i.e., gather data from files, save data to a file, thru email you can send data, return data to the user.

- You add, delete, modify elements within your database thru PHP.
- Access cookies variables and set cookies.
- Using PHP, you can restrict users to access some pages of your website.
- It can encrypt data.

5.1.2. Characteristics of PHP

Five important characteristics make PHP's practical nature possible:

- Simplicity;
- Efficiency;
- Security;
- Flexibility;
- Familiarity.

5.1.3. "Hello World" Script in PHP

Start with basic PHP scripts at first to get a feel for the language. As "Hello, World!" is a crucial example, let's start by writing a cute little script for it. As was previously stated, PHP is integrated into HTML. This means that you'll have PHP statements like this one mixed in with your regular HTML (or XHTML if you're really fancy):

```
<html>
<head>
<title>Hello World</title>
<body>
    <?php echo "Hello, World!";?>
</body>
</html>
```

It will produce the following result:

```
Hello, World!
```

You can see that the file that was sent from the server to your Web browser does not contain PHP code by looking at the HTML output of the example above. The only thing that is sent back to the client from the web server is pure HTML output; all PHP that is present on the page is processed and removed. One of the three unique markup tags that the PHP Parser recognizes must contain all PHP code.

```
<?php PHP code goes here ?>

<?    PHP code goes here ?>

<script language="php"> PHP code goes here </script>
```

FUNDAMENTALS OF WEB DEVELOPMENT

5.2. PHP – ENVIRONMENT SETUP

→Learning Objectives
- Understand PHP installation on Linux or Unix with Apache;
- Describe PHP installation on Mac OS X with Apache.

There are three essential components that must be installed on your computer before you can create and execute PHP Web pages.

1. **Web Server:** The most widely used web server software is Apache Server, which is freely available. However, PHP can be used with almost any web server software, including Microsoft's Internet Information Server (IIS).
2. **Database:** PHP is compatible with almost any database program, such as Sybase and Oracle, but MySQL is the most widely used free database.
3. **PHP Parser:** A parser needs to be installed in order to process PHP script instructions and produce HTML output that can be viewed in a web browser.

5.2.1. PHP ParserInstallation

Make sure your computer is configured correctly before continuing if you want to use PHP to develop web applications.

Type the following address into your browser's address box.

http://127.0.0.1/info.php

You have PHP and Webserver installed correctly if this brings up a page with information about your PHP installation. If not, you must follow the instructions to install PHP on your computer.

5.2.2. PHP Installation on Linux or Unix with Apache

If you plan to install PHP on Linux or any other variant of Unix, then here is the list of prerequisites:

- The PHP source distribution http://www.php.net/downloads.php The latest Apache source distribution http://httpd.apache.org/download.cgi.
- A working PHP-supported database, if you plan to use one (For example MySQL, Oracle etc.)
- Any other supported software to which PHP must connect (mail server, BCMath package, JDK, and so forth)
- An ANSI C compiler.
- Gnu make utility – you can freely download it at http://www.gnu.org/software/make
- Here are the instructions to install Apache and PHP5 on your Linux or Unix machine. Please ensure that you adjust the steps if you have different versions of PHP or Apache.
- If you haven't already done so, unzip and untar your Apache source distribution. Unless you have a reason to do otherwise,/usr/local is the standard place.

```
gunzip -c apache_1.3.x.tar.gz
tar -xvf apache_1.3.x.tar
```

- Build the Apache Server as follows:

```
cd apache_1.3.x
./configure --prefix=/usr/local/apache --enable-so
make
make install
```

- Unzip and untar your PHP source distribution. Unless you have a reason to do otherwise,/usr/local is the standard place.

```
gunzip -c php-5.x.tar.gz
tar -xvf php-5.x.tar
cd php-5.x
```

- Configure and build your PHP, assuming you are using MySQL database.

```
./configure --with-apxs=/usr/sbin/apxs \
            --with-mysql=/usr/bin/mysql
make
make install
```

Install the php.ini file. Edit this file to get configuration directives:

> **Keyword**
>
> **Address Box** – It is a rectangular box toward the top of a browser window where a user can type a web address.

```
cd ../../php-5.x
cp php.ini-dist /usr/local/lib/php.ini
```

- Tell your Apache server where you want to serve files from, and what extension(s) you want to identify PHP files. .php is the standard, but you can use .html, .phtml, or whatever you want.
    - Go to your HTTP configuration files (/usr/local/Apache/conf or whatever your path is)
    - Open httpd.conf with a text editor.
    - Search for the word DocumentRoot (which should appear twice) and change both paths to the directory you want to serve files out of (in our case,/home/httpd). We recommend a home directory rather than the default/usr/local/Apache/htdocs because it is more secure, but it doesn.t have to be in a home directory. You will keep all your PHP files in this directory.
- Add at least one PHP extension directive, as shown in the first line of code that follows. In the second line, we.ve also added a second handler to have all HTML files parsed as PHP.

```
AddType application/x-httpd-php .php
AddType application/x-httpd-php .html
```

Restart your server. Every time you change your HTTP configuration or php.ini files, you must stop and start your server again.

```
cd ../bin
./apachectl start
```

- Set the document root directory permissions to world-executable. The actual PHP files in the directory need only be world-readable (644). If necessary, replace/home/httpd with your document root below:

```
chmod 755 /home/httpd/html/php
```

- Open a text editor. Type: Save this file in your Web server's document root as info.php.
- Start any Web browser and browse the file. You must always

> **Keyword**
>
> **PHP 5** – It was released 4 years after the introduction of PHP 4 to the Internet scene, aimed to bring a brand-new functionality to the PHP language.

use an HTTP request (http://www.testdomain.com/info.php or http://localhost/info.php or http://127.0.0.1/info.php) rather than a filename (/home/httpd/info.php) for the file to be parsed correctly

Did you know?

According to recent research, nearly 80% of developers choose PHP as their server-side scripting language. Although it is by no means a new language, it remains an in-demand skill for web developers and professionals in the space. That's thanks to its widespread use, many PHP scalable frameworks, and active—and growing—community.

5.2.3. PHP Installation on Mac OS X with Apache

Users of Mac computers can choose to install from a source or a binary. Actually, Apache and PHP were most likely already preinstalled on your OS X. This build is probably fairly old, and it probably doesn't have many of the less popular additions.

Still, if all you want is a quick laptop Apache + PHP + MySQL/PostgreSQL setup, this is definitely the easiest way to go. The only things left to do are edit your Apache configuration file and activate the Web server.

So just follow the steps given below:

- Open the Apache config file in a text editor as root.

   ```
   sudo open -a TextEdit /etc/httpd/httpd.conf
   ```

- Edit the file. Uncomment the following lines:

   ```
   Load Module php5_module
   AddModule mod_php5.c
   AddType application/x-httpd-php .php
   ```

- You may also want to uncomment the block or otherwise tell Apache which directory to serve out of.
- Restart the Web server

   ```
   sudo apachectl graceful
   ```

- Open a text editor. Type: Save this file in your Web server's document root as info.php.
- Start any Web browser and browse the file. You must always use an HTTP request (http://www.testdomain.com/info.php or http://localhost/info.php or http://127.0.0.1/info.php) rather than a filename (/home/httpd/info.php) for the file to be parsed correctly

You should see a long table of information about your new PHP installation message Congratulations!

5.2.4. PHP Installation on Windows NT/2000/XP with IIS

Because it uses a precompiled binary rather than a source build, installing PHP on a Windows server with IIS is considerably easier than on a Unix system.

If you plan to install PHP on Windows, then here is the list of prerequisites:

- A working PHP-supported Web server. Under previous versions of PHP, IIS/PWS was the easiest choice because a module version of PHP was available for it; but PHP now has added a much wider selection of modules for Windows.

- A correctly installed PHP-supported database like MySQL or Oracle etc. (if you plan to use one).

- The PHP Windows binary distribution (download it atwww.php.net/downloads.php).

- A utility to unzip files (search http://download.cnet.com for PC file compression utilities).

- Now here are the steps to install Apache and PHP 5 on your Windows machine. If your PHP version is different, then please take care accordingly.

Did you get it?

1. What are essential components that must be installed on your computer before you can create and execute PHP Web pages.
2. How to install PHP on Windows NT/2000/XP with IIS.

5.3. PHP – SYNTAX OVERVIEW

→Learning Objectives
- Make Canonicals with PHP;
- Describe ASP-style tags.

5.3.1. Escaping to PHP

The ability to distinguish PHP code from other page elements is required by the PHP parsing engine. The process of accomplishing this is called "escaping to PHP." To accomplish this, there are four methods:

1. Canonical PHP Tags: The most universally effective PHP tag style is:

```
<?php...?>
```

If you use this style, you can be positive that your tags will always be correctly interpreted.

2. Short-Open (SGML-Style) Tags: Short or short-open tags look like this:

```
<?...?>
```

As one might expect, short tags are the shortest option. In order for PHP to recognize the tags, you need to do one of two things:

- Choose the – enable-short-tags configuration option when you're building PHP.
- Set the short_open_tag setting in your php.ini file to on. This option must be disabled to parse XML with PHP because the same syntax is used for XML tags.

3. ASP-Style Tags: ASP-style tags mimic the tags used by Active Server Pages to delineate code blocks. ASPstyle tags look like this:

```
<%...%>
```

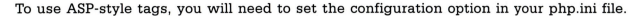

To use ASP-style tags, you will need to set the configuration option in your php.ini file.

4. HTML Script Tags: HTML script tags look like this:

```
<script language="PHP">...</script>
```

5.3.2. Commenting PHP Code

The part of a program that is only visible to humans is called a comment, and it is removed before the program's output is shown. PHP offers two comment formats: Single-line comments and double-line comments. Single-line comments are typically used for brief notes or explanations pertaining to the local code. These are some illustrations of one-line comments.

```
<?
# This is a comment, and
# This is the second line of the comment
// This is a comment too. Each style comments only
print "An example with single line comments";
?>
```

1. Multi-Lines Printing: Here are the examples to print multiple lines in a single print statement:

```
<?
# First Example
print <<<END
This uses the "here document" syntax to output
multiple lines with $variable interpolation. Note
that the here document terminator must appear on a
line with just a semicolon no extra whitespace!
END;
# Second Example
print "This spans
multiple lines. The newlines will be
output as well";
?>
```

2. Multi-Lines Comments: Pseudocode algorithms and more thorough explanations are typically provided by them when needed. The commenting style is multilinear, just like in C. These are some instances of multi-line comments.

```
<?
/* This is a comment with multiline
    Author : Mohammad Mohtashim
    Purpose: Multiline Comments Demo
    Subject: PHP
*/
print "An example with multi line comments";
?>
```

5.3.3. PHP Is Whitespace Insensitive

Whitespace is the text you type that is usually not visible on the screen. Examples of this include carriage returns (also known as end-of-line characters), tabs, and spaces. It hardly ever matters how many whitespace characters you use in a row because PHP is whitespace insensitive. Many of these characters are identical to one whitespace character. For instance, the PHP statements that assign the sum of 2 + 2 to the variable $four are equivalent to each other.

```
$four = 2 + 2; // single spaces
$four <tab>=<tab2<tab>+<tab>2 ; // spaces and tabs
$four =
2+
2; // multiple lines
```

5.3.4. PHP Is Case Sensitive

Yeah, it is true that PHP is a case sensitive language. Try out the following example:

```
<html>
<body>
<?
$capital = 67;
print("Variable capital is $capital<br>");
print("Variable CaPiTaL is $CaPiTaL<br>");
?>
</body>
</html>
```

This will produce the following result:

```
Variable capital is 67
Variable CaPiTaL is
```

5.3.5. Statements Are Expressions Terminated by Semicolons

Any expression in PHP that has a semicolon (;) after it is a statement. A valid PHP program is any series of statements that are enclosed in PHP tags. This PHP statement, which assigns a string of characters to a variable named $greeting, is typical.

```
$greeting = "Welcome to PHP!";
```

5.3.6. Expressions Are Combinations of Tokens

PHP's smallest building blocks are called indivisible tokens, and they include characters (dot two) and numbers (3.14159). variables ($two), constants (TRUE), and the special terms like if, else, while, for, and so on that comprise the syntax of PHP itself.

5.3.7. Braces Make Blocks

While expressions can be combined, statements cannot be combined in the same way. However, a sequence of statements can be placed in any location where a statement is expected by using curly braces to enclose them. The two statements in question are identical.

```
if (3 == 2 + 1)
   print("Good - I haven't totally lost my mind.<br>");


if (3 == 2 + 1)
{
   print("Good - I haven't totally");
   print("lost my mind.<br>");
}
```

> **Keyword**
>
> **PHP Statement** – Any PHP script is built out of a series of statements. A statement can be an assignment, a function call, a loop, a conditional statement or even a statement that does nothing (an empty statement). Statements usually end with a semicolon.

5.3.8. Running PHP Script From Command Prompt

Yes, you can use the command prompt to run your PHP script. Presuming your test .php file contains the following content.

```
<?php
   echo "Hello PHP!!!!!";
?>
```

Now run this script as command prompt as follows:

```
$ php test.php
```

It will produce the following result

```
Hello PHP!!!!!
```

Did you get it?

1. What do you mean by having PHP as whitespace insensitive?
2. How to execute PHP code using command line?

5.4. PHP – VARIABLE TYPES

→Learning Objectives
- Understand variables in PHP;
- Describe integers;
- Discuss about PHP local variables.

The main way to store information in the middle of a PHP program is by using a variable. Here are the most important things to know about variables in PHP.

- All variables in PHP are denoted with a leading dollar sign ($).
- The value of a variable is the value of its most recent assignment.
- Variables are assigned with the = operator, with the variable on the left-hand side and the expression to be evaluated on the right.
- Variables can, but do not need, to be declared before assignment.
- Variables in PHP do not have intrinsic types – a variable does not know in advance
- whether it will be used to store a number or a string of characters.
- Variables used before they are assigned have default values.
- PHP does a good job of automatically converting types from one to another when necessary.
- PHP variables are Perl-like.

PHP has a total of eight data types which we use to construct our variables:

i. **Integers:** These are whole numbers, without a decimal point, like 4195.
ii. **Doubles:** These are floating-point numbers, like 3.14159 or 49.1.
iii. **Booleans:** These have only two possible values either true or false.
iv. **NULL:** This is a special type that only has one value: NULL.
v. **Strings:** These are sequences of characters, like 'PHP supports string operations.'
vi. **Arrays:** These are named and indexed collections of other values.
vii. **Objects:** These are instances of programmer-defined classes, which can package up both other kinds of values and functions that are specific to the class.

viii. Resources: These are special variables that hold references to resources external to PHP (such as database connections).

The next two types, arrays, and objects are compound types; unlike the simple types, the compound types are able to package up other arbitrary values of arbitrary types. The first five types are simple types.

5.4.1. Integers

Like 4195, they are whole numbers without a decimal point. They are the most basic kind, and they match both positive and negative simple whole numbers. Integers can be utilized in expressions like this one or assigned to variables.

```
$int_var = 12345;
$another_int = -12345 + 12345;
```

An integer can have three different formats: hexadecimal (base 16), octal (base 8), and decimal (base 10). Hexadecimals have a leading 0x, octal integers are specified with a leading 0, and decimal format is the default.

For most common platforms, the largest integer is (2**31.1) (or 2,147,483,647), and the smallest (most negative) integer is (2**31.1) (or 2,147,483,647).

5.4.2. Doubles

They like 3.14159 or 49.1. By default, doubles print with the minimum number of decimal places needed. For example, the code:

```
$many = 2.2888800;
$many_2 = 2.2111200;
$few = $many + $many_2;
print(.$many + $many_2 = $few<br>.);
```

It produces the following browser output:

```
2.28888 + 2.21112 = 4.5
```

5.4.3. Boolean

True or false are the only two possible values for them. PHP provides a couple of constants especially for use as Booleans: TRUE and FALSE, which can be used like so:

```
if (TRUE)
    print("This will always print<br>");
else
    print("This will never print<br>");
```

5.4.3.1. Interpreting Other Types as Booleans

The following guidelines can be used to determine the "truth" of any value that isn't already Boolean:

- If the value is a number, it is false if exactly equal to zero and true otherwise.
- If the value is a string, it is false if the string is empty (has zero characters) or is the string "0" and is true otherwise.
- Values of type NULL are always false.
- If the value is an array, it is false if it contains no other values, and it is true otherwise. For an object, containing a value means having a member variable that has been assigned a value.
- Valid resources are true (although some functions that return resources when they are successful will return FALSE when unsuccessful).
- Don't use double as Booleans.

Each of the following variables has the truth value embedded in its name when it is used in a Boolean context.

```
$true_num = 3 + 0.14159;
$true_str = "Tried and true"
$true_array[49] = "An array element";
$false_array = array();
$false_null = NULL;
$false_num = 999 - 999;
$false_str = "";
```

5.4.4. NULL

The unique type of NULL has just one value, NULL. You can assign a variable the NULL value by doing so simply:

```
$my_var = NULL;
```

Convention dictates that the special constant NULL be capitalized, but in reality, case makes no difference—you could have typed: instead.

```
$my_var = null;
```

A variable that has been assigned NULL has the following properties:

- It evaluates to FALSE in a Boolean context.
- It returns FALSE when tested with IsSet() function.

5.4.5. Strings

They are sequences of characters, like "PHP supports string operations." Following are valid examples of string:

```
$string_1 = "This is a string in double quotes";
$string_2 = "This is a somewhat longer, singly quoted string";
$string_39 = "This string has thirty-nine characters";
$string_0 = ""; // a string with zero characters
```

Whereas doubly quoted strings specifically interpret certain character sequences and substitute the values of variables, singly quoted strings are treated almost literally.

```
<?
$variable = "name";
$literally = 'My $variable will not print!\\n';
print($literally);
$literally = "My $variable will print!\\n";
print($literally);
?>
```

This will produce the following result:

```
My $variable will not print!\n
My name will print
```

Strings that are delimited by double quotes (as in "this") are preprocessed in both the following two ways by PHP:

- Certain character sequences beginning with backslash (\) are replaced with special characters.
- Variable names (starting with $) are replaced with string representations of their values.

The escape-sequence replacements are:

- \n is replaced by the newline character.

- \r is replaced by the carriage-return character.
- \t is replaced by the tab character.
- \$ is replaced by the dollar sign itself ($).
- \" is replaced by a single double-quote (").
- \\ is replaced by a single backslash (\).

5.4.5.1. Here Document

You can assign multiple lines to a single string variable using here document

```
<?php

$channel =<<<_XML_
<channel>
<title>What's For Dinner<title>
<link>http://menu.example.com/<link>
<description>Choose what to eat tonight.</description>
</channel>
_XML_;

echo <<<END
This uses the "here document" syntax to output
multiple lines with variable interpolation. Note
that the here document terminator must appear on a
line with just a semicolon. no extra whitespace!
<br />
END;

print $channel;
?>
```

This will produce the following result:

```
This uses the "here document" syntax to output

multiple lines with variable interpolation. Note
```

```
that the here document terminator must appear on a
line with just a semicolon. no extra whitespace!


<channel>
<title>What's For Dinner<title>
<link>http://menu.example.com/<link>
<description>Choose what to eat tonight.</description>
```

5.4.6. Variable Naming

Rules for naming a variable is:

- Variable names must begin with a letter or underscore character.
- A variable name can consist of numbers, letters, underscores but you cannot use characters like +, –, %, (,), &, etc.

There is no size limit for variables.

5.4.7. PHP – Variables

The range of availability that a variable has within the program that it is declared in is known as its scope. There are four different scope types for PHP variables:

- Local variables;
- Function parameters;
- Global variables;
- Static variables.

5.4.8. PHP Local Variables

A variable that is declared inside of a function is regarded as local, meaning that it can only be referred to within that function. A variable declared outside of that function will be regarded as totally distinct from the variable declared inside the function:

```
<?
$x = 4;
function assignx () {
```

FUNDAMENTALS OF WEB DEVELOPMENT

```
$x = 0;
print "\$x inside function is $x.
";
}
assignx();
print "\$x outside of function is $x.
";
?>
```

This will produce the following result.

```
$x inside function is 0.
$x outside of function is 4.
```

Remember
There are no artificial restrictions on the length of strings; you should be able to create strings of any length as long as memory allows.

5.4.9. PHP Function Parameters

To put it briefly, a function is a tiny program unit that can process input in the form of parameters, return a value, and do other tasks.

Function parameters are enclosed in parenthesis and declared following the function name. They are declared much like a typical variable would be:

```
<?
// multiply a value by 10 and return it to the caller
function multiply ($value) {
    $value = $value * 10;
    return $value;
}

$retval = multiply (10);
Print "Return value is $retval\n";
?>
```

This will produce the following result.

```
Return value is 100
```

5.4.10. PHP Global Variables

A global variable, as opposed to a local variable, is accessible from anywhere within the program. Nevertheless, a global variable needs to be specifically declared as global in the function that wants to change it before it can be changed. Conveniently, this is achieved by preceding the variable that needs to be identified as global with the keyword GLOBAL. When this keyword appears in front of an existing variable, PHP is instructed to use the variable with that name. Take the following as an illustration.

```
<?
$somevar = 15;
function addit() {
GLOBAL $somevar;
$somevar++;
print "Somevar is $somevar";
}
addit();
?>
```

This will produce the following result.

```
Somevar is 16
```

5.4.11. PHP Static Variables

Static scoping is the last kind of variable scoping that we cover. Static variables retain their value even after a function exits and can be used to store values even if the function is called again, unlike variables declared as function parameters that are destroyed upon the function's termination. All it takes to declare a variable static is to put the keyword STATIC before the variable name.

```
<?
function keep_track() {
   STATIC $count = 0;
   $count++;
   print $count;
   print "
";
```

> **Keyword**
>
> **Static Variable** – It possesses the property of preserving its actual value even after it is out of its scope. Thus, the static variables are able to preserve their previous value according to their previous scope, and one doesn't need to initialize them again in the case of a new scope.

```
}
keep_track();
keep_track();
keep_track();
?>
```

This will produce the following result.

```
1
2
3
```

Did you get it?

1. What are the ways to specify string in PHP?
2. What is the difference between global and $globals in PHP?

5.5. PHP – CONSTANTS

→Learning Objectives
- Describe constant() function;
- Explain PHP constants.

For a basic value, a constant is its name or identifier. A constant value cannot be altered while the script is running. A constant is case-sensitive by default. Constant identifiers are always written in uppercase by convention. A constant name consists of an underscore or letter at the beginning, followed by any number of underscores, letters, or numbers. A defined constant is unchangeable and undefined once defined. You must use the define() function to define a constant, and all you need to do is specify its name to get its value. You do not require a constant with a $, in contrast to variables. If you want to dynamically get the name of a constant, you can also use the function constant() to read the value of the constant.

5.5.1. constant() Function

The name of the function indicates that it will return the constant's value. When you wish to retrieve the value of a constant but are unsure of its name, i.e., it is either returned by a function or kept in a variable.

constant() example:

```php
<?php

define("MINSIZE", 50);

echo MINSIZE;
echo constant("MINSIZE"); // same thing as the previous line

?>
```

Only scalar data (Boolean, integer, float, and string) can be contained in constants.

Differences between constants and variables are:
- There is no need to write a dollar sign ($) before a constant, whereas in Variable one has to write a dollar sign.

- Constants cannot be defined by simple assignment; they may only be defined using the define() function.
- Constants may be defined and accessed anywhere without regard to variable scoping rules.
- Once the Constants have been set, may not be redefined or undefined.

5.5.2. Valid and Invalid Constant Names

```
// Valid constant names
define("ONE",     "first thing");
define("TWO2",    "second thing");
define("THREE_3", "third thing")
// Invalid constant names
define("2TWO",    "second thing");
define("__THREE__", "third value");
```

> **Keyword**
>
> **PHP Server** – It typically refers to a web server configured to interpret and execute PHP scripts. PHP (Hypertext Preprocessor) is a widely-used open-source server-side scripting language that is especially suited for web development and can be embedded into HTML.

5.5.3. PHP Magic Constants

PHP provides a large number of predefined constants to any script which it runs. There are five magical constants that change depending on where they are used. For example, the value of __LINE__ depends on the line that it's used on in your script. These special constants are case-insensitive and are as follows:

Table 5.1 lists a few "magical" PHP constants along with their description:

Table 5.1. PHP Constants Along with Their Description

Name	Description
__LINE__	The current line number of the file.
__FILE__	The full path and filename of the file. If used inside an include, the name of the included file is returned. Since PHP 4.0.2, __FILE__ always contains an absolute path whereas in older versions it contained relative path under some circumstances.
__FUNCTION__	The function name. (Added in PHP 4.3.0) As of PHP 5 this constant returns the function name as it was declared (case-sensitive). In PHP 4 its value is always lowercased.

__CLASS__	The class names. (Added in PHP 4.3.0) As of PHP 5 this constant returns the class name as it was declared (case-sensitive). In PHP 4 its value is always lowercased.
__METHOD__	The class method name. (Added in PHP 5.0.0) The method name is returned as it was declared (case-sensitive).

Source: https://www.tutorialspoint.com/php/php_tutorial.pdf.

Did you get it?

1. What do you understand by valid and invalid constant names?
2. Differentiate between constants and variables.

5.6. PHP – OPERATOR TYPES

→Learning Objectives

- Describe arithmetic operators;
- Understand PHP comparison operators;
- Define PHP conditional assignment operators.

Values and variables can be operated on using operators. The PHP language is compatible with the following operators.

- Arithmetic operators;
- Comparison operators;
- Logical (or relational) operators;
- Assignment operators;
- Conditional (or ternary) operators.

5.6.1. Arithmetic Operators

The following arithmetic operators are supported by PHP language: Assume variable A holds 10 and variable B holds 20 then:

Operator	Description	Example
+	Adds two operands	A + B will give 30
-	Subtracts second operand from the first	A - B will give -10
*	Multiply both operands	A * B will give 200
/	Divide the numerator by denominator	B / A will give 2
%	Modulus Operator and remainder of after an integer division	B % A will give 0
++	Increment operator, increases integer value by one	A++ will give 11
--	Decrement operator, decreases integer value by one	A-- will give 9

- *Example:* To grasp all of the arithmetic operators, try the example below. The PHP program can be copied and pasted into a test .php file, saved in the document root of your PHP server, and viewed with any web browser.

```php
<html>
<head><title>Arithmetical Operators</title><head>
<body>
<?php
    $a = 42;
    $b = 20;

    $c = $a + $b;
    echo "Addition Operation Result: $c <br/>";
    $c = $a - $b;
    echo "Subtraction Operation Result: $c <br/>";
    $c = $a * $b;
    echo "Multiplication Operation Result: $c <br/>";
    $c = $a / $b;
    echo "Division Operation Result: $c <br/>";
    $c = $a % $b;
    echo "Modulus Operation Result: $c <br/>";
    $c = $a++;
    echo "Increment Operation Result: $c <br/>";
    $c = $a--;
    echo "Decrement Operation Result: $c <br/>";
?>
</body>
</html>
```

This will produce the following result:

```
Addition Operation Result: 62
Subtraction Operation Result: 22
Multiplication Operation Result: 840
Division Operation Result: 2.1
```

```
Modulus Operation Result: 2
Increment Operation Result: 42
Decrement Operation Result: 43
```

5.6.2. PHP Comparison Operators

The PHP increment operators are used to increment a variable's value.

FUNDAMENTALS OF WEB DEVELOPMENT

Operator	Same as...	Description
++$x	Pre-increment	Increments $x by one, then returns $x.
$x++	Post-increment	Returns $x, then increments $x by one.
--$x	Pre-decrement	Decrements $x by one, then returns $x.
$x--	Post-decrement	Returns $x, then decrements $x by one.

5.6.3. PHP Logical Operators

The PHP logical operators are used to combine conditional statements.

Operator	Name	Example	Result
and	And	$x and $y	True if both $x and $y are true.
or	Or	$x or $y	True if either $x or $y is true.
xor	Xor	$x xor $y	True if either $x or $y is true, but not both.
&&	And	$x && $y	True if both $x and $y are true.
||	Or	$x || $y	True if either $x or $y is true.
!	Not	!$x	True if $x is not true.

5.6.4. PHP Conditional Assignment Operators

The PHP conditional assignment operators are used to set a value depending on conditions:

Operator	Name	Example	Result
?:	Ternary	$x = expr1 ? expr2: expr3	Returns the value of $x. The value of $x is expr2 if expr1 = TRUE. The value of $x is expr3 if expr1 = FALSE.
??	Null coalescing	$x = expr1 ?? expr2	Returns the value of $x. The value of $x is expr1 if expr1 exists and is not NULL. If expr1 does not exist, or is NULL, the value of $x is expr2. Introduced in PHP 7.

Did you get it?

1. What is the difference between == and === in PHP?
2. What are the conditional assignment operators in PHP?

5.7. PHP ARRAYS

→Learning Objectives
- Understand the concept of indexed or numeric arrays;
- Describe associative arrays;
- Discuss about multidimensional arrays.

PHP arrays are a kind of data structure that spares us the trouble of having to create separate variables for each type of data by allowing us to store multiple elements of the same data type under a single variable. Using an index or key, one can retrieve a list of elements with similar types by using the arrays. Let's say we wish to print five names after storing them. This can be accomplished with ease by using five distinct string variables. However, it would be extremely challenging for the user or developer to create so many different variables if the number increased to 100 instead of 5. Arrays come into play here, enabling us to store all of the elements in a single variable and provide convenient access through the use of keys or indexes. In PHP, an array is created with the array() function.

There are basically three types of arrays in PHP:

- **Indexed or Numeric Arrays:** An array with a numeric index where values are stored linearly.
- **Associative Arrays:** An array with a string index where instead of linear storage, each value can be assigned a specific key.
- **Multidimensional Arrays:** An array which contains single or multiple arrays within it and can be accessed via multiple indices.

5.7.1. Indexed or Numeric Arrays

Any kind of element can be stored in these kinds of arrays, but an index is always a number. The index starts at zero by default. These arrays can be created in two different ways as shown in the following example:

Example:

```
<?php
//One way to create an indexed array
```

```php
$name_one = array("Zack," "Anthony," "Ram," "Salim," "Raghav");
//Accessing the elements directly
echo "Accessing the 1st array elements directly:\n";
echo $name_one[2], "\n";
echo $name_one[0], "\n";
echo $name_one[4], "\n";
//Second way to create an indexed array
$name_two[0] = "ZACK";
$name_two[1] = "ANTHONY";
$name_two[2] = "RAM";
$name_two[3] = "SALIM";
$name_two[4] = "RAGHAV";
//Accessing the elements directly
echo "Accessing the 2nd array elements directly:\n";
echo $name_two[2], "\n";
echo $name_two[0], "\n";
echo $name_two[4], "\n";
?>
```

Output:

Accessing the 1st array elements directly:

Ram

Zack

Raghav

Accessing the 2nd array elements directly:

RAM

ZACK

RAGHAV

5.7.1.1. Traversing

We can traverse an indexed array using loops in PHP. We can loop through the indexed array in two ways. First by using for loop and secondly by using foreach. You can refer to PHP | Loops for the syntax and basic use.

```php
<?php
//One way to create an associative array
$name_one = array("Zack"=>"Zara," "Anthony"=>"Any,"
"Ram"=>"Rani," "Salim"=>"Sara,"
"Raghav"=>"Ravina");
//Second way to create an associative array
$name_two["zack"] = "zara";
$name_two["anthony"] = "any";
$name_two["ram"] = "rani";
$name_two["salim"] = "sara";
$name_two["raghav"] = "ravina";
//Accessing the elements directly
echo "Accessing the elements directly:\n";
echo $name_two["zack"], "\n";
echo $name_two["salim"], "\n";
echo $name_two["anthony"], "\n";
echo $name_one["Ram"], "\n";
echo $name_one["Raghav"], "\n";
?>
```

Output:

Looping using foreach:

Zack

Anthony

Ram

Salim

Raghav

The number of elements is 5

Looping using for:

ZACK

ANTHONY

RAM

SALIM

RAGHAV

5.7.2. Associative Arrays

These array types are comparable to indexed arrays, but they do not use linear storage; instead, each value can be assigned a user-defined string key.

```
<?php
//Creating an Associative Array
$name_one = [
"Zack" => "Zara,"
"Anthony" => "Any,"
"Ram" => "Rani,"
"Salim" => "Sara,"
"Raghav" => "Ravina,"
];
//Looping through an array using foreach
echo "Looping using foreach: \n";
foreach ($name_one as $val => $val_value) {
echo "Husband is ."$val." and Wife is ."$val_value."\n";
}
//Looping through an array using for
echo "\nLooping using for: \n";
```

```php
$keys = array_keys($name_one);
$round = count($name_one);
for ($i = 0; $i < $round; ++$i) {
echo $keys[$i]." ."$name_one[$keys[$i]]."\n";
}
?>
```

Output:

Accessing the elements directly:

zara

sara

any

Rani

Ravina

5.7.2.1. Traversing Associative Arrays

Loops can be used to traverse associative arrays in a manner akin to that of numeric arrays. There are two ways we can iterate through the associative array. Using the for loop first, and then the foreach second.

```php
<?php
//Defining a multidimensional array
$favorites = array(
array(
"name" => "Dave Punk,"
"mob" => "5689741523,"
"email" => "davepunk@gmail.com,"
),
array(
"name" => "Monty Smith,"
```

"mob" => "2584369721,"

"email" => "montysmith@gmail.com,"

),

array(

"name" => "John Flinch,"

"mob" => "9875147536,"

"email" => "johnflinch@gmail.com,"

)

);

//Accessing elements

echo "Dave Punk email-id is: ."$favorites[0]["email"], "\n";

echo "John Flinch mobile number is: ."$favorites[2]["mob"];

?>

Output:

Looping using foreach:

Husband is Zack and Wife is Zara

Husband is Anthony and Wife is Any

Husband is Ram and Wife is Rani

Husband is Salim and Wife is Sara

Husband is Raghav and Wife is Ravina

Looping using for:

zack zara

anthony any

ram rani

salim sara

raghav ravina

5.7.3. Multidimensional Arrays

These arrays are known as multi-dimensional arrays because they store another array at each index rather than just one element. Put differently, an array of arrays can be used to define multi-dimensional arrays. As the name implies, each element in this array has the ability to hold other arrays within it as well as other arrays. Multiple dimensions can be used to access arrays or sub-arrays in multidimensional arrays.

```php
<?php
//Defining a multidimensional array
$favorites = array(
"Dave Punk" => array(
"mob" => "5689741523,"
"email" => "davepunk@gmail.com,"
),
"Dave Punk" => array(
"mob" => "2584369721,"
"email" => "montysmith@gmail.com,"
),
"John Flinch" => array(
"mob" => "9875147536,"
"email" => "johnflinch@gmail.com,"
)
);
//Using for and foreach in nested form
$keys = array_keys($favorites);
for($i = 0; $i < count($favorites); $i++) {
echo $keys[$i]."\n";
foreach($favorites[$keys[$i]] as $key => $value) {
echo $key.":.".$value."\n";
}
```

echo "\n";

}

?>

Output

Dave Punk email-id is: davepunk@gmail.com

John Flinch mobile number is: 9875147536

5.7.3.1. Traversing Multidimensional Arrays

The for and foreach loops allow us to navigate the multidimensional array in a nested manner. In other words, there would be one for loop for the outer array and another for the inner array.

PHP is a scripting language that runs on servers that is specifically intended for web development. You can gain a comprehensive understanding of PHP by referring to this PHP Tutorial and PHP Examples.

Did you get it?

1. What are numeric arrays in PHP?
2. How the Arrays or sub-arrays in multidimensional arrays can be accessed using multiple dimensions?

FOCUS ON CAREERS

- **PHP Developer:** PHP is an open-source server-side scripting language used to create websites or applications that can help a business boost its online presence. A PHP developer can use a range of web development languages like HTML, CSS, and JavaScript to build interactive portals that meet the specific needs of users. They also troubleshoot errors in the code alongside managing databases and the security of the programs. A PHP developer also helps develop a highly functional Integrated Development Environment (IDE) that can reinforce both graphical user interface (GUI) and non-GUI applications.
- **Key Responsibilities of a PHP Developer:** PHP developers contribute to all stages of the product life cycle development and may undertake tasks such as:
    - develop layout and design of websites, programs, and applications.
    - create reusable, effective and scalable PHP code.
    - understand how web applications work, including security and session management.
    - develop plugins and extensions.
    - perform maintenance of the code and enhance it.
    - define and maintain a database.
    - integrate payment gateways on e-commerce portals.
    - work with Application Program Interface (API).
    - assist frontend developers with code integration.
    - liaise with the User Experience (UX) team.
    - formulate internal coding standards.
    - integrate data storage solutions.
    - possess knowledge of common web server exploits.
    - develop a workflow for projects.
- **Technical Skills Required to Become a PHP Developer:** For PHP developers to enjoy a rewarding career, they may require knowledge and technical skills such as:
    - HTML, CSS, and JavaScript;
    - PHP frameworks;

- Database languages;
- Web servers;
- Content management systems;
- Graphic design software.

PHP developers are in high demand due to the increasing digital-first approach adopted by businesses across industries. Organizations in all verticals are marking their online presence using a website or an application for mobile devices. From social media platforms to e-commerce websites and mobile applications, the requirement of a PHP developer remains essential to delivering a smooth functioning online portal.

Here is a list of few industries where PHP developers are in high demand:

- Information technology;
- Retail;
- Fast-moving consumer goods (FMCG);
- Telecom;
- Banking;
- Media and broadcast;
- Manufacturing;
- Energy;
- Real estate;
- Logistics.

A CLOSER LOOK

The Future of PHP: PHP has evolved over the years, adapting to changing web development trends and user demands. From its early days as a procedural scripting language, PHP gradually embraced object-oriented programming (OOP) paradigms, enhancing code modularity, reusability, and maintainability.

The release of PHP 7 in 2015 brought substantial performance improvements, making PHP faster and more efficient than ever before.

Additionally, PHP has a vast ecosystem of frameworks and libraries such as Laravel, Symfony, and WordPress, which have contributed to its popularity and ease of development.

These frameworks provide structure, security, and additional functionalities, making PHP a reliable choice for building complex web applications.

- **Relevance in the Modern Web:** Critics of PHP often argue that its syntax and quirks make it less elegant compared to newer languages such as Python, Ruby, or JavaScript. While it's true that PHP has its idiosyncrasies, it remains a highly capable language that continues to power millions of websites and applications worldwide.

Here are a few reasons PHP remains relevant in the modern web landscape:

1. **Mature and Proven:** PHP has a long-standing presence on the web, giving it a strong foundation and a wealth of documentation and community support. This maturity ensures stability and reliability, especially for large-scale projects and enterprise applications.
2. **Vast Codebase:** PHP boasts an extensive codebase, with countless libraries, frameworks, and plugins available for various purposes. This vast ecosystem enables developers to leverage existing solutions, speeding up development and reducing the need to reinvent the wheel.
3. **CMS Dominance:** PHP-based Content Management Systems (CMS) like WordPress, Drupal, and Joomla power a significant portion of websites on the internet. These platforms offer user-friendly interfaces, robust features, and a thriving community, making PHP the go-to choose for building dynamic websites and online applications.
4. **Web Performance:** With PHP 7's significant performance improvements, PHP can handle high-traffic websites and applications efficiently. The language's ability to integrate seamlessly with web servers like Apache and Nginx further

enhances its performance, ensuring fast and responsive web experiences.

Future Prospects and Adaptation: Despite the emergence of newer languages, PHP continues to evolve and adapt to changing requirements. The PHP community actively releases updates and improvements, ensuring the language remains competitive and relevant.

PHP 8, released in 2020, introduced numerous features and enhancements, including JIT compilation, union types, and match expressions, further boosting performance and developer productivity.

Moreover, efforts like PHP-FIG (PHP Framework Interoperability Group) foster collaboration between different PHP projects, encouraging standardization and interoperability.

This collaborative spirit ensures that PHP remains compatible with modern development practices and emerging technologies.

It has established a solid presence in the web development landscape, thanks to its robustness, versatility, and vast ecosystem.

PHP's continuous evolution, community support, and adaptation to new trends have kept it relevant even as newer languages emerge.

While it's essential for developers to stay informed about alternative technologies, PHP will likely remain a popular choice for web development, particularly for CMS-driven websites, e-commerce platforms, and enterprise applications. By embracing modern PHP frameworks, adopting best practices, and keeping pace with language updates, developers can continue to harness the power of PHP for years to come.

SUMMARY

- PHP is a versatile scripting language designed primarily for web development. Programmer Danish-Canadian programmer Rasmus Lerdorf originally created it in 1993, and it was made available in 1995.
- PHP interpreters, which can be implemented as modules, daemons, or Common Gateway Interface (CGI) executables, are typically used on web servers to process PHP code.
- PHP performs system functions, i.e., from files on a system it can create, open, read, write, and close them.
- Users of Mac computers can choose to install from a source or a binary. Actually, Apache and PHP were most likely already preinstalled on your OS X. This build is probably fairly old, and it probably doesn't have many of the less popular additions.
- The ability to distinguish PHP code from other page elements is required by the PHP parsing engine. The process of accomplishing this is called "escaping to PHP."
- The main way to store information in the middle of a PHP program is by using a variable.
- The range of availability that a variable has within the program that it is declared in is known as its scope.
- A variable that is declared inside of a function is regarded as local, meaning that it can only be referred to within that function.
- To put it briefly, a function is a tiny program unit that can process input in the form of parameters, return a value, and do other tasks.

MULTIPLE CHOICE QUESTION

1. **What does PHP stand for?**
   a. Personal Home Page
   b. Preprocessed Hypertext Processor
   c. PHP: Hypertext Preprocessor
   d. Public Hosting Platform

2. **Which of the following tags is used to start and end a PHP code block?**
   a. <?php ?>
   b. <script></script>
   c. <!– –>
   d. {{ }}

3. **In PHP, which function is used to print output to the screen?**
   a. echo

b. print
c. printf
d. display

4. Which symbol is used for concatenating strings in PHP?
   a. +
   b. .
   c. &
   d. ,

5. What does the PHP function strlen() do?
   a. Calculates the length of a string
   b. Converts a string to lowercase
   c. Reverses a string
   d. Trims whitespace from a string

6. Which of the following is used to comment out a single line of code in PHP?
   a. //
   b. /*
   c. #
   d. --

7. Which PHP superglobal variable is used to collect form data after submitting an HTML form?
   a. $_GET
   b. $_POST
   c. $_REQUEST
   d. $_SERVER

8. What does the PHP function isset() do?
   a. Checks if a variable is set and is not NULL
   b. Initializes a variable
   c. Checks if a variable is empty
   d. Destroys a variable

9. Which PHP function is used to establish a connection to a MySQL database?
   a. mysql_connect()
   b. mysqli_connect()
   c. pdo_connect()
   d. db_connect()

10. Which of the following is NOT a valid PHP data type?
    a. string

b. Boolean
   c. object
   d. byte

REVIEW QUESTIONS

1. How do you define a constant in PHP?
2. What is the meaning of 'escaping to PHP'? Explain.
3. How can PHP and JavaScript interact?
4. Differentiate between variables and constants in PHP.
5. How many types of arrays are there in PHP?

Answer to Multiple Choice Questions

1. (c); 2. (a); 3. (a); 4. (b); 5. (a); 6. (a); 7. (b); 8. (a); 9. (b); 10. (d)

REFERENCES

1. Basher, K., (2013). *MVC Patterns (Active and Passive Model) and its implementation using ASP.NET Web Forms.* CodeProject.
2. Berdonosov, V., Zhivotova, A., & Sycheva, T., (2015). TRIZ evolution of the object-oriented programming languages. *Electronic Notes in Theoretical Computer Science, 314*, 23–44.
3. Bergmann, S., & Priebsch, S., (2011). *Real-World Solutions for Developing High-Quality PHP Frameworks and Applications.* Wiley.
4. Eshkevar, L., Dos, S. F., Cordy, J. R., & Antoniol, G., (2015). *Are PHP Applications Ready for Hack?* (pp. 63–72). IEEE.
5. Herraiz, Rodriguez, D., Robles, G., & Gonzalez-Barahona, J. M., (2013). *The Evolution of the Laws of Software Evolution: A Discussion Based on a Systematic Literature Review* (pp. 28:1–28:28). ACM.
6. Hills, M., & Klint, P., (2014). *PHP AiR: Analyzing PHP Systems with Rascal* (pp. 454–457). IEEE.
7. Kyriakakis, P., & Chatzigeorgiou, A., (2014). Maintenance patterns of large-scale PHP web applications. *IEEE International Conference on Software Maintenance and Evolution*, 381–390.
8. Merlo, E., Letarte, D., & Antoniol, G., (2007). *SQL-Injection Security Evolution Analysis in PHP* (pp. 45–49). IEEE.
9. Nylén, H. *PHP Framework Performance for Web Development Between Codeigniter and CakePHP.* Bachelor Thesis. School of Computing Blekinge Institute of Technology, Sweden, 2012.

CHAPTER 6
Working with AJAX

LEARNING OBJECTIVES

After studying this chapter, you will be able to:

- Understand the concept of AJAX;
- Describe AJAX: rich internet applications;
- Define common AJAX attributes;
- Explain the technologies used in AJAX;
- Discuss on AJAX application server performance.

INTRODUCTORY EXAMPLE

AJAX – Examples: AJAX is used in several popular web applications and more. Some examples include:

- **Autocomplete:** Google was among the first websites to incorporate AJAX for auto suggestions to their users. As you type a search query in Google, you will notice that some suggestions will appear automatically, and you can choose between those by navigating through up and down keys.

Here, it uses AJAX to display results based on input via each keystroke. Autocomplete makes it easier for the user to wade easily through many inputs while filling out forms or launching a query.

- **Voting:** Websites such as Reddit use AJAX to handle voting and rating on main content displayed on the site. The users can vote and give their opinions on several stories in a short amount of time.
- **Instant Messaging:** AJAX has also found its applications to enjoy seamless instant messaging features in a chat room. Two main processes handled by AJAX include – sending and receiving messages to and from the server for real-time updates. In the background, AJAX reloads the page every time a user sends or received messages.
- **Update User Content:** Twitter has recently used AJAX for enhancing its platform and interface. Every time a new topic starts trending, or a user tweets, these are instantly updated without the need to reload the entire page. Twitter feed is loaded every other second to let the user know about real-time updates, trending topics, tweet activity, and more.
- **Login Forms:** AJAX helps update the log-in system in scenarios where a user wants to access a certain page and can log in directly without going to the original login page. As the user logs in, AJAX will send a request to the server and the page will get updated as required by the user.
- **External Widgets:** AJAX also finds applications in various Content Management Systems such as WordPress and scrips like Google AdSense. The AJAX can communicate with any server online and not just the server where the web page is located. It loads external content on the web page while the original content on the web page remains unchanged.
- **Maps:** Google Maps and Yahoo Maps use AJAX to make the navigation process easier for the user. Users can simply drag the map without the need to click on a button.
- **AJAX – Browser Support:** AJAX supports a limited number of browsers, some of which include:
  - Mozilla Firefox 1.0 and above;
  - Konqueror;
  - Opera 7.6 and above;
  - Microsoft Internet Explorer 5 and above;
  - Apple Safari 1.2 and above;
  - Netscape version 7.1 and above.

The reason that AJAX does not support every browser is that different browsers use different methods for the creation of a built-in JavaScript object, known as XMLHttpRequest.

Therefore, it is recommended to check your browser is it supports AJAX or not before writing the web application. However, one way to create a JavaScript object is using the try....catch blocks.

6.1. UNIT INTRODUCTION

AJAX is a collection of web development techniques that generates asynchronous web applications by utilizing a variety of client-side web technologies. Web applications can send and retrieve data asynchronously (in the background) from a server using AJAX, all without affecting how the page looks and behaves. AJAX enables dynamic content changes on web pages and, consequently, web applications, without requiring a page reload by separating the data interchange layer from the presentation layer. In actuality, JSON is frequently used in place of XML in modern implementations.

Programming concepts rather than technologies make up AJAX. It is possible to mark up and style information by combining HTML and CSS. JavaScript allows the webpage to be changed so that the user can interact with the dynamically displayed content. Web pages can load content onto the screen without requiring a page refresh by utilizing the built-in XMLHttpRequest object to perform AJAX searches. Neither AJAX nor its associated languages are new. It is actually the novel application of already-existing technologies.

The term AJAX has come to represent a broad group of Web technologies that can be used to implement a Web application that communicates with a server in the background, without interfering with the current state of the page. Jesse James Garrett explained that the following technologies are incorporated:

- HTML (or XHTML) and CSS for presentation;
- The document object model (DOM) for dynamic display of and interaction with data;
- JSON or XML for the interchange of data, and XSLT for XML manipulation;
- The XMLHttpRequest object for asynchronous communication;
- JavaScript to bring these technologies together.

6.2. CONCEPT OF AJAX

→Learning Objectives
- Explain the characteristics of an AJAX application;
- Discuss the impact of AJAX on user.

Web content that is dynamic and asynchronously created is commonly created using JavaScript and XML, which are referred to as AJAX. Although XML and JavaScript are not the only technologies that can be utilized with AJAX, web applications typically use them in tandem.

The dynamic scripting language used in web applications is called JavaScript. It enables web pages to communicate with clients asynchronously and lets users add more functionality to user interfaces. JavaScript minimizes client access to servers by operating primarily on the client side, much like in a browser.

The Document Object Model (DOM) of the page is updated by the server's response to an asynchronous request sent by a JavaScript function from the client. This answer is frequently provided as an XML document. This communication between the client and server is referred to as AJAX. It is not necessary for the server response to only be in XML; it may also be in JSON or another format. Web applications can be updated partially and asynchronously thanks to AJAX. Real-time rendering of highly responsive web pages is made possible by this functionality. Web applications that use AJAX have the ability to retrieve data from servers, process it, and display it without affecting how the current web page appears and is rendered on a client (like a browser).

Some of the advantages of using AJAX are as follows:

- Form data validation in real time, eliminating the need to submit the form for verification;
- Enhanced functionality for web pages, such as username and password prompts;
- Partial update of the web content, avoiding complete page reloads.

AJAX is an acronym for XML and Asynchronous JavaScript. Asynchronous refers to the ability to send requests via Hypertext Transfer Protocol (HTTP) to a server and handle other data while you wait for a response. It is a collection of related web development techniques that are used on the client side to create interactive web applications; it is not a new programming language. It's a method for making interactive web apps with already-existing standards like XML and JavaScript. AJAX is used by both platform-independent and browser-based applications.

Data can be moved from a web page to a server using AJAX, and web applications can send and receive data from servers without affecting the current page or making the user wait for the page to reload. This is achieved by means of a specific type of HTTP request. When a web page's contents change, non-AJAX websites have to reload the entire thing. Numerous online applications, including Gmail, Yahoo, Facebook, Twitter, and YouTube, are powered by AJAX technology. AJAX makes use of the Document Object Model (DOM) for content display, CSS for presentation, and XHTML for content.

6.2.1. Characteristics of an AJAX Application

The term "AJAX" describes a collection of tools and methods that enhance the interactivity of web pages and simulate desktop applications. AJAX applications differ from classic web applications in the following ways:

- AJAX makes boundary between web page and application. In classic web application, web page is rendered by browser to display the result and in AJAX application, the server sends HTML page to browser that allows making page to be interactive.
- With AJAX, a web page feels like a desktop application. It responds fast and updates the page by fetching the data from the server in the background.
- In classic web applications web servers serve HTML pages. Some of the pages are static while others are created dynamically at server side. In AJAX applications servers do not need to convert data into HTML page. The server sends data directly to the client.
- Important characteristic of AJAX is in its first letter "A" – Asynchronous. Asynchronous means the user can interact with the application while the browser is communicating with the server.
- AJAX is scripting-based approach. Developers need to understand JavaScript and write code in JavaScript. JavaScript is hard to develop, maintain, test and debug.
- An AJAX application reduces network load and provides support for both synchronous and asynchronous communication. If user wants to create a secure application and if the browser does not support JavaScript, then we cannot use AJAX.

6.2.1.1. Browser Support

Not all browsers support AJAX. Here are some browsers which support AJAX:

- Mozilla Firefox 1.0 and above;
- Microsoft Internet Explorer 5 and above;
- Safari 1.2 and above;
- Netscape Navigator 7 and above.

6.2.1.2. What Can AJAX Do?

AJAX plays an important role in making web 2.0 promises a reality. Some of the features of web 2.0 are:

- We can use the Web as a platform;
- Software can be delivered as a service;
- Cost effective;
- Architecture with completely user interaction.

One of the most well-known AJAX-based applications is Google Maps, which lets users scroll the map in four directions and zoom in and out just like a desktop application. By double clicking the center, the user can drag the map around the screen with the mouse pointer.

Spell check, new mail check, and other features in Gmail rely on AJAX. AJAX is used by Yahoo's Flickr for the text editing and tagging interface. AJAX is used in the Yahoo front page as well. Windows Live is an example of an AJAX application. It offers functions like news, maps, email integration, instant messaging, and search.

> **Keyword**
>
> **XML** – It is a markup language and file format for storing, transmitting, and reconstructing arbitrary data.

6.2.1.3. Impact of AJAX on User

Existing AJAX applications can be divided into two types such as

- **Partially AJAXed:** It is used to provide functionalities like in.-Flickr; and
- **Fully AJAXed:** It is used for functionalities as well as user interface such as – Google Maps and Windows Live.
- The fully AJAXed applications are different from traditional web applications. In these applications
- A web page breaks down;
- Surfing site or using applications is not just clicking links and loading pages;
- URL remains unchanged in address bar, forward, backward, reload buttons are rendered meaningless.

> **Did you know?**
>
> The term AJAX was publicly used on 18 February 2005 by Jesse James Garrett in an article titled AJAX: A New Approach to Web Applications, based on techniques used on Google pages.

6.2.2. Examples

6.2.2.1. JavaScript Example

An example of a simple AJAX request using the GET method, written in JavaScript.

get-ajax-data.js:

```javascript
//This is the client-side script.
//Initialize the HTTP request.
let xhr = new XMLHttpRequest();
//define the request
xhr.open('GET,' 'send-ajax-data.php');
//Track the state changes of the request.
xhr.onreadystatechange = function () {
const DONE = 4;//readyState 4 means the request is done.
const OK = 200;//status 200 is a successful return.
if (xhr.readyState === DONE) {
if (xhr.status === OK) {
console.log(xhr.responseText);//'This is the output.'
} else {
console.log('Error: ' + xhr.status);//An error occurred during the request.
}
}
};
//Send the request to send-ajax-data.php
xhr.send(null);
```

end-ajax-data.php:

```php
<?php
//This is the server-side script.
//Set the content type.
header('Content-Type: text/plain');
//Send the data back.
echo "This is the output.";
?>
```

6.2.2.2. Fetch Example

An native JavaScript API is called fetch. "Fetch makes it easier to make web requests and handle responses than with the older XMLHttpRequest," claims the Google Developers

Documentation.

```
fetch('send-ajax-data.php')

.then(data => console.log(data))

.catch (error => console.log('Error:' + error));
```

6.2.2.3. ES7 Async/Await Example

```
async function doAjax1() {

try {

const res = await fetch('send-ajax-data.php');

const data = await res.text();

console.log(data);

} catch (error) {

console.log('Error:' + error);

}

}

doAjax1();
```

Fetch relies on JavaScript promises.

The fetch specification differs from AJAX in the following significant ways:

- The Promise returned from fetch() won't reject on HTTP error status even if the response is an HTTP 404 or 500. Instead, as soon as the server responds with headers, the Promise will resolve normally (with the ok property of the response set to false if the response isn't in the range 200–299), and it will only reject on network failure or if anything prevented the request from completing.
- fetch() won't send cross-origin cookies unless you set the credentials init option. (Since April 2018. The spec changed the default credentials policy to same-origin. Firefox changed since 61.0b13.)

Did you get it?

1. What is JavaScript real time example?
2. What do you understand by avaScript API?

6.3. AJAX: RICH INTERNET APPLICATIONS

→Learning Objectives
- Explain the features of AJAX;
- Understand architecture of Microsoft AJAX applications.

Richer and more interactive web applications can be created using AJAX. These applications are known as Rich Internet Applications (RIA). Web apps that offer desktop application functionality are known as RIAs. The degree to which users and interfaces interact is the main distinction between rich interfaces (RIAs) and conventional web applications. RIA makes use of controls to enhance user interaction by facilitating more effective error handling, user experience, and interactions.

RIAs fall into two basic categories:
- Object oriented-based approaches: Java and .Net; and
- Scripting-based approaches: AJAX and Flash.

6.3.1. Features of AJAX

AJAX's primary function is to speed up websites by allowing you to reload only the most crucial sections of them rather than the entire page.

6.3.1.1. Important Features of AJAX
- It make web page faster.
- Independent of server technology.
- Increase the Performance of web page.
- No need to pushing on a submit button and reloading the complete website.
- No need to reload the whole page only some part of page is reloaded which is required to reload.
- Apart from obtaining the XMLHTTP object, all processing is same for all browser types, because JavaScript is used.

- Using AJAX develop faster and more interactive web applications.
- Not require to completely reload page due to this server use less bandwidth.

6.3.1.2. Use Microsoft AJAX Features

Web forms applications that use AJAX features offer the following features:

- Familiar interactive UI elements such as progress indicators, tooltips, and pop-up windows.
- Improved efficiency for Web Forms application, because significant parts of a Web page's processing can be performed in the browser.
- Partial-page updates that refresh only the parts of the Web page that have changed.
- Client integration with ASP.NET application services for forms authentication, roles, and user profiles.
- Auto-generated proxy classes that simplify calling Web service methods from client script.
- The ability to customize server controls to include client capabilities.
- Support for the most popular browsers, which includes Microsoft Internet Explorer, Mozilla Firefox, and Apple Safari

> **Keyword**
>
> **Rich Internet Application**
> – It is a web application that has many of the characteristics of desktop application software.

6.3.2. Architecture of Microsoft AJAX Applications

A client-only solution or a client and server solution make up a Microsoft AJAX Web application. A client-only solution does not use any ASP; instead, it makes use of Microsoft AJAX Library. controls for NET servers. For example, script elements that reference the Microsoft AJAX Library .js files can be included in HTML. All processing for AJAX applications can be done on the client thanks to the Microsoft AJAX Library. Utilizing both ASP and the Microsoft AJAX Library is a client-server solution. controls for NET servers.

6.3.2.1. Microsoft AJAX Client Architecture

The client architecture includes libraries for component support, browser compatibility, networking, and core services.

Components Client components enable rich behaviors in the browser without postbacks. Components fall into three categories:

- Components, which are non-visual objects that encapsulate code;
- Behaviors, which extend the behavior of existing DOM elements;
- Controls, which represent a new DOM element that has custom behavior.

Depending on the kind of client behavior you desire, you can use a different kind of component. For instance, you can use a behavior that is attached to an existing text box to create a watermark for it.

1. **Browser Compatibility:** For the most popular browsers, the browser compatibility layer offers Microsoft AJAX scripting compatibility. This makes it possible for you to write the same script for any supported browser.

2. **Networking:** Communication between browser script and Web-based services and applications is handled by the networking layer. It also controls calls to asynchronous remote methods. You don't need to write any code to use the networking layer in many scenarios, like partial-page updates that use the UpdatePanel control.

   Role and profile information in client scripts, as well as server-based form authentication, are supported by the networking layer. Web apps that are not made with ASP can also benefit from this support. NET, provided that the program has access to the Microsoft AJAX Libraries.

3. **Core Services:** The ASP.NET AJAX client-script libraries. Included in NET is JavaScript (.js) files that offer functionality for object-oriented programming. A high degree of consistency and modularity in client scripting is made possible by the object-oriented features found in the Microsoft AJAX client-script libraries.

The following core services are part of the client architecture:

- Object-oriented extensions to JavaScript, such as classes, namespaces, event handling, inheritance, data types, and object serialization.
- A base class library, which includes components such as string builders and extended error handling.
- Support for JavaScript libraries that are either embedded in an assembly or are provided as standalone JavaScript (.js) files. Embedding JavaScript libraries in an assembly can make it easier to deploy applications and can help solve versioning issues.

4. **Debugging and Error Handling:** Among the fundamental services is the Sys. The Debug class offers techniques for presenting items at the conclusion of a webpage in a readable format. In addition, the class allows you to access the debugger, use assertions, and view trace messages. Useful exception details are provided by an extended Error object API that supports both release and debug modes.

5. **Globalization:** The AJAX server and client architecture in ASP.NET provides a model for localizing and globalizing client script. This lets you create applications with a single code base that support multiple locales' user interfaces (languages and cultures). For example, the AJAX architecture enables JavaScript code to

format Date or Number objects automatically according to culture settings of the user's browser, without requiring a postback to the server.

6.3.2.2. AJAX Server Architecture

The server pieces that support AJAX development consist of ASP.NET Web server controls and components that manage the UI and flow of an application. The server pieces also manage serialization, validation, and control extensibility. There are also ASP.NET Web services that enable you to access ASP.NET application services for forms authentication, roles, and user profiles.

1. Script Support: AJAX features in ASP.NET are commonly implemented by using client script libraries that perform processing strictly on the client. You can also implement AJAX features by using server controls that support scripts sent from the server to the client. You can also create custom client script for your ASP.NET applications. In that case, you can also use AJAX features to manage your custom script as static .js files (on disk) or as .js files embedded as resources in an assembly.

A model for release and debug modes is one of the features of AJAX. Release mode offers performance-optimized error checking and exception handling with reduced script size. More advanced debugging features, like type and argument checking, are available in debug mode. ASP.NET runs the debug versions when the application is in debug mode. This enables you to throw exceptions in debug scripts while minimizing the size of release code.

Script support for AJAX in ASP.NET is used to provide two important features:

- The Microsoft AJAX Library, which is a type system and a set of JavaScript extensions that provide namespaces, inheritance, interfaces, enumerations, reflection, and additional features; and
- Partial-page rendering, which updates regions of the page by using an asynchronous postback.

2. Localization: The Microsoft AJAX architecture builds on the foundation of the ASP.NET 2.0 localization model. It provides additional support for localized .js files that are embedded in an assembly or that are provided on disk. ASP.NET can serve localized client scripts and resources automatically for specific languages and regions.

3. Web Services: With AJAX functionality in an ASP.NET Web page, you can use client script to call both ASP.NET Web services (.asmx) and Windows Communication Foundation (WCF) services (.svc). The required script references are automatically added to the page, and they in turn automatically generate the Web service proxy classes that you use from client script to call the Web service.

You can also access ASP.NET Web services without using Microsoft AJAX server controls (for example, if you are using a different Web development environment). To do so, in the page, you can manually include references to the Microsoft AJAX Library, to script files, and to the Web service itself. At run time, ASP.NET generates the proxy classes that you can use to call the services.

WORKING WITH AJAX

4. Application Services: This in ASP.NET are built-in Web services that are based on ASP.NET forms authentication, roles, and user profiles. These services can be called by client script in an AJAX-enabled Web page, by a Windows client application, or by a WCF-compatible client.

5. Server Controls: AJAX server controls consist of server and client code that integrate to produce rich client behavior. When you add an AJAX-enabled control to an ASP.NET Web page, the page automatically sends supporting client script to the browser for AJAX functionality. You can provide additional client code to customize the functionality of a control, but this is not required.

6.3.3. How Does AJAX Work?

Because AJAX calls are asynchronous, they operate independently of the website as a whole and behind the scenes. The website does not stop working when a browser makes an AJAX call to the server because it is not stuck waiting for a response. As soon as the task is finished, the web service on the server will instead send the data back to the browser, where client-side scripts will process the response and present it to the user.

> **Keyword**
>
> AJAX Library – It is not a specific library itself but rather a set of web development techniques used to create asynchronous web applications.

For example: If you want to give a movie on Netflix a star rating, you can click the rating, it will show up immediately, and the rating gets stored in your profile, all without any other changes to the page. That's AJAX in action.

6.3.3.1. How AJAX Works?

AJAX makes use of the XMLHttpRequest object to interact with the server. With the help of the image shown below, let's attempt to comprehend how AJAX functions and flows (Figure 6.1).

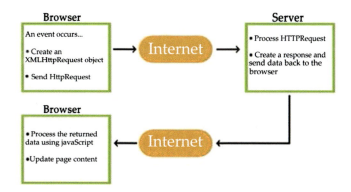

Figure 6.1. How AJAX works?

Source: https://www.pvpsiddhartha.ac.in.

As you can see in the above example, XMLHttpRequest object plays an important role:

> **Keyword**
>
> **Windows Communication Foundation** – It is a free and open-source runtime and a set of APIs in the .NET Framework for building connected, service-oriented applications.

- User sends a request from the UI and a JavaScript call goes to XMLHttpRequest object.
- HTTP Request is sent to the server by XMLHttpRequest object.
- Server interacts with the database using JSP, PHP, Servlet, ASP.net etc.
- Data is retrieved.
- Server sends XML data or JSON data to the XMLHttpRequest callback function.
- HTML and CSS data is displayed on the browser.

Did you get it?

1. What is AJAX client server architecture?
2. How does AJAX work?

6.4. COMMON AJAX ATTRIBUTES

→Learning Objectives
- Explain the concept of data processing;
- Define the term rendering;
- Describe events and JavaScript interactions.

The AJAX components work together to accomplish comparable tasks by sharing common attributes. These common characteristics are also shared by the majority of RichFaces components that have integrated AJAX support.

The majority of attributes come with default values, so the component can operate in its default state without requiring them to be explicitly set. If needed, these characteristics can be changed to modify the component's behavior.

6.4.1. Data Processing

The JSF 2 AJAX script serves as the foundation for the RichFaces AJAX script. As a result, the XMLHttpRequest object and the data from the requesting component's parent JSF form are submitted with every request. Values from the input element and auxiliary data, like state-saving data, are included in the form data.

6.4.1.1. Execute

JSF processing can be restricted to specified components thanks to the execute attribute. An id identifier of a particular component to process can be accessed via the execute attribute. Moreover, components can be found by utilizing Expression Language (EL).

Alternatively, the execute attribute accepts the following keywords:
- **@all:** Every component is processed.
- **@none:** No components are processed.
- **@this:** The requesting component with the execute attribute is processed. This is the default behavior for components.

- **@form:** The form that contains the requesting component is processed.
- **@region:** The region that contains the requesting component is processed. Use the <r:region> component as a wrapper element to specify regions.
- Some components make use of additional keywords.

6.4.1.2. bypassUpdates

The request processing lifecycle's Update Model phase is omitted if the bypassUpdates attribute is set to true. This is helpful when validating user input is necessary but updating the model is not. The execute attribute in RichFaces has the opposite functionality to this one.

6.4.2. Rendering

6.4.2.1. Render

A reference to one or more-page elements that require updating following an AJAX interaction can be found in the render attribute. It locates the components in the component tree by utilizing their id identifiers as a guide and the UIComponent .findComponent() algorithm.

To make locating components more effective, components can be referenced by their clientId identifier in addition to their id identifier. Example, "render example" shows both ways of referencing components. Each command button will correctly render the referenced panel grids, but the second button locates the references more efficiently with explicit clientId paths.

<h:form id="form1">

<r:commandButton value="Basic reference" render="infoBlock, infoBlock2"/>

<r:commandButton value="Specific reference" render=":infoBlock,:sv:infoBlock2"/>

</h:form>

<h:panelGrid id="infoBlock">

...

</h:panelGrid>

> **Remember**
> AJAX should be used judiciously to enhance user experience without compromising accessibility or functionality for users with older browsers or disabled JavaScript. Techniques like progressive enhancement and graceful degradation can help ensure a consistent experience across different environments.

```
<h:form id="sv">

<h:panelGrid id="infoBlock2">

...

</h:panelGrid>

</h:form>
```

The value of the render attribute can also be an expression written using JavaServer Faces' Expression Language (EL); this can either be a Set, Collection, Array, or String.

6.4.2.2. ajaxRendered

Every time an Ajax request is made, a component with ajaxRendered="true" will be re-rendered, even if it isn't referenced by the component making the request. When a status display or error message needs to be updated without being explicitly requested, this can be helpful.

The ajaxRendered attribute's functionality is the basis for the <r:outputPanel> component. The <r:outputPanel> component is designed to mark parts of the page for automatic updating.

6.4.2.3. limitRender

Only the components indicated in the render attribute will be updated, and RichFaces AJAX-enabled components and AJAX behaviors with limitRender="true" specified will prevent components with ajaxRendered="true" from re-rendering. This effectively causes other components' ajaxRendered attribute to be overridden.

Example describes two command buttons, a panel grid rendered by the buttons, and an output panel showing error messages. When the first button is clicked, the output panel is rendered even though it is not explicitly referenced with the render attribute. The second button, however, uses limitRender="true" to override the output panel's rendering and only render the panel grid.

```
<h:form id="form1">

<r:commandButton value="Normal rendering" render="infoBlock"/>

<r:commandButton value="Limited rendering" render="infoBlock" limitRender="true"/>

</h:form>
```

Keyword

Expression Language (EL) – It is a language for creating a computer-interpretable representation of specific knowledge and may refer to: Advanced Boolean Expression Language, an obsolete hardware description language for hardware descriptions.

```
<h:panelGrid id="infoBlock">

...

</h:panelGrid>

<r:outputPanel ajaxRendered="true">

<h:messages/>

</r:outputPanel>
```

6.4.3. Queuing and Traffic Control

6.4.3.1. requestDelay

The milliseconds that the request will wait in the queue before being sent to the server is indicated by the requestDelay attribute. The original request is replaced with the new one if a similar request is added to the queue before the delay is over.

6.4.3.2. ignoreDupResponses

The ignoreDupResponses attribute, when set to true, instructs the server to ignore responses for the request in the event that there is an identical request already pending. When an update is anticipated, this prevents the client from receiving needless updates. The request is still handled by the server, but the client is not updated if a similar request has already been queued.

6.4.4. Events and JavaScript Interactions

JSF offers global JavaScript. AJAX. onError along with jsf. AJAX. handlers (the JSSF) are defined using onEvent events. AJAX. All begin, succeed, and finish events use the onEvent event. At the component level, RichFaces adds event-specific attributes.

6.4.4.1. Onbeforesubmit

Prior to sending an AJAX request, the event listener is called by the onbeforesubmit event attribute. If the event listener specified for the onbeforesubmit event returns false, the request is canceled.

6.4.4.2. Onbegin

The onbegin event attribute invokes the event listener after an AJAX request is sent.

6.4.4.3. Onbeforedomupdate

The onbeforedomupdate event attribute invokes the event listener after an AJAX response has been returned but before the DOM tree of the browser is updated.

6.4.4.4. Oncomplete

The oncomplete event attribute invokes the event listener after an AJAX response has been returned and the DOM tree of the browser has been updated.

6.4.4.5. Data

The oncomplete event can handle additional data thanks to the data attribute. To access the managed bean's property, use JSF Expression Language (EL). The value of the property will be serialized into JavaScript Object Notation (JSON) and sent back to the client. The event can then be used to reference the property. data variable in the definitions of the event attributes. It is possible to serialize and use with data both simple types and sophisticated types, like arrays and collections.

```
<r:commandButton value="Update" oncomplete="showTheName(event.data.name)" data="#{userBean.name}"/>
```

6.4.4.6. Onerror

When an error occurs during AJAX communications, the event listener is triggered by the onerror event attribute.

6.4.4.7. Registering Event Callbacks with jQuery

RichFaces allows one to register callbacks for the events listed above using jQuery:

- **ajaxsubmit:** Triggered before an AJAX request is sent.
- **ajaxbegin:** Triggered after an AJAX request is sent.
- **ajaxbeforedomupdate:** Triggered after an AJAX response has been returned but before the DOM tree of the browser has been updated.
- **ajaxcomplete:** Triggered after an AJAX response has been returned and the DOM tree of the browser has been updated.

The event callback can be registered either on a form or a whole page:

```
<h:outputScript>

jQuery(document).ready(function() {

jQuery(#{r:element('form_id')}).on("ajaxsubmit," function() {

//the callback will be triggered before the form is submitted using JSF AJAX
```

```
console.log("ajaxsubmit");
});

jQuery(document).on("ajaxcomplete," function() {
//the callback will be triggered for each completed JSF AJAX for the current page
console.log("ajaxcomplete");
});
}
</h:outputScript>
```

Did you get it?

1. What is use of callback parameter of jQuery effect methods?

6.5. TECHNOLOGIES USED IN AJAX

→Learning Objectives
- Explain the steps of AJAX operation;
- Discuss about AJAX security.

AJAX is a web development technique that enables asynchronous data transmission and reception between the web browser and server to create interactive web applications.

AJAX solutions can leverage a wide range of technologies, but only three are necessary: JavaScript, DOM, and HTML/XHTML. It goes without saying that information display requires XHTML, but changing parts of an XHTML page without reloading it requires the DOM. JavaScript, the final component, is required to start the client-server connection and modify the DOM in order to update the webpage.

AJAX cannot function on its own. It is combined with other technologies to make websites that are interactive. AJAX is a collection of related technologies rather than a single technology, as will be explained later. AJAX uses the following technologies:

1. **JavaScript:** The object-based scripting language JavaScript is used to send requests to the web server. A JavaScript function is triggered when a page event takes place. It is a cross-platform programming language with loose typing. Websites that are interactive are made with it. Its primary uses include client-side validation, date and time display, pop-up window and dialog box display, and so forth. In server-side programming and desktop application development, it has become commonplace. It gives the application dynamic behavior.

2. **DOM:** It stands for Document Object Model, an HTML and XML document representation. It modifies the document's structure and permits Java Script interaction with web pages. It offers an API for modifying the style, structure, and content. It connects HTML and other markup languages with JavaScript and other scripting languages. Additionally, dynamic data display and data interaction are done with it. It's employed in the manipulation of HTML and XML documents.

3. **CSS:** It stands for Cascading Style Sheets. It describes how documents written in markup language are presented. It specifies how HTML element styles and contents should be displayed. The ability for users to create style sheets is a new feature added to HTML. Styles are kept in an external file. The website's pages can have their layout, colors, fonts, height, width, background images, and other elements changed using a CSS file. It allows for innovative website design. When working with web design, it is essential.

4. **XMLHttpRequest:** It is used to interact with client and server. It plays important role in AJAX web development technique. It can be used by JavaScript, VBScript, and other scripting languages to manipulate data to and from server using HTTP making connection between client and server side. It is used by many websites to create dynamic web applications. With AJAX, JavaScript communicates with server using XMLHttpRequest object to send request and get response from the server without refreshing the page.

   Syntax for creating XMLHttpRequest is as follows:

   Variable=new XMLHttpRequest ();

5. **HTML/XHTML and CSS:** These technologies are used for displaying content and style. It is mainly used for presentation

6.5.1. Steps of AJAX Operation

It has following stages:

- User visits the page by clicking the targeted link or typing URL in the web browser. When the page is loaded, the AJAX engine is also initialized. User interacts with AJAX engine to interact with web server.

- User requests from web browser and receive the response back. This can be done by an AJAX application which recalls the HTTP transaction which sends request to the server, server responds to the client and client and server close the connection.

- The client renders the document which may include some JavaScript. Communication with server takes place asynchronously to the user.

- JavaScript code creates XMLHttpRequest object which requests document from the web server.

- XMLHttpRequest indicates that data has arrived which is often called a callback. AJAX engine calls the callback functions to receive server response. Data is exchanged with server without reloading the page.

- The callback function updates the browser using DOM objects, HTML and CSS data. The callback function processes the data and displays it. AJAX applications are terminated once the request is completed

6.5.1.1. XMLHttpRequest

Interacting with the client and server is done with it. It has a significant impact on the AJAX web development methodology. Scripting languages such as JavaScript and VBScript can utilize HTTP to establish a connection between the client and server side and manipulate data to and from the server:

- It is used by many websites to create dynamic web applications.
- It communicates with server in the background.
- It updates the page with new data without reloading the page.
- It request and receive the data from web server.

Creating XMLHttpRequest object is as follows:

All modern browsers such as IE7, Firefox, Chrome, and Safari have built in XMLHttpRequest object.

variable variable_name = new XMLHttpRequest ();

OR

Old versions of Internet Explorer such as IE5 and IE6 use ActiveX objects as shown below:

variable variable_name= new ActiveXObject ("Microsft.XMlHTTP");

The following small example determines which object to use and how to create it:

If(window.XMLHttpRequest)

{

request=new XMLHttpRequest();

}

else if(window.ActiveXObject)

{

request=new ActiveXObject("Microsoft.XMLHTTP");

}

6.5.1.2. XMLHttpRequest Object Methods

open (method,URL):

open (method, URL, async), open (method, URL, async, userName),

open (method, URL, async, username, password), Specifies the method, URL and other attributes of the request.

Method represents types of the request such as GET, POST or HEAD and other Http methods such as PUT and DELETE. URL Specifies location or path of the file async specifies true (asynchronous) or false(synchronous), "true" means script processes after the send() method without waiting for response and "false" means script waits for response before continuing the script processing.

- send(string): It is used to send the request.
- String: Use only POST method request.
- setRequestHeader(label, value): It is used to set label/value to HTTP header.
- getResponseHeader(headerName): It returns value of the specific HTTP header
- getAllResponseHeaders(): It returns complete set of HTTP headers.
- abort(): It cancels the request.

6.5.1.3. XMLHttpRequest Object Properties

readyState: It defines current state or holds the status of the XMLHttpRequest. It has some possible values from 0 to 4.

    0: The request is not initialized.
    1: The request has been setup. Server connection established.
    2: The request has been sent.
    3: The request processing.
    4: The request is finished, and response is ready.

- **Onreadystatechange:** It stores the name of the function that will process the response from the server and will be called automatically each time the readyState property changes.
- **Status:** It returns status as a number, e.g., 404: page not found 200: OK
- **responseText:** It returns returned data as string of characters.
- **responseXml:** It returns data as XML file. It returns XML document object of data from server.
- **statusText:** It returns the status as a string. (e.g., "Not Found" or "OK").

6.5.2. AJAX Security

The asynchronous nature of AJAX can introduce security vulnerabilities if not implemented properly. Here are some security considerations when working with AJAX:

- JavaScript code is open source. Unauthorized user/hacker can use code for inferring server-side weaknesses and can easily penetrate into the system.
- It is combination of both JavaScript and XML which have security issues that AJAX helps to facilitate.
- The client code can be easily modified by attacker because it is open-source code.
- The AJAX engine uses JavaScript to capture and transfer user commands into

function calls which are sent in plain visible text to the server which may reveal database details.
- JavaScript code is downloaded from server side and executed at client side which compromises the client by mal-intended code.
- All the client-side validation must be backed up by server-side validation.
- AJAX applications use the same server-side security schemes of regular web applications.
- JavaScript code is open source. Unauthorized user/hacker can use code for inferring server-side weaknesses and can easily penetrate into the system.
- It is combination of both JavaScript and XML which have security issues that AJAX helps to facilitate.
- The client code can be easily modified by attacker because it is open-source code.
- The AJAX engine uses JavaScript to capture and transfer user commands into function calls which are sent in plain visible text to the server which may reveal database details.
- JavaScript code is downloaded from server side and executed at client side which compromises the client by mal-intended code.
- All the client-side validation must be backed up by server-side validation.
- AJAX applications use the same server-side security schemes of regular web applications.

6.5.3. AJAX Issues

AJAX is a strong technique used to create dynamic and interactive web applications, but it also has some issues and challenges. Like all technologies, it has its advantages and disadvantages. Thus, a few of the frequent problems with AJAX are as follows:

1. **Cross-Domain Requests:** Requests in AJAX typically comply with the same-origin policy. For security reasons, this policy limits requests to the same domain; if you attempt to make an AJAX request in a different domain, you will receive a CORS error. Therefore, in order to fix this error, you must reconfigure your system and use proxy servers or JSONP to enable cross-domain requests.
2. **Security Vulnerability:** Cross-Site Request Forgery (CSRF) and Cross-Site Scripting (XSS) are two methods that can be used to attack AJAX requests. Therefore, we must use input validation, output encoding, and CSRF protect tokens to prevent these kinds of vulnerabilities.
3. **Browser Support:** There is a browser compatibility issue because certain browser versions do not support AJAX functions. Therefore, before using AJAX, please make sure your browser can make and support AJAX requests.
4. **Performance Impact:** Performance will suffer if the AJAX request is not appropriately optimized. The page loading time can be slowed down and the server load can be increased if we transfer an excessive amount of data, make

pointless requests, make frequent requests, or process data inefficiently on the server. Thus, always submit a legitimate request that is optimized.

5. **Search Engine Optimization (SEO):** Since older web crawlers cannot run JavaScript, indexing AJAX-driven content can be difficult for search engines. It will have an impact on how well the website ranks and is found by search engines.

6. **Testing and Debugging:** Debugging AJAX codes is challenging because of the asynchronous nature of the request. Therefore, in order to solve this problem, we need to use effective debugging tools that can locate the problems and fix them.

7. **JavaScript Dependency:** In general, JavaScript is required for AJAX. Thus, we won't be able to use AJAX features if JavaScript is turned off in the web browser. To improve your experience, always have JavaScript enabled in your web browser.

8. **Code Complexity:** Complexity increases in AJAX codes when dealing with asynchronous flow and response management. Therefore, to get around this problem, always write code that is clear, maintainable, and well-organized, with each concern kept in its own piece of code for ease of understanding by developers.

9. **Dependency Management:** Since AJAX is implemented using a variety of web technologies, as is well known, it is dependent on third-party libraries and frameworks. The largest problem with AJAX is thus managing dependencies and updating them on time, particularly when using multiple components or plugins.

6.5.4. Uses of AJAX in Technologies

AJAX is a concept rather than a programming language or tool. A client-side script called AJAX allows data to be sent and received between a server and database without requiring a postback or a full-page refresh. "The method of exchanging data with a server and updating parts of a web page without reloading the entire page" is the best definition of AJAX that you have read. The term "AJAX" refers primarily to a collection of JavaScript methods that allow you to dynamically connect to a web server without loading multiple pages. More specifically, it refers to using JavaScript to dynamically communicate with a web server through XmlHttpRequest objects.

6.5.4.1. Benefits of AJAX

There are four main benefits of using AJAX in web applications:

1. **Callbacks:** In order to retrieve and/or save data without sending the full page back to the server, AJAX is used to execute a callback, which is a brief round trip to and from the server. Network consumption is reduced, and operations happen more quickly by transmitting all form data to the server instead of executing a full postback. In places where bandwidth is limited, this can

significantly enhance network efficiency. The majority of the time, not much data is sent to or from the server. The server does not have to process every form element when callbacks are used. The server's processing is kept to a minimum by sending only the data that is required. Processing the ViewState, processing every form element, returning images to the client, or returning an entire page to the client are not necessary.

2. **Making Asynchronous Calls:** You can call a web server asynchronously with AJAX. This saves the client browser from having to wait for all data to be received before enabling the user to take further action.

3. **User-Friendly:** Because a page postback is being eliminated, AJAX enabled applications will always be more responsive, faster, and more user-friendly.

4. **Increased Speed:** Enhancing a web application's speed, functionality, and usability is the primary goal of AJAX. Netflix's movie rating system is an excellent illustration of AJAX in action. When a user rates a movie, their individual rating is immediately saved to their database without requiring them to reload or refresh the page. Without resubmitting the entire page to the server, these movie ratings are being stored in their database.

6.5.5. Technical Aspects of AJAX

In the client-side JavaScript, create an XMLHttpRequest object to perform AJAX callbacks. Direct calls to server-side objects, such as pages and web services, can be made using the XMLHttpRequest object. Data will be saved and/or returned by these webpages and web services.

Originally, Asynchronous JavaScript and XML stood for AJAX. "Asynchronous" refers to the fact that various events are taking place separately from one another. The client can use the web application while the request is being processed, as long as it initializes an AJAX callback to the server. This eliminates the need for the client to wait for a response. After finishing, the client will receive a response from the server, which it can then process as needed.

6.5.5.1. What Advances Have Been Made to AJAX?

XML is a markup language used to define data, and JavaScript is the language used for client-side programming. Another markup language for defining data is JSON. When using JavaScript, JSON (JavaScript Object Notation) is far more user-friendly than XML. XML Web Services are being replaced by JSON Web Services in terms of JavaScript and AJAX.

An additional significant development for JavaScript and AJAX is the JavaScript object library known as jQuery. This program is an open-source, free wrapper for JavaScript. Writing client-side JavaScript to navigate, modify, and perform asynchronous AJAX callbacks on a page is made simple with jQuery. AJAX callbacks are now considered standard programming practices for creating and developing web applications, thanks to the use of jQuery and JSON Web Services.

Microsoft developed the AJAX Control Toolkit, a collection of controls that can be dragged and dropped onto web forms in the same way as html and server controls. It is integrated into Visual Studio. The purpose of these controls is to be used with AJAX callbacks. They can also be applied as standard client and/or server controls, though. For example, Asp.Net does not come with the Tabs controls. However, the AJAX Control Toolkit does. The Tab control can postback to the server just like server controls.

6.5.5.2. Where AJAX Should Be Used?

Anywhere in a web application where a small amount of data could be saved or retrieved without posting back the entire page, AJAX should be used. Data validation on save actions is a good illustration of this. Altering the values in a drop-down list box depending on additional inputs, like state and college list boxes, is an additional example. Only colleges and universities in that state will appear in the college list box once the user selects a state. When the client needs to save or retrieve session values from the server based on a user preference, like the height, width, or position of an object, is another excellent example. When the width is changed, the session variable could be set for the new width by making a callback to the server. In this manner, the object's width can be modified by the server using this session variable each time the page is refreshed. The object would return to its original default width if this were not the case.

Text hints and autocomplete text boxes are additional features. After the customer enters a few letters, a list of all values that begin with those letters is displayed below. To obtain all values that start with these characters, a callback is made to a web service. This wonderful feature, which is also a part of the AJAX Control Toolkit, would not be possible without AJAX. Recently, Segue used AJAX to support a client application that was experiencing issues because of its constrained bandwidth and page size. The combination resulted in an excessively long time for the application to retrieve and display data on the page. Occasionally, the web server would time out because it just lacked the resources to process the request. AJAX was the most effective fix for this problem. In order to retrieve the information about the selected item, we built JSON Web Services on the web server to address this issue. The data would be retrieved, converted to JSON, and returned as a JSON string by the JSON web service. When an item was chosen from the list box, the client would call the web service rather than posting back to the server. We made an asynchronous AJAX call to the web service using jQuery. Further client-side processing was carried out to display the data on the page after the client received the data back from the web service. As soon as the item was selected, the details appeared on the page immediately. There was no postback, refresh, or page flicker.

Did you get it?

1. What advances have been made to AJAX?
2. Explain the technical aspects of AJAX

6.6. AJAX APPLICATION SERVER PERFORMANCE

→Learning Objectives
- Discuss the client-side performance of an AJAX application;
- Describe The HTML application.

AJAX is the term used to refer to a collection of technologies that enhance the responsiveness of web applications. These technologies include HTML and CSS, dynamic HTML, client-side scripting (in JavaScript or Java), the DOM model for dynamic displays, XML for data exchange, and XMLHttpRequest for synchronous and asynchronous data retrieval. Crane is an excellent source. Google Maps and Gmail are two mature commercial examples of AJAX usage; AjaxPatterns uses AJAX to classify more than fifty websites. With the increasing support of XMLHttpRequest objects in more recent browser versions, AJAX is being used more often in web programming. On the other hand, not much research on the functionality of real AJAX apps have been released.

The AJAX performance evaluation case study published by White is one that is frequently referenced. This AJAX application increased performance by 73%, transferring on average 27% of the bytes compared to the traditional HTML application. The task times taken by users to complete the work also showed improvements in performance for the AJAX application. The effects of users' training and skill levels, which may have a significant impact on the outcomes reported, were not evaluated in this report, though. This is particularly valid given that the user interfaces of the two applications are different. However, compared to the HTML application, the AJAX application needed fewer bytes to complete the tasks, and users completed the given work faster. These time savings equate to a direct reduction in labor expenses.

6.6.1. The Application

The client-side performance of an AJAX application with the same user interface as a real-world HTML application was compared by Smullen and Smullen. Data was gathered through experimentation on how well each person performed when given the identical set of 110 tasks. Both the AJAX and HTML applications' performance metrics were calculated. By gathering information on a statistically significant sample size and including server performance results, the current study expands on previous research.

232 FUNDAMENTALS OF WEB DEVELOPMENT

The user enters one or more selection criteria (department, course/section, meeting days, start/end times, location, instructor, open/closed, etc.), and the application provides a list of courses that match the parameters along with more details about each course (such as title and enrollment status). The three-tier model used by the application allows for communication between the client and the database server, web server, and web server. Instead of being a "test" application, it is a production tool that instructors and students use on a daily basis. The application uses PHP 5.05 and custom database code to connect to the legacy SIS database, and the web server is Apache. All of the returned pages are XHTML 1.1 validated.

6.6.2. The HTML Application

The HTML form used to prepare a query is found on the first page a user loads. This page has a lot of "branding" overhead because the University uses a common style sheet, navigation, and layout for all of its pages. These shared components total 15573 bytes and are made up of two graphical images, a CSS style sheet, and JavaScript that supports the navigation links on the shared page. These are static elements that are linked to the HTML page. Instead of loading each query and response, they are downloaded once and cached for the majority of browsers.

The HTML page with the query form (27KB) and common elements (15.2KB) would load first for a normal user. A query is created by the user and sent to a server application. The SIS is queried by the server application. The format of the data that was taken out of the SIS is XML. After reading the XML data, the server process transforms it with XSLT to create XHTML. The client receives an XHTML response from the web server.

The page that appears in response to a query includes links to the previously mentioned common elements, an HTML-formatted list of courses that answer the query (or a message if no results are found), and the HTML form required to submit another query. Because of this, the response page for a query that returns nothing is roughly 27 KB (including the linked common elements).

6.6.3. The AJAX Application

The HTML application has an AJAX version coded. JavaScript is used by the AJAX version to control the XML handler and user interface. The AJAX version's "look and feel" was carefully designed to match that of the HTML version. The presentation page structure, graphics, and common navigation elements are all the same for both AJAX and HTML applications because they appear to the user the same.

The Sarissa libraries (0.9 version. 6.1) were employed in the AJAX application's coding. Sarissa is a free and open-source collection of ECMAScript-based cross-browser libraries for creating AJAX apps. It is an exemplar of the kinds of implementation libraries found in real-world AJAX applications. For this application, 57KB of code and libraries were downloaded to the client in order to implement the AJAX interface.

WORKING WITH AJAX

For a number of reasons, the AJAX application exclusively makes synchronous AJAX XMLHttpRequest calls for this investigation. Selecting courses is a sequential process by nature. The choice of next course is frequently influenced by the choice of previous courses. Performance analysis of asynchronous AJAX will be done in progress and published in a later paper. There was no need for asynchronous calls because the AJAX application mimics the "look and feel" of the HTML application. This application does not use event-triggered processing, preload data, or take advantage of AJAX capabilities to improve user experience. Thus, this application can be seen as a worst-case scenario for AJAX, with all of the overhead and minimal benefits aside from partial page refreshes.

The AJAX application made use of the already-existing server application. The central IT team was adamant about not changing a live system for this test. The current production server application responds to an AJAX XMLHttpRequest with the existing XML output because the query results from the server application are available in XML form; it bypasses the XSLT transform and sends the XML to the client. The XML data generated by the production server process is retrieved by the AJAX application, and the AJAX client processes it for display.

6.6.4. Data Collection

A browser loads an HTML page, along with any graphical elements, style sheets, or other linked elements, when it contacts a standard web application. When a client submits a form or clicks a link on the HTML page, it engages with the user interface and sends an HTTP request message to the web server. The browser receives a fresh HTML page from the web server. The browser's previous page has been replaced with this one.

An HTML page loads into the browser when a browser contacts an AJAX application. This page includes the XML handler for formatting and presenting the results, the JavaScript required to run the user interface and make XMLHttpRequest calls, and any additional components required for the user interface, like style sheets and HTML code. In order to interact with the user interface on the browser page, the client clicks links, fills out forms, or initiates events. When a user interface event occurs, the JavaScript code responds by typically sending an XMLHttpRequest message to the web server. The web browser receives XML data from the web server. The JavaScript code handles and displays this XML data to the user. The only area of the browser page that is updated is the part that shows the results. 42 points2 KB are needed for the HTML application's initial load (15 points2 KB for the common elements—graphics, CSS, navigation, JavaScript—and 27 points2 KB for the HTML page containing the form). Each response file that follows is an entire XHTML page that includes the form, the HTML presentation, and the query results. If the browser supports caching, only one load of the common elements is required.

The initial load of the AJAX application requires 99.2KB overhead (15.2KB common elements – graphics, CSS, navigation JavaScript, 27KB for the HTML presentation and form, and 57KB AJAX JavaScript code). All of these elements need to be loaded only once if the browser supports caching. This initial load could be made smaller if the AJAX application were not reproducing the graphics and look-and-feel of the existing HTML application. After loading the AJAX application, each response is an XML file containing the query result data and other information produced by the server application.

All information was gathered by sending queries to the live servers. Thirteen thousand two hundred and sixty questions were asked both through the AJAX form and the production HTML form. The HTML form and the AJAX form both had records of the number of bytes returned for each query. The common elements loaded from the client cache are not included in the size of each response; the effects of caching these common elements were investigated. The HTML values varied from 27KB (no courses) in a query to 1.9MB (all courses for fall semester) in a query. The byte values of the AJAX response varied from 7.6KB to 1.1MB.

A given query will always return the same number of bytes, regardless of the load on the servers. This is known as deterministic behavior. The time it took to process each request was taken from the Apache web server log in order to gauge the impact of using AJAX on the servers (and consequently the application's perceived responsiveness to the user). Two clients collected a small sample of these times, and an analysis of them revealed that they varied greatly because of the exogenous load placed on the servers. For both the HTML and AJAX applications, a set of 121 queries were repeated in order to lower the variance of the service times.

Did you get it?

1. How to load html response on browser using AJAX call?
2. What is client-side AJAX?
3. What is client-side vs server-side performance?

A CLOSER LOOK

AJAX Call Function: An AJAX call starts with the end user performing an action on the front end of a website (for example, clicking a button). When that action is performed, a JavaScript event is triggered, and its listener calls a function.

Inside the function, the AJAX call is fired, and, with the help of XML, the information is packaged, and the request is sent to a server script.

Inside the script, the request is processed with the help of a server-side scripting language like PHP, Java, Ruby, Python etc.

The response is sent back to the client, and a callback function updates the corresponding content part with the received data.

```
//rails-ujs
Rails.ajax({
  type: "POST",
  url: "/things",
  data: mydata,
  success: function(repsonse){...},
  error: function(repsonse){...}
})

//jQuery
$.ajax({
  type: "POST",
  url: "/things",
  data: mydata,
  success: function(data, textStatus, jqXHR){...},
  error: function(jqXHR, textStatus, errorThrown){...}
})

//axios
axios({
  method: 'POST',
  url: '/things',
  data: mydata,
  headers: {
    'X-CSRF-Token': document.querySelector("meta[name=csrf-token]").content
  }
})
.then(function(response) {...},
.catch(function(error) {...}
})
```

```
//rails-ujs
Rails.ajax({
  type: "POST",
  url: "/things",
  data: mydata,
  success: function(repsonse){...},
  error: function(repsonse){...}
})

//jQuery
$.ajax({
  type: "POST",
  url: "/things",
  data: mydata,
  success: function(data, textStatus, jqXHR){...},
  error: function(jqXHR, textStatus, errorThrown){...}
})

//axios
axios({
  method: 'POST',
  url: '/things',
  data: mydata,
  headers: {
    'X-CSRF-Token': document.querySelector("meta[name=csrf-token]").content
  }
})
.then(function(response) {...},
.catch(function(error) {...}
})
```

ROLE MODEL

JESSE JAMES GARRETT: BEST KNOWN FOR COINING THE TERM "AJAX"

Jesse James Garrett is a prominent figure in the field of user experience (UX) design. He is best known for coining the term "AJAX" (Asynchronous JavaScript and XML) in his seminal article "AJAX: A New Approach to Web Applications," which was published in 2005. This article played a significant role in popularizing the use of AJAX in web development, revolutionizing how web applications were built by enabling asynchronous data retrieval without requiring a full-page refresh.

Garrett is also known for his work in information architecture and user-centered design. He has contributed to the development of various design methodologies and frameworks aimed at creating more intuitive and user-friendly digital experiences. Garrett is often sought after as a speaker and consultant in the field of UX design, and his insights have helped shape the way designers approach their craft.

In addition to his contributions to the field of UX design, Garrett is the co-founder and Chief Creative Officer of Adaptive Path, a well-respected design consultancy firm. Through his work at Adaptive Path and his writings, Garrett has played a significant role in advancing the discipline of UX design and shaping the way digital products and services are designed and experienced.

6.7. SUMMARY

- AJAX is a collection of web development techniques that generates asynchronous web applications by utilizing a variety of client-side web technologies.
- AJAX enables dynamic content changes on web pages and, consequently, web applications, without requiring a page reload by separating the data interchange layer from the presentation layer.
- Web content that is dynamic and asynchronously created is commonly created using JavaScript and XML, which are referred to as AJAX.
- The Document Object Model (DOM) of the page is updated by the server's response to an asynchronous request sent by a JavaScript function from the client.
- The term "AJAX" describes a collection of tools and methods that enhance the interactivity of web pages and simulate desktop applications.
- Richer and more interactive web applications can be created using AJAX. These applications are known as Rich Internet Applications (RIA). Web apps that offer desktop application functionality are known as RIAs.
- Application services in ASP.NET are built-in Web services that are based on ASP.NET forms authentication, roles, and user profiles.
- AJAX makes use of the XMLHttpRequest object to interact with the server. With the help of the image shown below, let's attempt to comprehend how AJAX functions and flows.
- AJAX is a web development technique that enables asynchronous data transmission and reception between the web browser and server to create interactive web applications.

MULTIPLE CHOICE QUESTION

1. **What does AJAX stand for?**
   a. Asynchronous JavaScript and XML
   b. Advanced JavaScript and XML
   c. Automated JavaScript and XML
   d. Application JavaScript and XML

2. **Which of the following is NOT a benefit of using AJAX?**
   a. Improved user experience
   b. Reduced server load
   c. Faster page load times
   d. Higher security

3. Which HTTP request method is commonly used in AJAX requests to retrieve data?
   a. GET
   b. POST
   c. PUT
   d. DELETE
4. Which JavaScript object is commonly used to perform AJAX requests?
   a. XMLHttpRequest
   b. JSONParser
   c. AjaxRequest
   d. HTTPRequest
5. Which function is called when an AJAX request completes successfully?
   a. onDone()
   b. onSuccess()
   c. onComplete()
   d. onload()
6. Which of the following is true about AJAX?
   a. It requires the entire web page to reload.
   b. It allows asynchronous communication between the client and server.
   c. It can only be used with XML data.
   d. It cannot be used with JavaScript.
7. Which JavaScript method is used to send an AJAX request?
   a. sendRequest()
   b. open()
   c. create()
   d. ajax()
8. Which format is commonly used for exchanging data between the client and server in AJAX?
   a. XML
   b. JSON
   c. HTML
   d. CSV
9. Which of the following is NOT a commonly used JavaScript framework for simplifying AJAX development?
   a. jQuery
   b. AngularJS

c. React
   d. Bootstrap
10. Which HTTP status code indicates that an AJAX request was successful?
   a. 200
   b. 404
   c. 500
   d. 302

REVIEW QUESTIONS

1. What are all the features of AJAX?
2. How to use AJAX in JavaScript file?
3. What are the security threats that prevail with AJAX code?
4. Explain AJAX callback function.
5. What are the ready state of requests used with AJAX requests?

Answer to Multiple Choice Questions

1. (a); 2. (d); 3. (a); 4. (a); 5. (d); 6. (b); 7. (b); 8. (b); 9. (d); 10. (a)

REFERENCES

1. Culwin, F., & Faulkner, X., (2001). Browsing the web: Delay, determination, and satisfaction. In: *HICSS '01: Proceedings of the 34th Annual Hawaii International Conference on System Sciences* (p. 5018). Washington, DC, USA. IEEE Computer Society.
2. David, P. H., (2006). Ajax and record locking. *Dr. Dobb's Journal, 31*(10), 45–51.
3. Gomez, C., Arcia-Moret, A., & Crowcroft, J., (2017). TCP in the internet of things: From ostracism to prominence. *IEEE Internet Computing,* 1–15.
4. Guarda, T., Fernanda, M., et al., (2017). Internet of things challenges. *Proceedings of the 12th Iberian Conference on Information Systems and Technologies* (pp. 628–630).
5. Hart, J. K., & Martinez, K (2015). Toward an environmental internet of things. *Earth and Space Science* (pp. 1–7). 10.1002/2014EA000044.
6. Junchang, M., (2006). Dept. of Comput. Sci. & Eng., Beijing Inst. of Technol.; ZhiminGu; "finding shared fragments in large collections of web pages for fragment-based web caching." *Network Computing and Applications, 2006; NCA 2006, Fifth IEEE International Symposium.*
7. Lowry, P., Madariaga, S., Moffit, K., Moody, G., Spaulding, T., & Wells, T., (2006). A theoretical model and empirical results linking website interactivity and usability satisfaction. HICSS '06. *Proceedings of the 39th Annual Hawaii International Conference on System Sciences, 6*, 123a.

8. Mendes, C., Osaki, R., & Costa, C., (2017). Internet of things in automated production. *EJERS, European Journal of Engineering Research and Science, 2*(10).
9. Murray, G., (2006). *Asynchronous JavaScript Technology and XML (AJAX) With Java 2 Platform, Enterprise Edition.* http://java.sun.com/developer/technicalArticles/J2EE/AJAX (accessed on 20 April 2024).
10. Nadimpalli, M., (2017). Internet of things – future outlook. *International Journal of Innovative Research in Computer and Communication Engineering, 5*(6).
11. Qurashi, U. S., & Anwar, Z., (2012). *AJAX based attacks: Exploiting Web 2.0.* Emerging Technologies (ICET), 2012 International Conference.
12. Ricciardi, S., Amazonas, J. R., Palmieri, F., & Bermudez-Edo, M., (2017). Ambient intelligence in the internet of things. *Hindawi Mobile Information Systems, 2017,* 3. Article ID 2878146.
13. Schulke, G., (2017). *The Internet of Things (IoT), for the CIO.* Article November 2017. Available:
14. https://www.researchgate.net/publication/321367288.
15. Shi, F., Li, Q., Zhu, T., & Ning, H., (2018). A survey of data semantization in internet of things. *Sensors,* vol. 18, 313. doi: 10.3390/s18010313.
16. Wang, S., Xu, Z., Cao, J., & Zhang, J., (2007). A middleware for web service-enabled integration and interoperation of intelligent building systems. *Automation in Construction, 16*, 112–121.
17. Weiguo, H., Liping, D., Peisheng, Z., & Xiaoyan, L., (2009). Using Ajax for desktop-like geospatial web application development. *Geoinformatics, 2009 17th International Conference.*
18. Zhiliang, X., (2017). Information sensing and interactive technology of internet of things. *IOP Conf. Series: Earth and Environmental Science 94, EEMS 2017.* IOP Publishing, 012039. doi: 10.1088/1755-1315/94/1/012039.

CHAPTER 7
Working with Databases

LEARNING OBJECTIVES

After studying this chapter, you will be able to:

- Describe databases and web development;
- Understand structured query language (SQL);
- Define database (APIs);
- Manage a MYSQL database;
- Connect to MySQL using PHP.

INTRODUCTORY EXAMPLE

Closing a Connection: When we establish a connection to MySQL database from a PHP script, we should also disconnect or close the connection when our work is finished. Here we have described the syntax of closing the connection to a MySQL database in all 3 methods described above. We have assumed that the reference to the connection is stored in $conn variable.

Using MySQLi object oriented procedure

$conn->close();

Using MySQLi procedural procedure

mysqli_close($conn);

Using PDO procedure

$conn = null;

7.1. UNIT INTRODUCTION

A database is a structured set of data or a particular kind of data store that is created with the aid of a database management system (DBMS), which is a piece of software that communicates with applications, end users, and the database itself in order to collect and process data. The essential tools needed to manage the database are also included in the DBMS. A database system is the culmination of the database, the DBMS, and the related applications. Frequently, the term "database" is also used in an ambiguous manner to refer to any DBMS, the database system, or a database-related application.

While large databases are hosted on computer clusters or cloud storage, smaller databases can be kept on a file system. Formal methods and practical factors are taken into account when designing databases. These factors include data modeling, effective data representation and storage, query languages, security and privacy of sensitive data, and distributed computing concerns like fault tolerance and concurrent access support.

Database management systems can be categorized by computer scientists based on the database models they support. In the 1980s, relational databases gained popularity. The great majority of these use SQL for writing and querying data, and they model the data as rows and columns in a series of tables. Since they employ various query languages, non-relational databases—also known as NoSQL—became well-liked in the 2000s.

7.2. DATABASES AND WEB DEVELOPMENT

→Learning Objectives
- Understand database management systems;
- Describe the concept of my-structured query language.

There are millions of data generated every day. Businesses also use databases to store their important data. Stored in a specific system, a database is a collection of ordered data. One function of the database management system is to process the data that is stored in the system. On the other hand, considering how many files are kept in it, it's comparable to an office.

Database management systems are tools that businesses use to manage data from databases (fetch, store, update, and optimize). One of the main justifications for businesses moving to database management systems is security. There are many different database management systems available today, and each one has specializations and unique features. Even so, there's still a lot of disagreement over which database management system is most widely used in terms of feature set, best data modeling tool, and licensing. Oracle has the highest-ranking score (1266.89) according to the survey 2022, followed by IBM, Microsoft, and many more.

1. **Oracle:** The main applications of Oracle DBMS, an efficient object-relational database management system with multiple models, are data warehousing and online transaction processing. Its most recent version, 12c, refers to cloud computing. We have Linux, UNIX, and Windows as supporting systems. This version processes data very quickly, uses less memory, is more secure, and has larger databases. Owing to its exceptional functionality and dependability, major corporations like JPMorgan Chase, Citigroup, and UnitedHealth frequently utilize it.

   Features:
   - Easy backup and recovery.
   - Deploying a database is possible, be it a public cloud, or even a private cloud, and data center.
   - Has a single database for all data types.

- Uses encryption techniques, data masking, key management, and monitoring activities to safeguard the database.

2. **MySQL (My-Structured Query Language):** It is a free, open-source relational and again a multi-model database management system. A reliable, cost-effective tool that is implemented to enhance the security and scalability of the database. Its functionality includes high-speed data processing and data recovery increases its popularity. It supports Windows, Linux, Mac, and Ubuntu. Large organizations such as Google, Adobe, Facebook, and WordPress use this tool for the database management system.

   Features:
   - Provides technical support to the users and developers.
   - Supports client-server architecture.
   - Easy integration with other engines like Apache.
   - Responsive and open community support.

3. **Microsoft SQL Server:** An efficient and effective relational database management system is Microsoft SQL Server. It offers effective workload management and allows multiple users to access the same database. It builds customized containers that let users mix and match group views and scripts. The data is safe, secure, and modifiable. Linux and Windows are supported operating systems. MSLGROUP (France) and Penguin Random House LLC (United States) are two businesses that use this tool.

   Features:
   - Easy backup and recovery.
   - Highly secure and consistent.
   - Setting up a new database is easy.
   - Can create tables and designs without syntax.
   - Supports analytics, transaction processing applications, and business intelligence.

4. **PostgreSQL:** An advanced relational database management system that is free and open-source is called PostgreSQL. This tool's ability to export and import data is one of its primary features. Integrating functionalities such as managing and expanding intricate data tasks. It has a large number of plug-ins to improve functionality. It is compatible with Python and JSON programming languages. On Linux

> **Keyword**
>
> **Database Management Systems** – These are software systems used to store, retrieve, and run queries on data.

and Windows operating systems, it is compatible. Use of this tool is seen in large corporations like Instagram, Uber, and Netflix.

Features:
- Keeps a large amount of data secure.
- Supports ACID property.
- Compatible with data integrity.
- Has inheritance feature from the parent table.

5. **MongoDB:** MongoDB is a document-oriented, NoSQL, cross-platform, open-source database management system. A description of the table schema is not necessary for this tool. The majority of developers who work with large volumes of data storage favor this tool. Both self-managed infrastructure and a fully managed cloud service are offered for this. It is compatible with Windows, Linux, and macOS. Additionally, companies like Adobe, ADP, Barclays, and AstraZeneca are utilizing this tool.

Features:
- Authentication and Indexing.
- Has licensing options for both, cloud, and local devices.
- Supports programming languages like C, C#, Java, and JavaScript.
- Supports sharding (method for distributing a single dataset across multiple databases)

6. **Redis:** Using an in-memory dataset, Redis (Remote Dictionary Server) is an open-source database tool that can be used as a cache, streaming engine, and message broker. Replication, transactions, and Lua scripting are all integrated into it. It is an ANSI C-coded key-value database management system that is NoSQL in nature. This facilitates partial resynchronization, auto-reconnection, and asynchronous replication. Linux and Windows are supported operating systems.

Features:
- Highly available;
- Persistent and extensible;
- Provides automatic data partitioning;
- Clustering (hash-based sharding).

7. **IBM Db2:** DB2 was the previous name for the database management tool IBM Db2. It excels because it supports handle frameworks and data science languages like Python.

> **Keyword**
>
> **Data Processing** – It is the collection and manipulation of digital data to produce meaningful information.

It instantly saves a sizable amount of data. It can modernize the management of both structured and unstructured data in both local and cloud environments thanks to AI-powered capabilities. There are various Linux, UNIX, and Windows versions that this tool supports.

Features:
- High availability;
- Scalable and secure;
- Data retrieval is quick;
- Table or range partitioning.

8. **SQLite:** An open-source relational database management system, SQLite is written in C. This tool allows you to resize files with less metadata and at smaller sizes. It is the most widely used database engine because it is dependable and typically utilized for mobile applications. It can serve as a temporary dataset and handle HTTP requests with low to medium traffic. It works with Linux, Mac, Windows, and Solaris.

Features:
- Backup API;
- Null handling;
- Partial indexes;
- Standalone CLI (command line interface);
- Multi-threaded programs.

> **Keyword**
>
> **JSON** – It is a text format that is completely language independent but uses conventions that are familiar to programmers of the C-family of languages, including C, C++, C#, Java, JavaScript, Perl, Python, and many others.

Did you get it?

1. What is the difference between MySQL and Microsoft SQL Server?
2. What is Redis server used for?

7.3. STRUCTURED QUERY LANGUAGE (SQL)

→Learning Objectives
- Discuss the data types and constraints in MySQL;
- Define SQL for data definition.

Designed for managing data stored in relational database management systems (RDBMS) or for stream processing in relational data stream management systems (RDSMS), SQL is a domain-specific programming language. It works especially well when managing structured data, i.e., data that includes relationships between variables and entities.

When SQL was first introduced in the 1970s, it had two key advantages over previous read-write APIs like VSAM or ISAM. It first presented the idea of using a single command to access multiple records. Second, it does away with the requirement to indicate the path to a record, i.e., both in and out of an index.

SQL is a multi-state language that was initially built on relational algebra and tuple relational calculus. It can be loosely divided into four sublanguages: data query language (DQL), data definition language (DDL), data control language (DCL), and data manipulation language (DML). Data query, data manipulation (insert, update, and delete), data definition (creation and modification of schemas), and data access control are all included in the scope of SQL. SQL contains procedural elements as well as declarative language (4GL) elements.

Edgar F. was used in the first commercial languages, including SQL. The relational model of Codd. His seminal 1970 paper "A Relational Model of Data for Large Shared Data Banks" included a description of the model. Although SQL did not fully follow Codd's relational model, it did become the most popular database language (Figure 7.1).

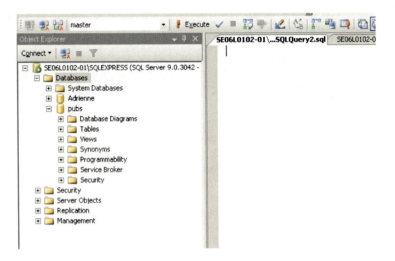

Figure 7.1. Example of Microsoft SQL server.

Source: https://www.mssqltips.com/.

In 1986, the American National Standards Institute (ANSI) and the International Organization for Standardization (ISO) both adopted SQL as a standard. [Since then, the standard has undergone numerous revisions to add common extensions and a wider range of features. Even though there are standards, very few implementations follow them exactly, and most SQL code needs to be modified in some way in order to be ported to other database systems.

In a DBMS, the SQL database language is used to:

- Create the database and table structures;
- Perform basic data management chores (add, delete, and modify);
- Perform complex queries to transform raw data into useful information.

> **Keyword**
>
> **RDBMS** – It is a type of database management system (DBMS) that stores data in a row-based table structure which connects related data elements.

7.3.1. Data Types and Constraints in MySQL

We are aware that a database is made up of one or more relations, and that each relation is composed of attributes (columns) within a table. There is a data type for every attribute. Constraints can be specified for every attribute in a relation.

7.3.1.1. Data Type of Attribute

The type of data value that an attribute can have been indicated by its data type. The operations that can be carried out on an attribute's data depend on its data type. For instance, numeric data can undergo arithmetic operations, but character data cannot (Table 7.1).

Table 7.1. Commonly Used Data Types in MySQL

Data Type	Description
CHAR(n)	Specifies character type data of length n where n could be any value from 0 to 255. CHAR is of fixed length, means, declaring CHAR (10) implies to reserve spaces for 10 characters. If data does not have 10 characters (for example, 'city' has four characters), MySQL fills the remaining 6 characters with spaces padded on the right.
VARCHAR(n)	Specifies character type data of length 'n' where n could be any value from 0 to 65535. But unlike CHAR, VARCHAR is a variable-length data type. That is, declaring VARCHAR (30) means a maximum of 30 characters can be stored but the actual allocated bytes will depend on the length of entered string. So 'city' in VARCHAR (30) will occupy the space needed to store 4 characters only.
INT	INT specifies an integer value. Each INT value occupies 4 bytes of storage. The range of values allowed in integer type are –2147483648 to 2147483647. For values larger than that, we have to use BIGINT, which occupies 8 bytes.
FLOAT	Holds numbers with decimal points. Each FLOAT value occupies 4 bytes
DATE	The DATE type is used for dates in 'YYYY-MM-DD' format. YYYY is the 4-digit year, MM is the 2-digit month and DD is the 2-digit date. The supported range is '1000-01-01' to '9999-12-31.'

Source: https://ncert.nic.in.

7.3.1.2. Constraints

Certain kinds of limitations on the data values that an attribute can have been called constraints. They are employed to guarantee the dependability and correctness of data. However, it is not mandatory to define constraint for each attribute of Table 7.2.

Table 7.2. *Commonly Used SQL Constraints*

Constraint	Description
NOT NULL	Ensures that a column cannot have NULL value
NOT NUL	Ensures that a column cannot have NULL values where NULL means missing/unknown/not applicable value.
UNIQUE	Ensures that all the values in a column are distinct/unique
DEFAULT	A default value specified for the column if no value is provided.
PRIMARY KEY	The column which can uniquely identify each row or record in a table
FOREIGN KEY	The column which refers to value of an attribute defined as primary key in another table.

Source: https://ncert.nic.in.

> **Keyword**
>
> **Data Definition Language (DDL)** – It is a computer language used to create and modify the structure of database objects in a database

7.3.2. SQL for Data Definition

Relation schema definition, schema modification, and relation deletion are all possible with SQL commands. These are referred to as Data Definition Language (DDL) and are used to specify the set of relations along with their schema, data type for each attribute, constraints, and authorizations pertaining to access and security.

The create statement is the first step in data definition. A database and its tables (relationships) are created using this statement. The number of tables, the columns (attributes) in each table, and the data type of each column should all be known before building the database. We choose the relation schema in this manner.

7.3.2.1. CREATE Database

To create a database, we use the CREATE DATABASE statement as shown in the following syntax:

CREATE DATABASE databasename;

To create a database called StudentAttendance, we will type following command at MySQL prompt.

MySQL> CREATE DATABASE StudentAttendance; Query OK, 1 row affected (0.02 sec)

A DBMS can manage multiple databases on one computer. Therefore, we need to select the database that we want to use. Once the database is selected, we can proceed with creating tables or querying data. Write the following SQL statement for using the database:

MySQL> USE StudentAttendance; Database changed

Initially, the created database is empty. It can be checked by using the Show tables command that lists names of all the tables within a database.

MySQL> SHOW TABLES;

Empty set (0.06 sec)

7.3.2.2. CREATE Table

After creating database StudentAttendance, we need to define relations (create tables) in this database and specify attributes for each relation along with data types for each attribute. This is done using the CREATE TABLE statement.

Syntax:

CREATE TABLE tablename(

attributename1 datatype constraint,

attributename2 datatype constraint,

:

attributenameN datatype constraint);

It is important to observe the following points with respect to the Create Table statement:

- N is the degree of the relation, means there are N columns in the table.
- Attribute name specifies the name of the column in the table.
- Datatype specifies the type of data that an attribute can hold.
- Constraint indicates the restrictions imposed on the values of an attribute. By default, each attribute can take NULL values except for the primary key.

Did you know?

After testing SQL at customer test sites to determine the usefulness and practicality of the system, IBM began developing commercial products based on their System R prototype, including System/38, SQL/DS, and IBM Db2, which were commercially available in 1979, 1981, and 1983, respectively.

7.3.3. SQL for Data Manipulation

A table is created without any data; only its structure is created. The INSERT statement is used to insert records into the table. SQL data manipulation statements can also be used to update or remove table records.

Using a database to manipulate data involves retrieving (accessing) already-existing data, adding new data, removing existing data, or changing existing data.

7.3.3.1. INSERTION of Records

INSERT INTO statement is used to insert new records in a table. Its syntax is:

INSERT INTO tablename

VALUES(value 1, value 2,…);

Here, value 1 corresponds to attribute 1, value 2 corresponds to attribute 2 and so on.

> **Remember**
> Note that we need not to specify attribute names in insert statement if there are exactly same number of values in the INSERT statement as the total number of attributes in the table.

7.3.3.2. SQL for Data Query

As of right now, we have learned how to store, process, and create databases. Since data can be more easily retrieved from databases in the future in any format we choose, we are interested in storing information in them. For retrieving data from multiple tables in a MySQL database (or any other RDBMS), the Structured Query Language (SQL) offers effective mechanisms. The particular specifications for the data to be retrieved are entered by the user in SQL commands known as queries. A SQL query statement, also known as the SELECT statement, is used to extract data from a database's tables.

SELECT Statement

The SQL statement SELECT is used to retrieve data from the tables in a database and the output is also displayed in tabular form.

Syntax:

SELECT attribute1, attribute2,…

FROM table_name

WHERE condition

Here, attribute1, attribute2,… are the column names of the table table_name from which we want to retrieve data. The FROM clause is always written with SELECT clause as it specifies the name of the table from which data is to be retrieved. The WHERE clause is optional and is used to retrieve data that meet specified condition(s).

7.3.3.3. Querying Using Database Office

Various organizations keep databases to hold data in tabular form. Let's look at an organization's database called Office, which contains numerous related tables like Department and Employee. Each employee in the database has a department assigned to them, and the Department number (DeptId) is kept in the EMPLOYEE table as a foreign key.

7.3.4. Data Updation and Deletion

SQL data manipulation also includes data deletion and update. We will use these two techniques for data manipulation.

7.3.4.1. Data Updation

We may need to make changes in the value(s) of one or more columns of existing records in a table. For example, we may require some changes in address, phone number or spelling of name, etc. The UPDATE statement is used to make such modifications in the existing data.

Syntax:

UPDATE table_name

SET attribute1 = value1, attribute2 = value2,…

WHERE condition;

The STUDENT Table has NULL value for GUID for student with roll number 3. Also, suppose students with roll numbers 3 and 5 are siblings. So, in STUDENT table, we need to fill the GUID value for student with roll number 3 as 101010101010. In order to update or change GUID of a particular row (record), we need to specify that record using WHERE clause, as shown below:

```
MySQL> UPDATE STUDENT
    -> SET GUID = 101010101010
    -> WHERE RollNumber = 3;
Query OK, 1 row affected (0.06 sec)
Rows matched: 1  Changed: 1  Warnings: 0
```

We can then verify the updated data using the statement SELECT * FROM STUDENT.

7.3.4.2. Data Deletion

The DELETE statement is used to delete one or more record(s) from a table.

Syntax:

DELETE FROM table_name

WHERE condition;

Suppose the student with roll number 2 has left the school. We can use the following MySQL statement to delete that record from the STUDENT table.

MySQL> DELETE FROM STUDENT WHERE RollNumber = 2; Query OK, 1 row affected (0.06 sec)

Did you get it?

1. What are commonly used data types in MySQL?
2. What is data manipulation command in SQL?

7.4. DATABASE APIS

→Learning Objectives
- Understand the concept of application programming interface (API);
- Understand the function of (API).

An Application Programming Interface, or API, acts as a mediator or messenger between computer programs so they can safely exchange data. A website that lets users book flights and compare costs from several airlines is a popular example of an API. The program makes requests for information from several outside APIs, which link to the real data source (such as databases). The client user interface (UI) presents the data in a single view after the API sends the response to the application that made the request.

7.4.1. What Is an API?

A database or web server is not what an API is. It does, however, offer safe access to both. The API forwards requests for information (data) from clients or applications to the relevant source and then sends the response back to the client (Figure 7.2).

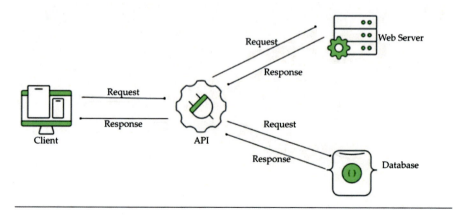

Figure 7.2. What API is and what does it do?

Source: https://www.mongodb.com.

7.4.1.1. So, What Exactly Is an API?

A fundamental tenet of object-oriented programming (OOP), interface is employed by numerous programming languages. Interface keeps the implementation hidden from external parties (i.e., third-party services and apps), but permits them to utilize an application's features, nonetheless. Essentially, this means that if you wanted to use a functionality, you would know what the method accomplished but not how it worked! An API's interface is a lot like this; you hide the inner workings of your program by only exposing a portion of the functionality through the API (Figure 7.3).

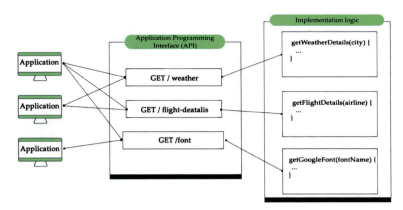

Figure 7.3. Example to show an API.

Source: https://www.mongodb.com.

7.4.2. How Does an API Work?

Companies can create APIs for their internal use or to share with the public. For example, social media plugins and programming language APIs are used by developers and web users. Any individual can create an API to share their content with more people. There is no front end of an API, and the requests are usually sent through a web server over the internet. There are different types of APIs.

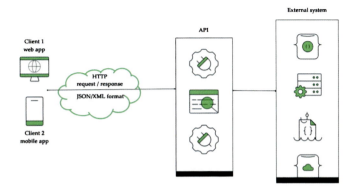

Figure 7.4. How applications use API to exchange data?

Source: https://www.mongodb.com.

The REST (Representational State Transfer) architecture is used by the majority of web APIs, and it delivers requests and responses over the HTTP protocol (Figure 7.4).

The API works as follows:

- The client places a request from their device, using the HTTP GET, PUT, POST, or DELETE methods. The request is sent via HTTP to the URI (Uniform Resource Identifier). The requests include the request method, headers, and body—for example, in XML, JSON, or other formats.
- If the request is not valid, the API will not call the program but return an error.
- If the request is valid, the API makes a call to the required service.
- Once the API receives the response from the service, it sends the response back to the requesting application (client) via HTTP.

Did you get it?

1. What is an API?
2. How applications use API to exchange data?

7.5. MANAGING A MYSQL DATABASE

→Learning Objectives
- Manage MySQL databases from the command line;
- Discuss the tools for managing MySQL database servers.

MySQL databases can be managed within the Databases section of hPanel. To access it, go to Websites → Manage, search for Databases Management on the sidebar and click on it:

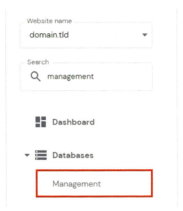

Once there, you can choose a website from the left drop-down menu to show its associated databases:

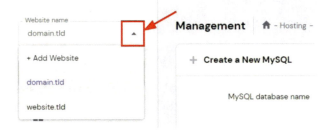

You will be presented with the List of Current MySQL Databases and Users section. Please note that all new databases will be assigned to the selected domain; if a database is not yet assigned to a website, you can do so by clicking on Assign:

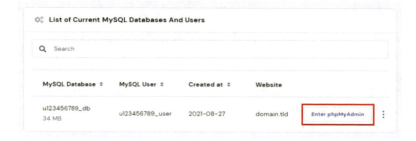

To access your database contents via phpMyAdmin, click on Enter phpMyAdmin:

If you need more options, select your desired database, and click the : button:

You will be able to do the following actions:

- Repair the database – it will analyze and optimize your database tables, ensuring that the database is working perfectly fine;
- Change the current database password;
- Change various permissions;
- Delete the database completely.

7.5.1. Manage MySQL Databases From the Command Line

One of the most widely used relational database management systems is MySQL. There are numerous frontends for managing MySQL servers, such as PhpMyAdmin, MySQL

Workbench, and even Adminer. Nonetheless, it is evident that using the command line is the most effective method of managing a MySQL server.

The MySQL DBMS is bundled with the MySQL command-line tool, which is a basic SQL shell solution that allows for input line editing. Both interactive and non-interactive use are supported.

When a query is interactive, the results are shown as an ASCII table. When using the system in a non-interactive manner, the output is shown in a tabular format. Command options can be used to modify the output format.

For Linux servers, you must first log in to your server via SSH. You must use Remote Desktop in order to connect to a Windows server. You can also use a direct connection to access your MySQL database. Use these instructions to establish a command-line connection to MySQL:

1. Once the command line is available, enter the following, where USERNAME is your database username:

   MySQL-u USERNAME-p

2. You'll be prompted for a password, enter your password. You should then see the "MySQL>" prompt.

3. You can see a list of databases by typing in this command:

   show databases;

4. To perform database tasks, you need to tell MySQL which database you want to use. To access a particular database, type the following command, where DBNAME is the database, you want to access:

   use DBNAME;

5. Once you've run this command you have access to your database. Next, you can execute queries, get a listing of MySQL tables and much more. By the way, typing "help" will get you a list of commands you can use, while typing "\q" will get you out of MySQL.

7.5.1.1. Adding New Users and Creating a New Database

You can add users and databases when you are logged in as the root user in MySQL. To log in as root, and create new users and databases, follow these steps:

1. Log into MySQL with root privileges using the following command:

   MySQL-u root-p

2. You'll be prompted for your root password, fill it in and press return to proceed.

3. Creating a database is straight forward, you just need the following command. When entering it, replace username with your user you would like to add. Do that with password too. This is the command you need to enter:

   GRANT ALL PRIVILEGES ON *.* TO 'username'@'localhost' IDENTIFIED BY 'password';

4. Note that the command we listed above will give the new user you create blanket permissions. Instead of granting all privileges you can limit the user. One example is the SELECT permission. To limit the user to permissions as specified by SELECT only you need to enter the following command:

    GRANT SELECT ON *.* TO 'username'@'localhost';

5. Type \q to exit MySQL so that you can log in with the user that you have just created.

6. It's simple to log in to MySQL with your new user, just enter the login command we specified previously, typing the new user's name instead of Username:

    MySQL-u username-p

7. The user we create have all privileges assigned to them, including the ability to create a database. Create a database with the following command, using the name of your database instead of DBNAME.

    CREATE DATABASE dbname;

8. Want to start using this newly created database? Run the following command, again replacing DBNAME with the name of your database:

    USE dbname;

9. MySQL now knows which database you want to work with. You can create a database table by running the following command, for example:

    CREATE TABLE example (id smallint unsigned not null auto_increment, name varchar(50) not null, constraint pk_example primary key (id));

    INSERT INTO example (id, name) VALUES (null, 'Sample data');

7.5.1.2. Scripting in SQL

You don't need to run every single SQL command one command at a time, as in our previous example. Instead, you can execute several commands all in one go by making use of a SQL script file.

This is how you use a SQL script file to create a new database, and to populate your new database:

1. Just like we did in the previous example we start by creating a new user for your database. These are the commands you need:

MySQL-u root-p

GRANT ALL PRIVILEGES ON *.* TO 'username'@'localhost' IDENTIFIED BY 'password';

\q

2. Next, create a new file on your computer, and call it sql. You can use any text editor you like to use, as long as the file is stored in plain text.

3. Copy and paste the following into your text file:

```
CREATE DATABASE dbname;

USE dbname;

CREATE TABLE tablename (id smallint unsigned not null auto_increment, name varchar(20) not null, constraint pk_example primary key (id));

INSERT INTO tablename (id, name) VALUES (null, 'Sample data');
```

4. Before you save your file, change dbname into the name of your database and tablename into the name of the table you want to add to your new database.

Remember, you can modify this script to make as many tables as you like, and even to create multiple databases all in one go. Note that our example creates a very basic table: you might want to add more complex requirements by expanding on the script.

5. Save the changes to your file and close your text editor.

6. Processing your script is easy. Type the following command in, replacing username with the name of the user you created in the first step.

```
MySQL-u username-p < example.sql
```

Note that MySQL will execute commands in a script one line at a time, in other words one statement at a time. In our example file, once MySQL has finished executing the entire file you will notice that a new database and a new table is created. Finally, the table will contain any data that you have specified in the INSERT statement.

7.5.2. Tools for Managing MySQL DataBase Servers

Database management is a challenging task that may require a team effort, contingent on the database's size. The management of user access, data backup and recovery, and data storage and organization are just a few of the many duties involved in database administration. The database server may be the most important component that affects each of those duties.

Like anything else related to database administration and management, there are a plethora of tools available to make the job easier. Especially when it comes to database server administration, selecting the appropriate tool is crucial.

7.5.2.1. MySQL Essentials

Owned by Oracle, MySQL is an open-source relational database that has been available for more than 20 years. MySQL is widely considered the most secure and suitable database platform, with scalability and customization to meet almost any business requirement, by developers and database administrators (DBAs).

A relational database, as opposed to a flat-file database, has numerous data tables arranged in rows and columns. Structured query language (SQL) is a user-friendly programming interface that relational databases use to organize and store data. The key fields in the data structure connect every element to every other. Compared to flat-file databases, relational databases are more functional and adaptable.

MySQL-powered databases are used by numerous businesses of all sizes in their web and mobile applications. Since MySQL is an open-source project, anyone can participate in its development and support. A number of significant tech companies, including Amazon Web Services, support and utilize MySQL.

Among the most widely used relational databases worldwide are MySQL databases. With its Community Edition, MySQL provides a free database based on the needs of the user. Different commercial licenses are available from MySQL for users who require additional features and services. MySQL is user-friendly and compatible with a variety of operating systems, including Windows, Linux, and Mac. It is referred to as a secure database and is compatible with numerous programming languages, including C++, Java, and PHP.

7.5.2.2. MySQL Server Basics

A database developer will most likely download the MySQL software locally to their computer when they create a MySQL database. A new database is created and connected to a server by the developer, who typically uses the operating system's command line interface. Keeping data locally on a computer is frequently impractical or not feasible, depending on the volume of data the database will hold. A MySQL database server is useful in this typical situation.

A MySQL database server is where an established database connects to store and handle entered or gathered data, just like any other server. When a database is first set up and configured, the database developer creates the client-server relationship that MySQL server connections follow.

7.5.2.3. Five Tools for Server Management

To manage and administer a database, a plethora of graphical user interface (GUI) tools and applications are available. When choosing a tool, it's equally important to look for one that supports a strong method of managing your database server. Since the server houses all of your data, efficient administration and user-friendliness are crucial. Most significantly, each tool offers a targeted strategy, or options designed especially for database server management.

1. **MySQL Workbench:** It is unlikely that DBAs and developers will ever stop using the command line interface as their preferred method of communication. On the other hand, the MySQL Workbench is an alternative. This tool offers a graphical user interface (GUI) for managing, creating, and designing MySQL databases. The Workbench has a Community Edition and a Commercial Edition, just like MySQL.

Database administrators and developers can configure servers specifically for a database server using the MySQL Workbench. The MySQL Workbench offers numerous command-line functions that enable a graphical approach to developing and interacting with a database server. Database administrators can monitor server health and performance with the help of the tool's visual performance dashboard.

2. **SQL Server Management Studio:** Any database that uses SQL can be managed with ease using the complete environment offered by SQL Server Management Studio (SSMS). This covers a number of different database management systems in addition to MySQL. Database administrators and developers can design, create, and oversee every facet of a SQL server with SSMS. One of SMSS's advantages is that it combines script and graphical editors, making SQL servers accessible to all users regardless of experience or ability level.

    A DBA or developer can connect MySQL data to an SQL Server instance within SSMS using the Microsoft SQL Server Management Studio. The MS SQL Server Linked Server tool is used to complete this process. DBAs and developers can run commands from various data sources, like MySQL, and combine them with the SQL Server database by using linked servers.

3. **phpMyAdmin:** A free software tool called phpMyAdmin functions incredibly well with MySQL databases. PHP is the programming language used to create phpMyAdmin, as the name suggests. The ability of the tool to manage tasks like server maintenance over the internet is one of its design strengths. Numerous operations for MySQL databases are supported by phpMyAdmin. Adding or modifying tables, controlling user permissions, and backing up data are just a few examples of frequently performed tasks. The interface is used to complete all of these tasks. Developers and DBAs can also set up and manage several servers with phpMyAdmin.

4. **dbForge Studio for MySQL:** dbForge Studio is an all-inclusive and potent MySQL tool. An extensive array of server management and administration tools are available through the user-friendly GUI. dbForge Studio provides tools for database development, administration, and data query in addition to this potent feature.

    For MySQL databases, dbForge Studio is a well-liked option among DBAs and developers. Even though the front-facing GUI tool has many features, a junior DBA or developer can still use it. SQL Server is a tool specifically designed for server management, administration, and development within the studio.

5. **MySQL Monitoring:** One powerful tool from Application Manager is MySQL Monitoring. Its ability to monitor is one of its best qualities. With this capability, DBAs can respond to application-generated alerts and optimize server performance in the event that something goes wrong. Furthermore, the application offers comprehensive performance factor metrics and can be set up to automatically notify users of any server outage. No matter the size or scope, a large number of transactions are processed daily by many MySQL databases. MySQL Monitoring's

FUNDAMENTALS OF WEB DEVELOPMENT

performance reporting capabilities offer valuable insights into database usage and can identify potential issues in the database before they cause disruptions to operations. With the help of this kind of data, DBAs can take prompt action and proactively resolve problems.

Did you get it?

1. Add new users and creating a new database.
2. What are tools for server management?

7.6. CONNECT TO MYSQL USING PHP

→Learning Objectives

- Understand the ways to connect to MySQL database using PHP;
- Identify potential errors with MySQLi and PDO.
- A PHP script needs to connect to a MySQL database in order to access and add content to the database. Prerequisites
- Special CREATE privileges;
- A MySQL database;
- A MySQLi or PDO extension.

7.6.1. Two Ways to Connect to MySQL Database Using PHP

There are two popular ways to connect to a MySQL database using PHP:

- With PHP's MySQLi extension;
- With PHP data objects (PDO).

The guide also includes explanations for the credentials used in the PHP scripts and potential errors you may come across using MySQLi and PDO.

7.6.1.1. Option 1: Connect to MySQL with MySQL Improved Extension

The only database type supported by MySQLi is MySQL. It offers an object-oriented and procedural interface, enabling access to new features found in MySQL systems. Client-side prepared statements are not supported; only server-side prepared statements are.

The MySQLi extension is included PHP version 5 and newer.

The PHP script for connecting to a MySQL database using the MySQLi procedural approach is the following:

```
<?php

$servername = "localhost";
```

268 FUNDAMENTALS OF WEB DEVELOPMENT

```php
$database = "database";
$username = "username";
$password = "password";
//Create connection
$conn = mysqli_connect($servername, $username, $password, $database);
//Check connection
if ($conn->connect_error) {
die("Connection failed: ."$conn->connect_error);
}
echo "Connected successfully";
mysqli_close($conn);
?>
```

- **Credentials Explained:** The first part of the script is four variables (server name, database, username, and password) and their respective values. These values should correspond to your connection details.

```
2    $servername = "localhost";
3    $database = "database";
4    $username = "username";
5    $password = "password";
```

Next is the main PHP function mysqli_connect(). It establishes a connection with the specified database.

```
7    // Create connection
8
9    $conn = mysqli_connect($servername, $username, $password, $database);
```

Following is an "if statement." It is the part of the code that shows whether the connection was established. When the connection fails, it gives the message Connection failed. The die function prints the message and then exits out of the script.

```
13   if ($conn->connect_error) {
14
15   die("Connection failed: " . $conn->connect_error);
16   }
```

The connection is successful, it displays "Connected successfully."

```
18    echo "Connected successfully";
```

When the script ends, the connection with the database also closes. If you want to end the code manually, use the mysqli_close function.

```
19    mysqli_close($conn);
20
21    ?>
```

7.6.1.2. Option 2: Connect to MySQL with PDO

An extension called PHP Data Objects (PDO) acts as an interface for database connections. It is not restricted to MySQL and is capable of executing any database function, unlike MySQLi. Compared to MySQL, it is more universal and permits flexibility across databases. PDO facilitates prepared statements that are client-side or server-side.

The PHP code for connecting to a MySQL database through the PDO extension is:

<?php

$servername = "localhost";

$database = "database";

$username = "username";

$password = "password";

$charset = "utf8mb4";

try {

$dsn = "mysql:host=$servername;dbname=$database;charset=$charset";

$pdo = new PDO($dsn, $username, $password);

$pdo->setAttribute(PDO::ATTR_ERRMODE, PDO::ERRMODE_EXCEPTION);

echo "Connection Okay";

return $pdo

}

catch (PDOException $e)

{

echo "Connection failed: ." $e->getMessage();

}

?>

- **Credentials Syntax:** First, we have five variables (server name, database, username, password, and charset) and their values. These values should correspond to your connection details.

The server name will be localhost. If connected to an online server, type in the server name of that server.

The variable charset tells the database in which encoding it will be receiving and sending data. The recommended standard is utf8mb4.

```
2   $servername = "localhost";
3   $database = "database";
4   $username = "username";
5   $password = "password";
6   $charset = "utf8mb4";
```

7.6.1.3. Try and Catch Blocks

PDO's great asset is that it has an exception class to take care of any potential problems in database queries. It solves these problems by incorporating try and catch blocks.

If a problem arises while trying to connect, it stops running and attempts to catch and solve the issue. Catch blocks can be set to show error messages or run an alternative code.

```
8   try
9       $dsn = "mysql:host=$servername;dbname=$database;charset=$charset";
10      $pdo = new PDO($dsn, $username, $password);
11      $pdo->setAttribute(PDO::ATTR_ERRMODE, PDO::ERRMODE_EXCEPTION);
12      echo "Connection Okay";
13
14      return $pdo
15
16
17  catch (PDOException $e)
```

This try and catch block's first parameter is DSN, or data(base) source name. It is essential because it specifies the name and type of the database in addition to any other relevant details. We're using a MySQL database in this example. PDO does, however, support a variety of database kinds. Replace the "MySQL" portion of the syntax with the name of the database you are using if you are using a different one.

```
8   try {
9       $dsn = "mysql:host=$servername;dbname=$database;charset=$charset";
```

Next is the PDO variable. This variable is going to establish a connection to the database. It has three parameters:

- The data source name (dsn);

- The username for your database; and
- The password for your database.

```
10    $pdo = new PDO($dsn, $username, $password);
```

Following is the setAttribute method adding two parameters to the PDO:

- PDO::ATTR_ERRMODE;
- PDO::ERRMODE_EXCEPTION.

This method instructs the PDO to run an exception in case a query fails.

Add the echo "Connection Okay." To confirm a connection is established.

```
12    echo "Connection Okay";
```

Return the PDO variable to connect to the database.

```
13
14    return $pdo
15
```

After returning the PDO variable, define the PDOException in the catch block by instructing it to display a message when the connection fails.

```
17    catch (PDOException $e)
18    {
19        echo "Connection failed: ". $e->getMessage();
```

7.6.2. Potential Errors with MySQLi and PDO

7.6.2.1. Incorrect Password

There must be a match between the password in the database and the PHP code. A connection cannot be made to the database if the two are not the same. An error message stating that the connection has failed will appear.

Possible solutions:

- Check the database details to ensure the password is correct;
- Ensure there is a user assigned to the database.

7.6.2.2. Unable to Connect to MySQL Server

If the host name is not recognized, PHP might not be able to establish a connection with the MySQL server. Ensure that localhost is selected as the server name.

When attempting to troubleshoot any errors, be sure to refer to the error_log file for assistance. The file can be found in the same folder as the script that is executing.

Did you get it?

1. How to connect to MySQL with MySQL improved extension?
2. Write down the steps to connect MySQL with PDO.

FOCUS ON CAREERS

SQL Developer: In today's digital information age, the quality and accessibility of data are more important than ever. As a result, SQL developers are in high demand across a wide range of industries, from health care to retail to finance.

An SQL Developer is a hybrid database engineer and software developer who uses structured query language (SQL) to manipulate data, implement database-driven solutions, and build applications. SQL developers design relational databases and write code that interacts with stored data to complete functional requirements for a business.

An SQL developer is a database professional who often works alongside business analysts, database administrators, and other IT professionals to help companies create and maintain databases to control and manipulate their data.

- **What Does an SQL Developer Do?:** The role of an SQL developer is to develop and manage SQL databases by planning, developing, and maintaining the databases. SQL developers use structured query language (SQL) to create and modify database tables using CRUD SQL commands. CRUD is an acronym for create, read, update, delete and refers to the four operations developers perform on database tables to manipulate the data.

    As an SQL developer, you'll:
    - Optimize database performance
    - Create complex functions and stored procedures
    - Analyze queries, develop security protocols, and resolve problems
    - Design database architecture and create dashboards
    - Write complex queries for applications and business intelligence reporting

Some queries and application functionality can be simple, such as a command to pull up all records related to a specific customer in an e-commerce database. Code can also be complex, involving multiple tables linked via a web of interconnected relationships, such in supply chain enterprise resource planning (ERP).

SQL developers' code allows users to interact with the information stored in databases, access metrics that show key business insights and provide decision support to the organization.

- **Skills Needed to be an SQL Developer:** SQL developers must possess a combination of workplace and technical skills. These skills are necessary to thrive in an SQL developer role.

- **Proficiency in SQL:** The first and most apparent SQL developer competency is proficiency in SQL (Structured Query Language). SQL is the programming language used to interface with databases.
- **Knowing How to Use a Database Management System:** Besides knowing the language, SQL developers need to be familiar with one of the major database management systems. These include MySQL, Microsoft SQL Server, and PostgreSQL.
- **Integrating Databases with Business Intelligence Software:** Business intelligence software is the umbrella term for applications that help companies analyze data. SQL developers often help connect databases with business intelligence software packages like Power BI and Tableau.

It might be an SQL developer's responsibility to modify the database schema to ensure that external applications can access data or even to build a new database from scratch to meet the needs of a business case.

- **Familiarity with Excel, Including Pivot Tables:** If you're working with data in Excel and want to summarize it using pivot tables, you'll need to know how to write SQL code. Pivot tables extract and arrange data into neat categories and subcategories for quick analysis. You can also add filters, charts, and other visualizations on top of this data—which means you'll need to learn how to write queries to use them effectively.
- **Database Design and Management:** Before writing programs, SQL developers must design a database. They are usually responsible for cataloging and organizing data into tables, specifying data types, primary and foreign keys, and other constraints. They may also develop processes to import data from external sources and migrate databases when moving to new technology, such as onto cloud database systems.
- **Experience in Programming Languages:** SQL developers should have strong programming fundamentals, including experience with one or more programming languages such as Java, .NET, C++, Python, or Ruby on Rails. Developers should also know web application development languages and tools to design front-end user interfaces (e.g., HTML, PHP).

A CLOSER LOOK

MySQL Cluster Internal Architecture: MySQL Cluster is tightly linked to the MySQL server, yet it is a separate product. Due to its distributed nature, MySQL Cluster has a far more complicated architecture than a standard MySQL database. This presentation and white paper will describe the internal architecture of the MySQL Cluster product and the different mechanisms and process that exists to insure the availability of the cluster. We will also take a close look at the data and message flow that takes place between the nodes in the cluster during different types of operations.

- **MySQL Cluster Features:** MySQL Cluster can be distinguished from many other clustering products in that it offers five nines availability with a shared-nothing architecture. Most clustering products use a shared-disk architecture. Using a shared-nothing architecture allows the cluster to run on commodity hardware, thus greatly reducing costs compared to shared-disk architecture. Having a shared-nothing architecture does, however, come with a different cost, namely, a more complex way of ensuring high availability and synchronization of the nodes which is mainly seen as increased network traffic.

  MySQL Cluster also provides ACID transactions with row level locking using the READ-COMMITTED isolation level. MySQL Cluster is, in general, an in-memory database, however non-indexed data can be stored on disk and the disks are also used for checkpointing to ensure durability through system shutdown. MySQL cluster provides unique hash indexes as well as ordered T-tree indexes. It also supports several online features, including a native online backup, and the ability perform certain ALTER TABLE operations with the tables unlocked (most storage engines require table locks for all ALTER TABLE operations).

- **Architecture:** The MySQL Cluster architecture can be divided into several layers. The first is the application layer where the applications that communicate with the MySQL servers reside. These applications are normal MySQL clients from a MySQL server perspective and all communication with the lower layers of the cluster is handled by the MySQL servers.

  The second layer is the SQL layer where the MySQL servers reside, called SQL or API nodes in the cluster. The number of MySQL servers is completely independent of the number of data nodes, which allows great flexibility in a cluster's configuration. In particular as the number of SQL nodes can be increased without shutting down the cluster. In addition to MySQL servers, other programs that communicate directly with the data nodes (such as restoration programs or programs to view the clustered tables) are also considered API nodes.

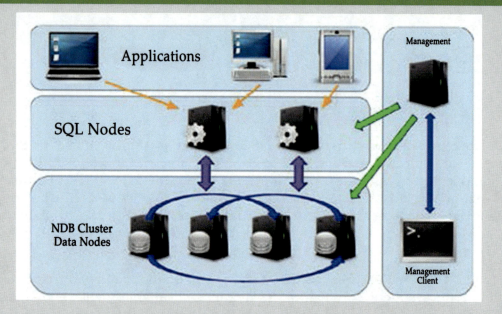

- **Partitioning:** Let's take a closer look at the data managed by the data nodes. Each table in the cluster is partitioned based on the number of data nodes. This means that if the cluster has two data nodes, each table is partitioned in two parts, and if the cluster has four data nodes, each table is partitioned into four parts. The partitioning is done based on the hash value of the primary key, by default. The partitioning function can be changed if needed, but for most cases the default is good enough. Each data node holds the so called primary replica or fragment for a partition, allowing the data to be distributed evenly between all the data nodes. To ensure the availability (and redundancy) of the data, each node also holds a copy of another partition, called a secondary replica. The nodes work in pairs so that the node holding the secondary partition of another node's primary partition, will reciprocate and give its own primary partition as a secondary partition to the same node partner. These pairs are called node groups and there will be #nodes/2 node groups in the cluster. This means that for a cluster with 2 data nodes, each node will contain the whole database, but for a cluster with 4 nodes, each node will only contain half of the data.

- **Heartbeat Circle:** Because of the shared-nothing architecture, all nodes in the cluster must always have the same view of who is connected to the cluster. Detecting failed nodes is extremely important. In MySQL Cluster this can either be handled through TCP close or through the heartbeat circle.

- **Network Partitioning Protocol:** The network partitioning protocol is fundamental to guaranteeing the availability of the cluster. The largest problem derives from the fact that a network failure is indistinguishable from a node crash, from another node's perspective. This means that precautions must be in place so that a split-brain scenario cannot occur when the cause of the communication failure is a network failure and not an actual node crash. When there is a network partitioning, the network partitioning protocol is launched on both sides of the split and it guarantees that, in the event of an even split, there will only be one running "cluster" remaining.

- **Durability:** Since the MySQL Cluster is generally an in-memory database some measures have to be taken so that a cluster shutdown is possible without incurring data loss. The data nodes use two procedures to maintain data on disk. The first is the REDO log. When a transaction takes place on a node, the transaction is stored in a REDO log buffer which is synchronously flushed to disk at even intervals. The disk based REDO log will only contain the transactions that were committed at the point in time the flush took place. The flushing takes place through a global checkpoint or GCP.

Transactions MySQL Cluster provides synchronous replication between the data nodes, which means that the replication is synchronous from the client's perspective. In order to achieve this, a complex algorithm is used called the two-phase commit protocol (2PC). In the 2PC, a transaction is committed through two phases: a prepare phase and a commit phase. During the prepare phase, the nodes perform the requested operations and are ready to commit the transaction. During the commit phase, the transaction is committed and the changes cannot be undone anymore.

SUMMARY

- A database is a structured set of data or a particular kind of data store that is created with the aid of a database management system (DBMS), which is a piece of software that communicates with applications, end users, and the database itself in order to collect and process data.
- Database management systems are tools that businesses use to manage data from databases (fetch, store, update, and optimize).
- The main applications of Oracle DBMS, an efficient object-relational database management system with multiple models, are data warehousing and online transaction processing.
- MySQL (My-Structured Query Language), is a free, open-source relational and again a multi-model database management system.
- An efficient and effective relational database management system is Microsoft SQL Server. It offers effective workload management and allows multiple users to access the same database.
- An advanced relational database management system that is free and open-source is called PostgreSQL.
- Using an in-memory dataset, Redis (Remote Dictionary Server) is an open-source database tool that can be used as a cache, streaming engine, and message broker.
- Designed for managing data stored in relational database management systems (RDBMS) or for stream processing in relational data stream management systems (RDSMS), SQL is a domain-specific programming language.
- The MySQL DBMS is bundled with the MySQL command-line tool, which is a basic SQL shell solution that allows for input line editing. Both interactive and non-interactive use are supported.

MULTIPLE CHOICE QUESTION

1. **Which PHP function is commonly used to establish a connection to a MySQL database?**
    a. mysqli_connect()
    b. mysql_connect()
    c. pdo_connect()
    d. db_connect()

2. **Which MySQL extension is preferred for new development in PHP as of PHP 7.0?**
    a. mysqli
    b. MySQL
    c. pdo_mysql
    d. mysqlnd

3. What does the "SELECT" statement do in MySQL?
   a. Inserts data into a table
   b. Updates data in a table
   c. Retrieves data from a table
   d. Deletes data from a table
4. Which function is used to execute an SQL query in PHP using the mysqli extension?
   a. mysql_query()
   b. mysqli_query()
   c. pdo_query()
   d. db_query()
5. What does the "INSERT INTO" statement do in MySQL?
   a. Deletes data from a table
   b. Updates data in a table
   c. Inserts data into a table
   d. Retrieves data from a table
6. Which PHP function retrieves the next row from a result set returned by a SELECT statement?
   a. mysql_fetch_array()
   b. mysqli_fetch_array()
   c. pdo_fetch_array()
   d. db_fetch_array()
7. What does the "UPDATE" statement do in MySQL?
   a. Inserts data into a table
   b. Deletes data from a table
   c. Updates data in a table
   d. Retrieves data from a table
8. Which function is used to fetch all rows from a result set as an associative array in PHP using mysqli?
   a. mysqli_fetch_assoc()
   b. mysql_fetch_assoc()
   c. pdo_fetch_assoc()
   d. db_fetch_assoc()
9. Which PHP function is used to close a connection to a MySQL database?
   a. mysql_close()
   b. mysqli_close()
   c. pdo_close()
   d. db_close()

10. What does the "DELETE FROM" statement do in MySQL?
    a. Updates data in a table
    b. Inserts data into a table
    c. Deletes data from a table
    d. Retrieves data from a table

REVIEW QUESTIONS

1. What do you understand by structured query language (SQL)?
2. What are the components of a SQL system?
3. Which database is best for API?
4. What is the difference between LIKE and REGEXP operators in MySQL?
5. How to use PHP with MYSQL database?

Answer to Multiple Choice Questions

1. (a); 2. (a); 3. (c); 4. (b); 5. (c); 6. (b); 7. (c); 8. (a); 9. (b); 10. (c)

REFERENCES

1. Baik, C., Jagadish, H. V., & Li, Y., (2019). Bridging the semantic gap with SQL query logs in natural language interfaces to databases. In: *2019 IEEE 35th International Conference on Data Engineering (ICDE)* (pp. 374–385).

2. Bhalotia, G., Hulgeri, A., Nakhe, C., Chakrabarti, S., & Sudarshan, S., (2002). Keyword searching and browsing in databases using BANKS. In: *Proceedings 18th International Conference on Data Engineering* (pp. 431–440). San Jose, CA, USA. https://doi.org/10.1109/ ICDE.2002.994756.

3. Blunschi, L., Jossen, C., Kossman, D., Mori, M., & Stockinger, K., (2020). *SODA: Generating SQL for Business Users.* arXiv:1207.0134 [cs] [Online].

4. Brad, F., Iacob, R. C. 4., Hosu, I. A., & Rebedea, T., (2020). Dataset for a neural natural language interface for databases (NNLIDB). In: *Proceedings of the Eighth International Joint Conference on Natural Language Processing* (Vol. 1: Long Papers, pp. 906–914), Taipei, Taiwan [Online].

5. Dong, L., & Lapata, M., (2016). *Language to Logical Form with Neural Attention.* arXiv:1601.01280 [cs].

6. Ge, R., & Mooney, R., (2005). A statistical semantic parser that integrates syntax and semantics. In: *Proceedings of the Ninth Conference on Computational Natural Language Learning (CoNLL-2005)* (pp. 9–16). Ann Arbor, Michigan.

7. Nayak, N. R., Dash, P. K., & Bisoi, R., (2019). A hybrid time frequency response and fuzzy decision tree for non-stationary signal analysis and pattern recognition. *International Journal of Automation and Computing, 16*(3), 398–412.

8. Popescu, A. M., Etzioni, O., & Kautz, H., (2003). Towards a theory of natural language interfaces to databases. In: *Proceedings of the 8th International Conference on Intelligent User Interfaces* (pp. 149–157). New York, NY, USA.
9. Sasaki, H., Yamamoto, S., Agchbayar, A., & Nkhbayasgalan, N., (2020). Extracting problem linkages to improve knowledge exchange between science and technology domains using an attention-based language model. *Engineering, Technology & Applied Science Research, 10*(4), 5903–5913.
10. Sun, C., (2018). *A Natural Language Interface for Querying Graph Databases*. M.S. thesis, Massachusetts Institute of Technology.
11. Xu, X., Liu, C., & Song, D., (2017). *SQLNet: Generating Structured Queries from Natural Language Without Reinforcement Learning*. arXiv:1711.04436 [cs] [Online].
12. Yaghmazadeh, N., Wang, Y., Dillig, I., & Dillig, T., (2017). SQLizer: Query synthesis from natural language. *Proceedings of the ACM on Programming Languages* (Vol. 1, No. OOPSLA, pp. 1–63).

CHAPTER 8
Error Handling

LEARNING OBJECTIVES

After studying this chapter, you will be able to:

- Understand the concept of handling errors;
- Discuss how to handle external errors;
- Explain the concept of exceptions.

INTRODUCTORY EXAMPLE

PHP Error Reporting: PHP has built-in error reporting functions that can be used to display or log errors. The two main functions are error_reporting() and ini_set().

Use the error_reporting() function to set the error reporting level:

error_reporting(E_ALL);//Show all errors

error_reporting(E_ERROR | E_WARNING | E_PARSE);//Show only errors, warnings, and parse errors

error_reporting(E_ALL & ~E_NOTICE);//Show all errors, except for notices\

Use the ini_set() function to configure PHP's error handling settings:

ini_set('display_errors,' 1);//Display errors on the screen

ini_set('log_errors,' 1);//Log errors to a file

ini_set('error_log,' '/path/to/error.log');//Set the path to the error log file

8.1. UNIT INTRODUCTION

The process of responding to and recovering from error conditions in your program is known as error handling. For the purpose of propagating, catching, manipulating, and throwing recoverable errors at runtime, Swift offers excellent support. It is not always guaranteed that an operation will run through to completion or yield a useful result. Optionals are used to indicate that a value is not present, but when an operation fails, it's frequently helpful to know why it failed so that your code can react appropriately.

In programming, errors come in two basic flavors:

- External errors—When a program component behaves differently than expected, the code may take an unexpected turn. An example of an external error would be a database connection that fails to establish even though the code expects it to.
- Code logic errors—These errors, commonly referred to as bugs, are errors in which the code design is fundamentally flawed due to either faulty logic ("it just doesn't work that way") or something as simple as a typo.
- These two categories of errors differ significantly in several ways:
- External errors will always occur, regardless of how "bug free" code is. They are not bugs in and of themselves because they are external to the program.
- External errors that aren't accounted for in the code logic can be bugs. For example, blindly assuming that a database connection will always succeed is a bug because the application will almost certainly not respond correctly in that case.
- Code logic errors are much more difficult to track down than external errors because by definition their location is not known. You can implement data consistency checks to expose them, however.

PHP comes with built-in error handling capabilities and a built-in severity system that limits the errors you can see to those that are serious enough to worry you. Three error severity levels exist for PHP:

- E_NOTICE;
- E_WARNING;
- E_ERROR.

E_NOTICE errors are minor, nonfatal errors designed to help you identify possible bugs in your code. In general, an E_NOTICE error is something that works but may not do what you intended. An example might be using a variable in a non-assignment expression before it has been assigned to, as in this case:

```php
<?php
    $variable++;
?>
```

This example will increment $variable to 1 (because variables are instantiated as 0/false/empty string), but it will generate an E_NOTICE error. Instead you should use this:

```php
<?php
    $variable = 0;
    $variable++;
?>
```

This check is designed to prevent errors due to typos in variable names. For example, this code block will work fine:

```php
<?
    $variable = 0;
    $variabel++;
?>
```

However, $variable will not be incremented, and $variabel will be. E_NOTICE warnings help catch this sort of error; they are similar to running a Perl program with use warnings and use strict or compiling a C program with –Wall.

Because E_NOTICE errors can result in rather large and repetitive logs, PHP turns them off by default. To help with code cleanup, we prefer to enable E_NOTICE warnings in applications during development and turn them off on production machines. Runtime errors with an E_WARNING status are not fatal. They signal that something went wrong, but they do not stop or alter the script's control flow. E_WARNING errors are produced by numerous external errors. Receiving an error when calling mysql_connect() via fopen() is one example.

Unrecoverable errors known as E_ERRORs stop the running script from continuing to execute. A couple of instances are failing a type hint in a function and trying to instantiate a class that doesn't exist. (Ironically, an E_WARNING error is all that results from giving a function the wrong amount of arguments.).

With the help of PHP's trigger_error() function, a user can create custom errors within a script. The user can cause one of three types of errors, all of which share the same semantics as the errors that were recently discussed.

- E_USER_NOTICE;
- E_USER_WARNING;
- E_USER_ERROR.

You can trigger these errors as follows:

```
while(!feof($fp)) {
  $line = fgets($fp);
  if(!parse_line($line)) {
    trigger_error("Incomprehensible data encountered", E_USER_NOTICE);
  }
}
```

If no error level is specified, E_USER_NOTICE is used. In addition to these errors, there are five other categories that are encountered somewhat less frequently:

- E_PARSE—The script has a syntactic error and could not be parsed. This is a fatal error.
- E_COMPILE_ERROR—A fatal error occurred in the engine while compiling the script.
- E_COMPILE_WARNING—A nonfatal error occurred in the engine while parsing the script.
- E_CORE_ERROR—A fatal runtime error occurred in the engine.
- E_CORE_WARNING—A nonfatal runtime error occurred in the engine

Furthermore, PHP reports errors at all levels using the E_ALL error category. The php.ini setting error_reporting allows you to regulate the amount of errors that trickle down to your script. A bit-field test set called error_reporting employs defined constants, like this one for all errors.

error_reporting = E_ALL

error_reporting uses the following for all errors except for E_NOTICE, which can be set by XOR'ing E_ALL and E_NOTICE:

error_reporting = E_ALL ~ E_NOTICE

Similarly, error_reporting uses the following for only fatal errors (bitwise OR of the two error types):

error_reporting = E_ERROR | E_USER_ERROR

It should be noted that eliminating E_ERROR from the error_reporting level merely stops an error handler from being called for it; it does not permit you to ignore fatal errors.

8.2. HANDLING ERRORS

→Learning Objectives
- Display errors;
- Describe the logging errors.

Having seen the types of errors that PHP can produce, you need to prepare yourself to handle them when they arise. PHP provides four choices for handling errors that fall within the error_reporting threshold:

- Display them;
- Log them;
- Ignore them;
- Act on them.

Each of these options plays a crucial role in a strong error-handling system; none is more significant than the others in terms of functionality or importance. Errors should generally be logged in a production environment, but in a development environment, errors should be displayed extensively. While it is safe to ignore certain errors, others require action. Your unique needs will determine the precise combination of error-handling strategies you use.

8.2.1. Displaying Errors

An error is sent to the standard output stream when you choose to display errors; on a Web page, this means that the error is sent to the browser. This php.ini setting allows you to turn this setting on and off: display_errors = On. For developers, display errors are very useful because they allow you to quickly see what went wrong with a script without having to tail a log file or do anything other than visit the website you are developing.

What's good for a developer to see, however, is often bad for an end user to see. Displaying PHP errors to an end user is usually undesirable for three reasons:

- It looks ugly;
- It conveys a sense that the site is buggy; and
- It can disclose details of the script internals that a user might be able to use for nefarious purposes.

It is imperative to emphasize the third point. Running your code in production with display_errors enabled is the fastest way to have security flaws discovered and exploited. We once observed a single instance where a malicious INI file was removed from a very popular website due to a few mistakes. The corrected file was copied out to the Web servers as soon as it was discovered, and we all concluded that the main damage had been done to our pride. We located and apprehended a cracker who had been nefariously altering the pages of other members a year and a half later. He promised to reveal all the vulnerabilities he had discovered in exchange for our not attempting to prosecute him. Apart from the usual array of JavaScript exploits (the website permitted a great deal of user-generated content), he had also created a few extremely ingenious application hacks by simply looking at the code that had been posted online for a few hours the previous year.

The main exploits he had were on unvalidated user input and nondefaulted variables (this was in the days before register_global).All our database connection information was held in libraries and not on the pages. Many a site has been seriously violated due to a chain of security holes like these:

- Leaving display_errors on.
- Putting database connection details (mysql_connect()) in the pages.
- Allowing nonlocal connections to MySQL

These three mistakes together put your database at the mercy of anyone who sees an error page on your site. You would (hopefully) be shocked at how often this occurs.

> **Did you know?**
>
> Software exception handling developed in the 1960s and 1970s. Exception handling was subsequently widely adopted by many programming languages from the 1980s onward.

8.2.2. Logging Errors

PHP internally supports both logging to a file and logging via syslog via two settings in the php.ini file. This setting sets errors to be logged:

log_errors = On

And these two settings set logging to go to a file or to syslog, respectively:

error_log =/path/to/filename

error_log = syslog

Logging gives you an auditable record of any errors that happen on your website. Debugging lines are frequently placed around the problematic area to aid in diagnosis.

In addition to the errors logged from system errors or via trigger_error(), you can manually generate an error log message with this:

error_log("This is a user defined error");

Alternatively, you can send an email message or manually specify the file. See the PHP manual for details. error_log logs the passed message, regardless of the error_reporting level that is set; error_log and error_reporting are two completely different entries to the error logging facilities.

If you have only a single server, you should log directly to a file. syslog logging is quite slow, and if any amount of logging is generated on every script execution (which is probably a bad idea in any case), the logging overhead can be quite noticeable. Syslog's centralized logging features, however, offer a practical means of combining real-time logs from several machines in one place for analysis and archiving if you are managing multiple servers. If you intend to use Syslog, you should refrain from logging excessively.

8.2.3. Ignoring Errors

With the @ syntax, PHP lets you selectively disable error reporting when you suspect it may happen. Therefore, you can use this to suppress any errors that may appear and open a file that might not exist:

$fp = @fopen($file, $mode);

You may want to just suppress errors that you know will happen but don't care about, as PHP's error facilities don't offer any flow control capabilities.

Consider a function that gets the contents of a file that might not exist:

$content = file_get_content($sometimes_valid);

If the file is not present, an E_WARNING error is displayed. You should suppress this warning if you are aware that this is a likely expected outcome; as it was anticipated, there isn't really a mistake. This can be accomplished by suppressing warnings on individual calls by using the @ operator:

$content = @file_get_content($sometimes_valid);

In addition, if you set the php.ini setting track_errors = On, the last error message encountered will be stored in $php_errormsg. This is true regardless of whether you have used the @ syntax for error suppression.

8.2.4. Acting on Errors

With PHP, you can use the set_error_handler() function to set custom error handlers. You define a function similar to this to set a custom error handler:

```php
<?php
require "DB/Mysql.inc";
function user_error_handler($severity, $msg, $filename, $linenum)
{
    $dbh = new DB_Mysql_Prod;
    $query = "INSERT INTO errorlog
    (severity, message, filename, linenum, time) VALUES(?,?,?,?, NOW())";
    $sth $dbh->prepare($query);
    switch ($severity) {
    case E_USER_NOTICE:
    $sth->execute('NOTICE', $msg, $filename, $linenum);
    break;
    case E USER WARNING:
    $sth->execute('WARNING', $msg, $filename, $linenum); break;
    case E_USER_WARNING:
    $sth->execute('WARNING', $msg, $filename, $linenum); break;
    case E_USER_ERROR: $sth->execute('FATAL', $msg, $filename, $linenum); echo "FATAL error $msg at $filename: $linenum<br>";
    break;
    default:
    echo "Unknown error at $filename: $linenum<br>"; break;
    }
}
?>
```

> **Remember**
>
> Remember that flow control is not offered by error handlers. When processing is finished and there is no fatal error, the script resumes where it left off; if there is a fatal error, the script exits after the handler has finished.

You set a function with this:

set_error_handler("user_error_handler");

When an error is detected, it will now be entered into a database table of errors and, if it is a fatal error, a message will be printed to the screen rather than being displayed or printed to the error log.

Did you get it?

1. What is the use of Error_reporting () function in PHP?
2. What is error function in PHP?

8.3. HANDLING EXTERNAL ERRORS

→Learning Objectives
- Describe external errors;
- Explain the primary cause of external.

Even though we have referred to the work we have done as error handling, not much handling has actually been done. We have acknowledged and dealt with the warning messages that our scripts have produced, but we haven't been able to modify the flow control in our scripts using those methods, so in essence, we haven't dealt with our errors at all. The key to handling errors adaptively is understanding the potential places for code failure and knowing what to do in those situations.

Connecting to or retrieving data from external processes is the primary cause of external failures.

Consider the following function, which is designed to return the passwd file details (home directory, shell, gecos information, and so on) for a given user:

```php
<?php
function get_passwd_info($user) {
    $fp = fopen("/etc/passwd", "r");
    while(!feof($fp)) {
        $line = fgets($fp);
        $fields = explode(";", $line);
        if($user == $fields[0]) {
            return $fields;
        }
    }
    return false;
}
?>
```

As it stands, this code has two bugs in it: One is a pure code logic bug, and the second is a failure to account for a possible external error. When you run this example, you get an array with elements like this:

```php
<?php
    print_r(get_passwd_info('www'));
?>
```

```
Array
    (
        [0] => www:*:70:70:World Wide Web Server:/Library/WebServer:/noshell
    )
```

This is because the first bug is that the field separator in the passwd file is:, not;. So this:

$fields = explode(";," $line);

needs to be this:

$fields = explode(":," $line);

The second bug is subtler. If you fail to open the passwd file, you will generate an E_WARNING error, but program flow will proceed unabated. If a user is not in the passwd file, the function returns false. However, if the fopen fails, the function also ends up returning false, which is rather confusing.

This simple example demonstrates one of the core difficulties of error handling in procedural languages (or at least languages without exceptions): How do you propagate an error up to the caller that is prepared to interpret it?

If you are utilizing the data locally, you can often make local decisions on how to handle the error. For example, you could change the password function to format an error on return:

```php
<?php
function get_passwd_info($user) {
    $fp = fopen("/etc/passwd", "r");
    if(!is_resource($fp)) {
        return "Error opening file";
    }
    while(!feof($fp)) {
        $line = fgets($fp);
        $fields = explode(":", $line);
        if($user == $fields[0]) {
            return $fields;
        }
    }
    return false;
}
?>
```

Alternatively, you could set a special value that is not a normally valid return value:

```php
<?php
function get_passwd_info($user) {
    $fp = fopen("/etc/passwd", "r");
    if(!is_resource($fp)) {
        return -1;


    }
    while(!feof($fp)) {
        $line = fgets($fp);
        $fields = explode(":", $line);
        if($user == $fields[0]) {
            return $fields;
        }
    }
    return false;
}
?>
```

You can use this sort of logic to bubble up errors to higher callers:

```php
<?php
function is_shelled_user($user) {
    $passwd_info = get_passwd_info($user);
    if(is_array($passwd_info) && $passwd_info[7] != '/bin/false') {
        return 1;
    }
    else if($passwd_info === -1) {
        return -1;
    }
    else {
        return 0;
    }
}
?>
```

When this logic is used, you have to detect all the possible errors:

```php
<?php
$v = is_shelled_user('www');
if($v === 1) {
    echo "Your Web server user probably shouldn't be shelled.\n";
}
else if($v === 0) {
    echo "Great!\n";
}
else {
    echo "An error occurred checking the user\n";
}
?>
```

If this seems nasty and confusing, it's because it is. One of the main reasons exceptions are implemented in programming languages is to eliminate the hassle of manually bubbling up errors through multiple callers. PHP5 allows you to use exceptions in PHP as well. To some extent, you can make this specific example work, but what if the function in question could legitimately return any number? How could you then pass the error up in a clear fashion? The worst part of the entire mess is that any complex error handling scheme you come up with won't just affect the functions that implement it; it will also affect anyone in its call hierarchy and requires understanding and handling.

Did you get it?

1. How to get exception code in PHP?
2. How to catch errors when using file_get_contents on an external URL.

8.4. EXCEPTIONS

→Learning Objectives
- Use exception hierarchies;
- Handle constructor failure.

Since PHP5 only supported the methods we've covered thus far, you can see that this presents some serious issues, particularly when writing larger applications. The main problem lies in giving errors back to library users. Think about the error checking you added to the passwd file reading function just now.

When you were building that example, you had two basic choices on how to handle a connection error:

- Handle the error locally and return invalid data (such as false) back to the caller.
- Propagate and preserve the error and return it to the caller instead of returning the result set.

You did not choose the first option in the passwd file reading function example because it would have been assuming that a library knows how an application wants it to handle an error. In a Web application, you might want to send the user back to an error page; however, if you are writing a database testing suite, you might want to propagate the error in high granularity back to the top-level caller.

Although the second approach is used in the example above, it is not significantly superior to the first one. The issue with it is that ensuring that errors can always be correctly propagated through an application requires a great deal of planning and foresight. How can an error string be distinguished from a string returned by a database query, for instance?

Additionally, error propagation must be done manually. The caller must be notified of the error at each stage, and they must then decide whether to handle it or pass it along. The last section demonstrated how challenging this is to manage.

This kind of situation is what exceptions are meant to handle. A flow-control structure is an exception, enabling you to halt a script's current execution path and unwind the stack to a predetermined point. There is an object designated as the exception that represents the error you encountered.

FUNDAMENTALS OF WEB DEVELOPMENT

Exceptions are objects. To help with basic exceptions, PHP has a built-in Exception class that is designed specifically for exceptions. Although it is not necessary for exceptions to be instances of the Exception class, there are some benefits of having any class that you want to throw exceptions derive from Exception, which we'll discuss in a moment. To create a new exception, you instantiate an instance of the Exception class you want and you throw it.

When an exception is raised, the current block of code's execution ends instantly, and the Exception object is saved. The code goes to the exception-handler block's location and runs the handler if one is set in the current scope. The caller's scope is examined for an exception-handler block and the execution stack is popped if no handler is set in the current scope. Until a handler is located or the main, or top, scope, is reached, this process is repeated.

Running this code:

```php
<?php

throw new Exception;

?>
```

returns the following:

```
> php uncaught-exception.php
```

Fatal error: Uncaught exception 'exception'! in Unknown on line 0

An error that is fatal is an uncaught exception. Consequently, exceptions present additional maintenance needs. In case exceptions are employed in a script as cautions or potentially non-fatal errors, all callers within that code block need to be aware that exceptions might be thrown and should be ready to handle them.

Exception handling consists of a block of statements you want to try and a second block that you want to enter if and when you trigger any errors there. Here is a simple example that shows an exception being thrown and caught:

```php
try {

throw new Exception;

print "This code is unreached\n";

}

catch (Exception $e) {

print "Exception caught\n";

}
```

In this case you throw an exception, but it is in a try block, so execution is halted and you jump ahead to the catch block. catch catches an Exception class (which is the class being thrown), so that block is entered. catch is normally used to perform any cleanup that might be necessary from the failure that occurred.

Here is an example that throws something other than an Exception class:

```php
<?php

class AltException {}

try {
        throw new AltException;
}
catch (Exception $e) {

        print "Caught exception\n";
}
?>
```

Running this example returns the following:

> php failed_catch.php

Fatal error: Uncaught exception 'altexception'! in Unknown on line 0

This example failed to catch the exception because it threw an object of class AltException but was only looking to catch an object of class Exception.

Here is a less trivial example of how you might use a simple exception to facilitate error handling in your old favorite, the factorial function. The simple factorial function is valid only for natural numbers (integers > 0). You can incorporate this input checking into the application by throwing an exception if incorrect data is passed:

```php
<?php

//factorial.inc

//A simple Factorial Function

function factorial($n) {

if(!preg_match('/^\d+$/,'$n) || $n < 0) {

throw new Exception;

} else if ($n == 0 || $n == 1) {

return $n;
```

```
}
else {
return $n * factorial($n - 1);
}
}
?>
```

Incorporating sound input checking on functions is a key tenant of defensive programming.

When you call factorial, you need to make sure that you execute it in a try block if you do not want to risk having the application die if bad data is passed in:

```
<html>
<form method="POST">
Compute the factorial of

    <input type="text" name="input" value="<?= $_POST['input'] ?>"><br>
<?php
include "factorial.inc";
if($_POST['input']) {
    try {
        $input = $_POST['input'];
        $output = factorial($input);
        echo "$_POST[input]! = $output";
    }
    catch (Exception $e) {
        echo "Only natural numbers can have their factorial computed.";
    }
}
?>
<br>
<input type=submit name=posted value="Submit">
</form>
```

8.4.1. Using Exception Hierarchies

If you would like to handle different errors in different ways, you can try using multiple catch blocks. For example, we can modify the factorial example to also handle the case where $n is too large for PHP's math facilities:

class OverflowException {}

class NaNException {}

function factorial($n)

```php
{
    if(!preg_match('/^\d+$/', $n) || $n < 0 ) {
        throw new NaNException;
    }
    else if ($n == 0 || $n == 1) {
        return $n;
    }
    else if ($n > 170 ) {
        throw new OverflowException;
    }
    else {
        return $n * factorial($n - 1);
    }
}
```

Now you handle each error case differently:

```php
<?php
if($_POST['input']) {
    try {
        $input = $_POST['input'];

        $output = factorial($input);
        echo "$_POST[input]! = $output";
    }
    catch (OverflowException $e) {
        echo "The requested value is too large.";
    }
    catch (NaNException $e) {
        echo "Only natural numbers can have their factorial computed.";
    }
}
?>
```

As it stands, you now have to enumerate each of the possible cases separately. This is both cumbersome to write and potentially dangerous because, as the libraries grow, the set of possible exceptions will grow as well, making it ever easier to accidentally omit one.

To handle this, you can group the exceptions together in families and create an inheritance tree to associate them:

class MathException extends Exception {}

class NaNException extends MathException {}

class OverflowException extends MathException {}

You could now restructure the catch blocks as follows:

<?php

```php
if ($_POST['input']) {
try {
$input $_POST['input'];
$output factorial ($input);
echo "$ POST [input)!= $output";
}
catch (OverflowException $e) {
echo "The requested value is too large.";
}
catch (MathException $e) {
echo "A generic math error occurred";
}
catch (Exception $e) {
echo "An unknown error occurred";
}
}
?>
```

In this case, if an OverflowException error is thrown, it will be caught by the first catch block. If any other descendant of MathException (for example, NaNException) is thrown, it will be caught by the second catch block. Finally, any descendant of Exception not covered by any of the previous cases will be caught.

This is the benefit of having all exceptions inherit from Exception: It is possible to write a generic catch block that will handle all exceptions without having to enumerate them individually. Catchall exception handlers are important because they allow you to recover from even the errors you didn't anticipate.

8.4.2. A Typed Exceptions Example

To the best of our knowledge, every exception has been attribute-free. This should cover the majority of your requirements if all you need to do is identify the kind of exception that was thrown and you took care when establishing our hierarchy. Obviously, exceptions would not have been implemented with full objects, but rather with strings, if strings were the only data you would ever be interested in passing up in an exception. But, you would prefer to have the flexibility to add any kind of arbitrary data that could be helpful to the caller handling the exception.

The base exception class itself is actually deeper than indicated thus far. It is a built-in class, meaning that it is implemented in C instead of PHP. It basically looks like this:

```
class Exception {
Public function construct ($message=false, $code=false) {
$this->file = _FILE_;
$this->line = LINE_
$this->message = $message; // the error message as a string
$this->code = $code; // a place to stick a numeric error code
}
public function getFile() {
return $this->file;
}
public function getLine() {
return $this->line;
}
public function getMessage() {
return $this->message;
}
public function getCode() {
return $this->code;
}
}
```

Tracking _ _FILE_ _ and _ _LINE_ _ for the last caller is often useless information. Imagine that you decide to throw an exception if you have a problem with a query in the DB_Mysql wrapper library:

```
class DB_Mysql {
    // ...
    public function execute($query) {
      if(!$this->dbh) {
        $this->connect();
```

```
        }
        $ret = mysql_query($query, $this->dbh);
        if(!is_resource($ret)) {
          throw new Exception;
        }
        return new MysqlStatement($ret);
      }
    }
```

Now if you trigger this exception in the code by executing a syntactically invalid query, like this:

<?php

require_once "DB.inc";

try {

$dbh = new DB_Mysql_Test;

// ... execute a number of queries on our database connection

$rows = $dbh->execute("SELECT * FROM")->fetchall_assoc();

}

catch (Exception $e) { print_r($e);

}

?>

you get this:

exception Object

(

[file] =>/Users/george/Advanced PHP/examples/chapter-3/DB.inc

[line] => 42

)

Line 42 of DB.inc is the execute() statement itself! If you executed a number of queries within the try block, you would have no insight yet into which one of them caused the error. It gets worse, though: If you use your own exception class and manually set $file and $line (or call parent::__construct to run Exception's constructor), you would actually end up with the first callers _ _FILE_ _ and _ _LINE_ _ being the constructor itself! What you want instead is a full backtrace from the moment the problem occurred.

You can now start to convert the DB wrapper libraries to use exceptions. In addition to populating the backtrace data, you can also make a best-effort attempt to set the message and code attributes with the MySQL error information:

```php
class MysqlException extends Exception {
  public $backtrace;
  public function __construct($message=false, $code=false) {
    if(!$message) {
      $this->message = mysql_error();
    }
    if(!$code) {
      $this->code = mysql_errno();
    }
    $this->backtrace = debug_backtrace();
  }
}
```

If you now change the library to use this exception type:

```php
class DB_Mysql {
  public function execute($query) {
    if(!$this->dbh) {
      $this->connect();
    }
    $ret = mysql_query($query, $this->dbh);
    if(!is_resource($ret)) {
      throw new MysqlException;
    }
    return new MysqlStatement($ret);
  }
}
```

and repeat the test:

```php
<?php
require_once "DB.inc";
try {
$dbh = new DB_Mysql_Test;
//...execute a number of queries on our database connection
$rows = $dbh->execute("SELECT * FROM")->fetchall_assoc();
}
catch (Exception $e) {
print_r($e);
}
?>
```

you get this:

```
mysqlexception Object
(
[backtrace] => Array
(
[0] => Array
(
[file] =>/Users/george/Advanced PHP/examples/chapter-3/DB.inc
[line] => 45
[function] => _ _construct
[class] => mysqlexception
[type] =>->
[args] => Array
(
)
)
```

```
    [1] => Array
    (
    [file] =>/Users/george/Advanced PHP/examples/chapter-3/test.php
    [line] => 5
    [function] => execute
    [class] => mysql_test
    [type] =>->
    [args] => Array
    (
    [0] => SELECT * FROM
    )
    )
   )
  )
 [message] => You have an error in your SQL syntax near " at line 1
 [code] => 1064
)
```

Compared with the previous exception, this one contains a cornucopia of information:

- Where the error occurred;
- How the application got to that point;
- The MySQL details for the error.

You can now convert the entire library to use this new exception:

```
class MysqlException extends Exception {
public $backtrace;
public function _ _construct($message=false, $code=false) {
if(!$message) {
$this->message = mysql_error();
}
if(!$code) {
```

```php
$this->code = mysql_errno();
}
$this->backtrace = debug_backtrace();
}
}
class DB_Mysql {
protected $user;
protected $pass;
protected $dbhost;
protected $dbname;
protected $dbh;
public function __construct($user, $pass, $dbhost, $dbname) {
$this->user = $user;
$this->pass = $pass;
$this->dbhost = $dbhost;
$this->dbname = $dbname;
}
protected function connect() {
$this->dbh = mysql_pconnect($this->dbhost, $this->user, $this->pass);
if(!is_resource($this->dbh)) {
throw new MysqlException;
}
if(!mysql_select_db($this->dbname, $this->dbh)) {
throw new MysqlException;
}
}
public function execute($query) {
if(!$this->dbh) {
```

```php
$this->connect();
}
$ret = mysql_query($query, $this->dbh);
if(!$ret) {
throw new MysqlException;
}
else if(!is_resource($ret)) {
return TRUE;
} else {
return new DB_MysqlStatement($ret);
}
}
public function prepare($query) {
if(!$this->dbh) {
$this->connect();
}
return new DB_MysqlStatement($this->dbh, $query);
}
}
class DB_MysqlStatement {
protected $result;
protected $binds;
public $query;
protected $dbh;
public function __construct($dbh, $query) {
$this->query = $query;
$this->dbh = $dbh;
if(!is_resource($dbh)) {
```

FUNDAMENTALS OF WEB DEVELOPMENT

```php
    throw new MysqlException("Not a valid database connection");
  }
}
public function bind_param($ph, $pv) {
  $this->binds[$ph] = $pv;
}
public function execute() {
  $binds = func_get_args();
  foreach($binds as $index => $name) {
    $this->binds[$index + 1] = $name;
  }
  $cnt = count($binds);
  $query = $this->query;
  foreach ($this->binds as $ph => $pv) {
    $query = str_replace(":$ph," "'."mysql_escape_string($pv)."'," $query);
  }
  $this->result = mysql_query($query, $this->dbh);
  if(!$this->result) {
    throw new MysqlException;
  }
}
public function fetch_row() {
  if(!$this->result) {
    throw new MysqlException("Query not executed");
  }
  return mysql_fetch_row($this->result);
}
public function fetch_assoc() {
```

```
return mysql_fetch_assoc($this->result);
}
public function fetchall_assoc() {
$retval = array();
while($row = $this->fetch_assoc()) {
$retval[] = $row;
}
return $retval;
}
}
?>
```

8.4.3. Cascading Exceptions

Sometimes you might want to handle an error but still pass it along to further error handlers. You can do this by throwing a new exception in the catch block:

```
<?php
try {
        throw new Exception;
}
catch (Exception $e) {
        print "Exception caught, and rethrown\n";
        throw new Exception;
}
?>
```

After catching the exception and printing its message, the catch block throws a new exception. This new exception is not handled by the catch block in the previous example, so it remains uncaught. Observe what happens as you run the code:

> php re-throw.php

Exception caught, and rethrown

Fatal error: Uncaught exception 'exception'! in Unknown on line 0

In fact, creating a new exception is not necessary. If you want, you can rethrow the current Exception object, with identical results:

```php
<?php
try {
        throw new Exception;
}
catch (Exception $e) {
        print "Exception caught, and rethrown\n";
        throw $e;
}
?>
```

Being able to rethrow an exception is important because you might not be certain that you want to handle an exception when you catch it. For example, say you want to track referrals on your Web site. To do this, you have a table:

CREATE TABLE track_referrers (

url varchar2(128) not null primary key,

counter int

);

The first time a URL is referred from, you need to execute this:

INSERT INTO track_referrers VALUES('http://some.url/,' 1)

On subsequent requests, you need to execute this:

UPDATE track_referrers SET counter=counter+1 where url = 'http://some.url/'

You could first select from the table to determine whether the URL's row exists and choose the appropriate query based on that. This logic contains a race condition though: If two referrals from the same URL are processed by two different processes simultaneously, it is possible for one of the inserts to fail.

A cleaner solution is to blindly perform the insert and call update if the insert failed and produced a unique key violation. You can then catch all MysqlException errors and perform the update where indicated:

<?php

include "DB.inc";

function track_referrer($url) {

$insertq = "INSERT INTO referrers (url, count) VALUES(:1,:2)";

$updateq = "UPDATE referrers SET count=count+1 WHERE url =:1";

$dbh = new DB_Mysql_Test;

```
try {
$sth = $dbh->prepare($insertq);
$sth->execute($url, 1);
}
catch (MysqlException $e) {
if($e->getCode == 1062) {
$dbh->prepare($updateq)->execute($url);
}
else {
throw $e;
}
}
}
?>
```

Alternatively, you can use a purely typed exception solution where execute itself throws different exceptions based on the errors it incurs:

```
class Mysql_Dup_Val_On_Index extends MysqlException {}
//...
class DB_Mysql {
//...
public function execute($query) {
if(!$this->dbh) {
$this->connect();
}
$ret = mysql_query($query, $this->dbh);
if(!$ret) {
if(mysql_errno() == 1062) {
throw new Mysql_Dup_Val_On_Index;
```

314 FUNDAMENTALS OF WEB DEVELOPMENT

```php
    else {
        throw new MysqlException;
    }
}
else if(!is_resource($ret)) {
    return TRUE;
} else {
    return new MysqlStatement($ret);
}
}
```

Then you can perform your checking, as follows:

```php
function track_referrer($url) {
    $insertq = "INSERT INTO referrers (url, count) VALUES('$url,' 1)";
    $updateq = "UPDATE referrers SET count=count+1 WHERE url = '$url'";
    $dbh = new DB_Mysql_Test;
    try {
        $sth = $dbh->execute($insertq);
    }
    catch (Mysql_Dup_Val_On_Index $e) {
        $dbh->execute($updateq);
    }
}
```

Both methods are valid; it's largely a matter of taste and style. If you go the path of typed exceptions, you can gain some flexibility by using a factory pattern to generate your errors, as in this example:

```php
class MysqlException {
    //...
    static function createError($message=false, $code=false) {
        if(!$code) {
```

```
$code = mysql_errno();
}
if(!$message) {
$message = mysql_error();
}
switch($code) {
case 1062:
return new Mysql_Dup_Val_On_Index($message, $code);
break;
default:
return new MysqlException($message, $code);
break;
}
}
}
```

There's also the added advantage of better readability. You get a suggestive class name instead of a mysterious constant. One should not undervalue the importance of readability aids. You just call this now, rather than throwing specific errors in your code.

```
throw MysqlException::createError();
```

8.4.4. Handling Constructor Failure

It's challenging to manage constructor failure in an object. PHP class constructors are restricted to returning an instance of the class they construct:

- You can use an initialized attribute in the object to mark it as correctly initialized;
- You can perform no initialization in the constructor;
- You can throw an exception in the constructor.

The first option is very inelegant, and we won't even consider it seriously. The second option is a pretty common way of handling constructors that might fail. In fact, in PHP4, it is the preferable way of handling this.

To implement that, you would do something like this:

```php
class ResourceClass {
protected $resource;
public function _ _construct() {
//set username, password, etc
}
public function init() {
if(($this->resource = resource_connect()) == false) {
return false;
}
return true;
}
}
```

When the user creates a new ResourceClass object, there are no actions taken, which can mean the code fails. To actually initialize any sort of potentially faulty code, you call the init() method. This can fail without any issues.

Constructor failure is typically handled best by the third option, which is further supported by the fact that more conventional object-oriented languages like C++ use this approach by default. Compared to PHP, C++ has slightly more significance for the cleanup done in a catch block surrounding a constructor call because memory management may be required. Fortunately, in PHP memory management is handled for you, as in this example:

```php
class Stillborn {
public function _ _construct() {
throw new Exception;
}
public function _ _destruct() {
print "destructing\n";
}
}
try {
$sb = new Stillborn;
```

}

catch(Stillborn $e) {}

Running this generates no output at all:

>php stillborn.php

>

The Stillborn class illustrates how an exception thrown inside the constructor prevents the object's destructors from being called. This is due to the fact that until the constructor is returned from, the object does not actually exist.

8.4.5. Installing a Top-Level Exception Handler

Installing a default exception handler that will be triggered if an exception reaches the top scope and is still uncaught is an intriguing feature of PHP. Unlike a typical catch block, this handler consists of a single function that can handle any type of uncaught exception (including exceptions that don't inherit from Exception).

When it comes to Web applications, the default exception handler comes in handy because it keeps users from seeing an error message or a partially loaded page in the event that an exception is not caught. You can gracefully exit out of any errors and reroute the user to the correct page if you use PHP's output buffering to postpone sending content until the page is completely generated.

To set a default exception handler, you define a function that takes a single parameter: function default_exception_handler($exception) {}

You set this function like so:

$old_handler = set_exception_handler('default_exception_handler');

The previously defined default exception handler (if one exists) is returned. User-defined exception handlers are held in a stack, so you can restore the old handler either by pushing another copy of the old handler onto the stack, like this:

set_exception_handler($old_handler);

or by popping the stack with this:

restore_exception_handler();

An example of the flexibility this gives you has to do with setting up error redirects for errors incurred for generation during a page. Instead of wrapping every questionable statement in an individual try block, you can set up a default handler that handles the redirection. Because an error can occur after partial output has been generated, you need to make sure to set output buffering on in the script, either by calling this at the top of each script:

```
ob_start();
```

or by setting the php.ini directive:

```
output_buffering = On
```

The former has the advantage of making it easier to turn on and off behavior in individual scripts and allowing for more portable code, as behavior is determined by the script's content and does not depend on nondefault .ini settings. The benefit of the latter is that it eliminates the need to add output buffering code to each script and enables output buffering in every script with a single setting.

The following is an example of a default exception handler that will automatically generate an error page on any uncaught exception:

```php
<?php
function redirect_on_error($e) {
  ob_end_clean();
  include("error.html");
}
set_exception_handler("redirect_on_error");
ob_start();
// ... arbitrary page code goes here
?>
```

In order to discard all content generated up to this point and return an HTML error page in the event that an uncaught exception is bubbled to the top calling scope, this handler depends on output buffering being enabled. You can further enhance this handler by adding the ability to handle certain error conditions differently. For example, if you raise an AuthException exception, you can redirect the person to the login page instead of displaying the error page:

```php
<?php
function redirect_on_error($e) {
  ob_end_clean();
  if(is_a($e, "AuthException")) {
    header("Location: /login/php");

  }
  else {
    include("error.html");
  }
}
set_exception_handler("redirect_on_error");
ob_start();
// ... arbitrary page code goes here
? >
```

8.4.6. Data Validation

An important reason for Web programming bugs is the absence of data validation for client-provided input. Verifying that the data you receive from a client is, in fact, in the format you anticipated receiving is known as data validation. Unvalidated data causes two major problems in code:

- Trash data; and
- Maliciously altered data.

Information that just does not fit the parameters of what it should be is considered trash data. Imagine a form for user registration where users can provide their location. If a user can enter his or her state free form, then you have exposed yourself to getting states like:

- New Yrok (typo);
- Lalalala (intentionally obscured).

Providing users with a choice of states via drop-down option boxes is a common strategy used to address this. This only addresses half of the issue, though: while it keeps users from unintentionally entering the wrong state, it does not shield them from malicious users manipulating their POST data to pass through a non-existent option.

To protect against this, you should always validate user data in the script as well. You can do this by manually validating user input before doing anything with it:

```php
<?php
$STATES = array('al' => 'Alabama,'
/*...*/,
'wy' => 'Wyoming');
function is_valid_state($state) {
global $STATES;
return array_key_exists($STATES, $state);
}
?>
```

Here's an example:

```php
class User {
  public id;
  public name;
  public city;
  public state;
  public zipcode;
  public function __construct($attr = false) {
    if($attr) {
      $this->name = $attr['name'];
      $this->email = $attr['email'];
      $this->city = $attr['city'];
      $this->state = $attr['state'];
      $this->zipcode = $attr['zipcode'];

    }
  }
  public function validate() {
    if(strlen($this->name) > 100) {
      throw new DataException;
    }
    if(strlen($this->city) > 100) {
      throw new DataException;
    }
    if(!is_valid_state($this->state)) {
      throw new DataException;
    }

    }
    if(!is_valid_zipcode($this->zipcode)) {
      throw new DataException;
    }
  }
}

?>
```

The validate() method fully validates all the attributes of the user object, including the following:

- Compliance with the lengths of database fields.
- Handling foreign key data constraints (for example, the user's U.S. state being valid).
- Handling data form constraints (for example, the zip code being valid).

To use the validate() method, you could simply instantiate a new User object with untrusted user data:

```
$user = new User($_POST);
```

and then call validate on it

```
try {
    $user->validate();
}
catch (DataException $e) {
    /* Do whatever we should do if the users data is invalid */
}
```

Again, the benefit of using an exception here instead of simply having validate() return true or false is that you might not want to have a try block here at all; you might prefer to allow the exception to percolate up a few callers before you decide to handle it.

Naturally, malicious data extends far beyond merely inserting spurious state names. Cross-site scripting attacks are the most well-known type of bad data validation attack. In order to commit a cross-site scripting attack, malicious HTML—typically client-side scripting tags like JavaScript tags—must be inserted into forms that users submit.

The following case is a simple example. If you allow users of a site to list a link to their home page on the site and display it as follows:

```
<a href="<?= $url ?>">Click on my home page</a>
```

When the page is rendered, this results in the following being displayed to the user:

```
<a href="'http://example.foo/" onClick=bad_javascript_func foo="">
  Click on my home page
</a>
```

This will cause the user to execute bad_javascript_func when he or she clicks the link. What's more, because it is being served from your Web page, the JavaScript has full access to the user's cookies for your domain. This is, of course, really bad because it allows malicious users to manipulate, steal, or otherwise exploit other users' data.

Needless to say, proper data validation for any user data that is to be rendered on a Web page is essential to your site's security. The tags that you should filter are of course regulated by your business rule. We prefer to take a pretty draconian approach to this filtering, declining any text that even appears to be JavaScript. Here's an example:

```php
<?php
$UNSAFE_HTML[] = "!javascript\s*:!is";
$UNSAFE_HTML[] = "!vbscri?pt\s*:!is";
$UNSAFE_HTML[] = "!<\s*embed.*swf!is";
$UNSAFE_HTML[] = "!<[^>]*[^a-z]onabort\s*=!is";

$UNSAFE_HTML[] = "!<[^>]*[^a-z]onblur\s*=!is";
$UNSAFE_HTML[] = "!<[^>]*[^a-z]onchange\s*=!is";
$UNSAFE_HTML[] = "!<[^>]*[^a-z]onfocus\s*=!is";
$UNSAFE_HTML[] = "!<[^>]*[^a-z]onmouseout\s*=!is";
$UNSAFE_HTML[] = "!<[^>]*[^a-z]onmouseover\s*=!is",
$UNSAFE_HTML[] = "!<[^>]*[^a-z]onload\s*=!is";
$UNSAFE_HTML[] = "!<[^>]*[^a-z]onreset\s*=!is";
$UNSAFE_HTML[] = "!<[^>]*[^a-z]onselect\s*=!is";
$UNSAFE_HTML[] = "!<[^>]*[^a-z]onsubmit\s*=!is";
$UNSAFE_HTML[] = "!<[^>]*[^a-z]onunload\s*=!is";
$UNSAFE_HTML[] = "!<[^>]*[^a-z]onerror\s*=!is";
$UNSAFE_HTML[] = "!<[^>]*[^a-z]onclick\s*=!is";

function unsafe_html($html) {
    global $UNSAFE_HTML;
    $html = html_entities($html, ENT_COMPAT, ISO-8859-1_
    foreach ($UNSAFE_HTML as $match) {
        if(preg_match($match, $html, $matches)) {
            return $match;
        }
    }
    return false;
}
?>
```

ERROR HANDLING

If you plan on allowing text to be directly integrated into tags (as in the preceding example), you might want to go so far as to ban any text that looks at all like client-side scripting tags, as in this example:

$UNSAFE_HTML [] = "!onabort\s*=!is";

$UNSAFE_HTML [] = "!onblur\s*=!is";

$UNSAFE_HTML [] 11 = !onchange\s*=!is";

$UNSAFE_HTML [] = "!onfocus\s*=!is";

$UNSAFE HTML [] = ! onmouseout\s*=!is";

$UNSAFE_HTML [] = "! onmouseover\s*=!is";

$UNSAFE_HTML [] = !onload\s*=!is";

$UNSAFE_HTML [] = "!onreset\s*=!is";

$UNSAFE_HTML [] !onselect\s*=!is"; =

$UNSAFE_HTML [] = "!onsubmit\s*=!is";

$UNSAFE_HTML [] = "! onunload\s*=!is";

$UNSAFE_HTML [] = "!onerror\s*=!is";

$UNSAFE_HTML [] = "!onclick\s*=!is";

It is often tempting to turn on magic_quotes_gpc in you php.ini file. magic_quotes automatically adds quotes to any incoming data. We do not care for magic_quotes. For one, it can be a crutch that makes you feel safe, although it is simple to craft examples such as the preceding ones that are exploitable even with magic_quotes on.

There is frequently the option to perform filtering and conversion either inbound (when the data is submitted) or outbound (when the data is displayed) when it comes to data validation, especially when the data is used for display. Filtering data as it is received is generally safer and more effective. When the data is shown in multiple locations, the likelihood of forgetting to perform inbound filtering is reduced and only needs to be done once. The following are two reasons you might want to perform outbound filtering:

- You need highly customizable filters (for example, multilingual profanity filters); and
- Your content filters change rapidly.

Did you get it?

1. Which version of PHP was added with exception handling?
2. How to install a top-level exception handler.

A CLOSER LOOK

Checkers and Handlers: If you doubt your own ability to see internal errors in the code, you may use various PHP error checkers. You can find them online (for example, PHP Code Checker) or download a specific software (such as Phan). A fresh pair of eyes is always useful, and a PHP error checker will make PHP show errors you did not notice.

An error handler is a custom function, which is called whenever a PHP error occurs. It is not challenging to create. You must note that a custom error handler must be able to handle at least two parameters passed into it (error message and level are required). The number of parameters might reach up to five, as there are three optional ones (file, line-number, and context) that might be included.

Let's look at the syntax example:

err_function(err_level,err_message, err_file,err_line,err_context)

```
<?php
$text1 = "Learning PHP";
$text2 = "ALL the PHP";
$var1 = 58;
$var2 = 4;
print "<h6>." $text1. $text2."</h6>";
print $var1 + $var2;
?>
```

The following table consist of the parameters you can add:

Parameter	Description
error_level	Required. A numeric value which is used to tell the level of the report.
error_message	Required. A string value which is outputted upon an error occurring.
error_file	Optional. The name of the file in which the error took place.
error_line	Optional. The number of the line on which the error took place.
error_context	Optional. Used to specify using which variables, files, functions the error occurred in.

CASE STUDY

Exception Handling in PHP: An exception is an unwanted event in the program that interrupts the normal flow of the instructions. It is the unexpected outcome of the program. The major difference between the error and exception is that the exception can be handled by the program, unlike error.

Exception handling is the process of handling the exception (run time errors) to induce the normal flow of the code execution. This is the set of actions we take to handle the unwanted behavior of the code. The main goal is to execute the program without any unexpected behavior and outcome of the code.

When an exception occurs in the program, It proceeds generally using these steps:

- The current code state is saved.
- The code implementation will switch to a custom exception handler function
- Then the handler resumes the execution from the saved code state, terminates the script execution/continues the execution from a different location in the code.

Need of Exception Handling in PHP: PHP provides different functionalities in exception handling. It can handle various runtime errors such as IOException, SQLException, ClassNotFoundException, and arithmetic exceptions.

The following keywords are used when we use exception handling in PHP – try, catch, throw, finally.

- **Try:** It is the block of code in which an exception is present. This piece of code raises the exception. Try block should have a catch or finally block. It contains more than one catch block too.
- **Throw:** The throw keyword is used to symbolize the occurrence of a PHP exception Then we try to find a catch statement to handle this exception.
- **Catch:** This is the block of code that is executed when the try block throws an exception. It is responsible for handling the exception in the try block. It is always used with the try block.
- **Finally:** The PHP 5.5 version introduced the "finally" statement in PHP. The "finally" block can be used after a catch block or in place of catch blocks. "Finally " term means that it will be executed no matter the exception is thrown or not. It generally executes the necessary parts of the program. We use it for many purposes like closing the files, closing the open databases connections, etc.

The Basic syntax which we use when handle the exceptions using try and catch is given below:

- Multiple exceptions use multiple try-catch blocks for the implementation and execution of the code. It is used when you want to show the customized message or you wanted to perform some unique operation when the exception is thrown.
- In the single program, multiple exceptions can be there like arithmetic exceptions, IO exceptions. We will help you to understand the concept of Multiple exceptions firstly by flowchart representation and then by executing the program.

Flowchart to Describe the Working of Multiple Exceptions: Now here is an example for the multiple exceptions using the program.

We will implement the code that divides a number by the number in the denominator.

We have the chance to get the two types of exceptions by dividing the number by zero or by dividing the number by a negative number.

We can work with the multiple cases of exceptions

The code below shows the implementation.

Here we are writing the code when we divide a number by the denominator there are two chances of exceptions one is by dividing it to zero or by a negative number. In the program, we are using multiple catches to solve the exceptions.

Using Multiple Try-Catch with Multiple Exception Types: PHP supports the use of more than one nested catch block to handle their thrown exceptions. This provides us the permission to alter our code based on the type of exception thrown. This is useful for customizing how you display an error message. We can handle different types of exceptions using the catch blocks.

The syntax is given below:

```
try {
    // run your code here
}
catch (Exception $e) {
    // code to handle the Exception
}
catch (Exception $e) {
    // code to handle the Exception
}
```

- **Use of Try-Catch-Finally:** Introduced in PHP version 5.5, Sometimes we can also use a "finally" section. Finally is useful in many cases it is not just limited to exception handling, it is used to perform the necessary tasks, and in the cases where the execution is independent of exceptions.

The "finally" block is always used when the try-catch block exits. It ensures that finally block is executed in any situation.

Example for using try-catch-finally:

```
try {
    print "this is our try block n";
    throw new Exception();
}
catch (Exception $e) {
    print "Exception occurs caught here yeah!!!!|n";
}
finally {
    print "this part is always executed n";
}
```

Explanation of the working of flowchart

Firstly, we check If the exception occurs or not and if occurs it will be handled by the catch block. There are two chances:

- The exception will be handled; and
- The exception will not be handled.

If the exception is handled by the catch block then the "finally" block will be executed too.

If the exception is not handled, then also the "finally" block will be executed itself.

- **Conclusion of Exception Handling in PHP:** The concept of exception is almost similar in all the languages. Exception Handling ensures the normal execution of the programs and we can handle it using try, catch, throw, and finally keywords in PHP.

SUMMARY

- The process of responding to and recovering from error conditions in your program is known as error handling.
- PHP comes with built-in error handling capabilities and a built-in severity system that limits the errors you can see to those that are serious enough to worry you.
- An error is sent to the standard output stream when you choose to display errors; on a Web page, this means that the error is sent to the browser.
- PHP internally supports both logging to a file and logging via syslog via two settings in the php.ini file.
- Logging gives you an auditable record of any errors that happen on your website. Debugging lines are frequently placed around the problematic area to aid in diagnosis.
- Since PHP5 only supported the methods we've covered thus far, you can see that this presents some serious issues, particularly when writing larger applications.
- When the user creates a new ResourceClass object, there are no actions taken, which can mean the code fails.
- Installing a default exception handler that will be triggered if an exception reaches the top scope and is still uncaught is an intriguing feature of PHP.

MULTIPLE CHOICE QUESTION

1. **What function is used to customize error handling in PHP?**
   a. setErrorHandler()
   b. handleErrors()
   c. customizeErrors()
   d. setCustomErrorHandler()

2. **Which of the following PHP error levels represents non-fatal errors?**
   a. E_ERROR
   b. E_WARNING
   c. E_PARSE
   d. E_NOTICE

3. **What PHP function is used to trigger an error condition?**
   a. error_trigger()
   b. trigger_error()
   c. raise_error()
   d. generate_error()

4. Which PHP function is used to log errors to a file?
   a. log_error()
   b. error_log()
   c. write_error_log()
   d. save_error()
5. Which PHP directive is used to set the error reporting level?
   a. error_level
   b. report_errors
   c. error_reporting
   d. set_error_level
6. What does the "@" symbol do in PHP error handling?
   a. Suppresses error messages
   b. Raises a fatal error
   c. Logs the error to a file
   d. Outputs error message to the browser
7. What is the default error reporting level in PHP?
   a. E_ERROR
   b. E_ALL
   c. E_NOTICE
   d. E_WARNING
8. Which error type indicates a syntax error in PHP?
   a. E_ERROR
   b. E_WARNING
   c. E_PARSE
   d. E_NOTICE
9. Which PHP function is used to restore the previous error handler after custom error handling?
   a. restore_error_handler()
   b. revert_error_handler()
   c. reset_error_handler()
   d. previous_error_handler()
10. What PHP function can be used to check if an error has occurred?
    a. has_error()
    b. check_error()
    c. error_occurred()
    d. error_get_last()

REVIEW QUESTIONS

1. Which version of PHP was added with Exception handling? Discuss.
2. Create a custom error handler for PHP.
3. Discuss the ways to handle PHP errors
4. What is the purpose of error handling in PHP, and why is it important for web development?
5. What are some best practices for error handling in PHP applications, especially in terms of security and user experience?

Answer to Multiple Choice Questions

1. (a); 2. (b); 3. (b); 4. (b); 5. (c); 6. (a); 7. (b); 8. (c); 9. (c); 10. (d)

REFERENCES

1. Antonija, M., Brent, M., & Michael, M., (2002). Using evaluation to shape its design: Results and experiences with SQL-tutor. *User Modeling and User-Adapted Interaction, 12*, 243–279.
2. Barbara, K., et al., (2012). Attack-defense trees. *Proc. of FAST 2010* (Vol. 24, No. 1). Published by Oxford University Press.
3. Brain, C., & Jacob, W. *Secure Programming with Static Analysis.* 9th Chapter: "Web Applications."
4. Halevy, A. Y., Mumick, I. S., Sagiv, Y., & Shmueli, O., (2001). Static analysis in datalog extensions. *Journal of the ACM, 48*, 971–1012.
5. Internet Security Auditors, S. L., (2006). *MX Injection- Capturing and Exploiting Hidden Mail Server.* [Online].
6. Stefan, B., & Christian, G., (2004). *Detecting Logical Errors in SQL Queries.* Technical Report, University of Halle.
7. Stefan, B., & Christian, G., (2004). Semantic errors in SQL queries: A quite complete list. In: *Fourth International Conference on Quality Software (QSIC'04).* IEEE Computer Society Press, To Appear.

Index

A

Absolute positioning 108
ACID transactions 275
Active server pages 15
AJAX callbacks 229, 230
AJAX engine 224, 226, 227
AJAX functionality 214, 215
AJAX server 213, 214, 215
AJAX web development methodology 225
American National Standards Institute (ANSI) 249
Animated graphic image 61
Animationiteration event 143
Apache server 164
API nodes 275
Arithmetic operators 184
ASP.NET application 212, 214
Associative arrays 187
Asynchronous replication 246
Asynchronous web applications 205
AuthException exception 318

B

Basic visual formatting model 80
Border attribute 65
Business analysts 273

C

CamelBack notation 151
Cascading style sheets (CSS) 34
Central processing unit 21
Client-side scripting tags 321
Client-side web technologies 205
Cluster hosting 22
Codd's relational model 248
Code execution 325
Code logic errors 285
Coding languages 3
Coding standards 195
Common gateway interface (CGI) 15, 161
Connection error 297
Constant identifiers 181
Content management systems 196
CORS error 227
Cross-site request forgery (CSRF) 227
CSS box model 94, 114, 116
CSS grid 98
CSS grouping selector 82
CSS reference 92

D

Database administration 263
Database connection 306
Database management system (DBMS) 243
Database system 243

Data manipulation 254
Data processing 245
Data recovery 245
Data validation 321
DB wrapper libraries 305
Debugger 150
Debugging 149, 150, 151
Debugging tools 150
Declaration block 82
Declarative language 248
Desktop application software 212
Desktop computers 3
dir attribute 51, 52
Distributed computing 243
Document object model 45
Document object oodel (DOM) 121
DOM programming 129, 133
DOM-related libraries 139
Dynamic programming language 122

E

Email integration 208
Embedded styles 86, 88
Error handling 211
Error message 271
Event object 136
Exception hierarchies 297
Expression language (EL) 217
External style sheets 86
Extreme programming 146

F

Fatal errors 287
File transfer protocol 4
Fixed positioning 106, 109
Flexbox 100
Function parameters 177, 178

G

Gopher protocol 4
Graphical user experience 122
Graphic design software 196
Grid hosting 23

Grid layout 102

H

Help desk software 11
Home page 3
Hosting service 21
HTML elements 31, 32, 34, 36, 45, 46, 47, 49, 68, 71, 72
HTML tags 31, 34, 36, 38, 48, 60, 72
HTML templates 2
Hypertext preprocessor 161

I

Inline styles 87
INSERT statement 253, 263
Instant messaging 208
Integrated development environment (IDE) 149
Internal stylesheet 86
International Organization for Standardization (ISO) 249
Internet Explorer 5, 6
Internet information server (IIS) 163
IP addresses 23

J

JavaScript 34, 36, 68, 71
JavaScript function 206, 223, 237
JavaScript Object Notation (JSON) 154

L

Login page 204

M

Mac computers 166, 199
Malicious data 321
Markup languages 81
Media-specific style sheets 80
Model-view-controller (MVC) 16, 17, 154
Mozilla Firefox 122
Multidimensional arrays 187
MySQL statement 255

INDEX

N

Network partitioning protocol 276
Network protocol 155
Node interface 131, 132, 133
Non-relational databases 243

O

Object-oriented languages 316
Object-oriented programming (OOP) 257
Online data 4
Open-source database 246

P

Page layout strategies 98
Pair programming 144, 145
Personal computers 5
PHP comparison operators 184
PHP conditional assignment operators 184, 186
PHP data objects (PDO) 267
PHP memory management 316
PHP Parser 162, 163
PHP parsing engine 168, 199
Programming interface 127
Pseudocode algorithms 169

Q

Quality assurance (QA) 13, 14
Query languages 243

R

Regular expressions 121
Relational databases 243
Relational data stream management systems (RDSMS) 248
Relative positioning 107
Remote desktop 261
Rich internet applications (RIA) 211
Roman numerals 55
Run time errors 325

S

Script processing 226
Semantic value 57
Server-side validation 227
Session management 195
SIS database 232
Social media platforms 13
Social networking 3
Software program 4
SQL server management studio (SSMS) 265
Standard markup language 34
Static scoping 179
Static web page 1
Sticky positioning 110
Structural semantics 34

T

the DOM hierarchy 132
Two-phase commit protocol (2PC) 277

U

Uniform resource locator (URL) 61
Unix system 167
Unordered list 55

V

Virtual private server (VPS) 22
Visual appearance 57
Visual Studio 230

W

Warning messages 293
Web applications 203
Web-based applications 13
Web browser 10
Web content 81
Web development environment 214
Web development process 13
Web framework 15
Webpage behavior 121
Web server software 163
Website 1, 3, 4, 6, 7, 8, 9, 10, 11, 12, 13, 14, 16, 17, 19, 20, 21, 22, 23, 24, 25, 27, 28, 29
Web technologies 205
Whitespace 170

Window objects 129
Windows operating system 5
World Wide Web Consortium (W3C) 34, 48, 70
World Wide Web (WWW) 4, 27

X

XML documents 127, 128, 156
XML manipulation 205

Printed in the United States
by Baker & Taylor Publisher Services